总主编 刘世伟

New Century College English Course(1)

新世纪英语教程 1

(修订版)

主　编　段三伏　王玉芝
副主编　杨新焕　赵伶萍　罗梦华　杨崇建
　　　　张荣斌
编　委　杨新焕　赵伶萍　何满成　李伊沙
　　　　肖腊梅

北京大学出版社
PEKING UNIVERSITY PRESS

图书在版编目(CIP)数据

新世纪英语教程(1)(修订版)/刘世伟总主编.—北京：北京大学出版社,2004.8
ISBN 978-7-301-07701-6

Ⅰ.新… Ⅱ.刘… Ⅲ.英语－高等学校：技术学校－教材 Ⅳ.H31

中国版本图书馆CIP数据核字(2004)第076966号

书　　　名：新世纪英语教程(1)(修订版)
著作责任者：刘世伟　总主编
责 任 编 辑：黄瑞明
标 准 书 号：ISBN 978-7-301-07701-5/H·1094
出 版 发 行：北京大学出版社
地　　　址：北京市海淀区成府路205号　100871
网　　　址：http://www.pup.cn　电子信箱：zbing@pup.pku.edu.cn
电　　　话：邮购部62752015　发行部62750672　编辑部62767315　出版部62754962
印　刷　者：北京飞达印刷有限责任公司
经　销　者：新华书店
　　　　　　787毫米×1092毫米　16开本　17印张　442千字
　　　　　　2004年8月第1版　2005年5月第2版
　　　　　　2011年10月第7次印刷(总第8次印刷)
定　　　价：28.00元(配有光盘)

未经许可,不得以任何方式复制或抄袭本书之部分或全部内容。
版权所有,侵权必究
举报电话：(010)62752024　电子信箱：fd@pup.pku.edu.cn

前　　言

《新世纪英语教程》由全国高职高专英语教材编写组编写，供招收高中毕业生、中专毕业生和职高毕业生的三年制高等职业学院和高等普通专科学校的学生以及英语自学者使用。

《新世纪英语教程》根据教育部高等教育司《高职高专教育英语课程教学基本要求》，按照建构主义学习理论编写，贯彻听说领先的原则，重在培养学生实际使用英语进行交际的能力，同时培养学生较强的阅读能力，并兼顾写作、翻译等各项能力的发展，使学生具备以英语为工具，捕捉和获取所需信息的能力，为学习各种专业英语打下坚实基础。

本套教材共分四册，同时配有学习指导、同步练习、电子教案和学习光盘。教材语言材料大部分选自原文，具有较强的思想性、科学性、知识性、趣味性和实用性。第一、二册的内容以共核英语语言为主(Common Core English)为主，第三、四册适当增加科普内容的比例。学生学完第三册后可以达到《高职高专教育英语课程教学基本要求》所规定的 B 级要求，学完第四册后可以达到《高职高专教育英语课程教学基本要求》所规定的 A 级要求。编排体例采用主题教学(Theme-based)模式：从不同侧面围绕一个激发学生兴趣和思考的共同主题，把听说读写译等各种技能的训练合理安排在一个单元内，教学活动包括：听力理解、交际技巧、课文选读结合主体预演和课文理解、阅读技巧、快速阅读、翻译训练、应用写作等，从而将教与学有机结合，课内外连成一片，使学生真正做到听得懂、说得出、用得活。

教材每册有 8 个单元，每单元有听力、交际技巧、课文选读(分为 Text A 和 Text B)和课文理解、阅读技巧、翻译技巧、实践与提高几个部分。听力部分旨在培养学生的听力理解能力。交际技巧以诗歌朗读作为热身练习，过渡到日常会话，重在培养学生的交际能力。课文选读有两篇意义相关、语言结构相同的课文，为实践与提高提供了阅读、写作和翻译各项练习的中心材料。阅读技巧着重讲清并解决一个阅读方面的难题。翻译技巧讲解翻译的基本问题，主要是语言结构和短语、习语的练习。实践与提高则强调对阅读、写作和翻译各种技能的培养，包括两篇快速阅读和一篇完型填空，内容与课文相近但难度稍浅，旨在培养学生快速获取信息的能力。写作技巧从课文选读重点句型的模仿入手，重在掌握日常应用文的写作。每单元提供的练习形式多且数量大，教师可根据教学的实际情况进行取舍。

本套教材每册的教学课时建议为 72 课时，每个单元的教学课时为 8 课时，另外每 4 个单元后有一个复习材料，每个复习材料的教学课时为 4 课时。

本套教材承英国东伦敦大学语言中心高级讲师，英国文化教育委员会理事 Amanda Maitland 女士，美国阿拉巴马州立大学教育学院 Louise Lee 博士审阅并提出宝贵修改意见，在此一并表示感谢。

由于时间仓促，书中疏漏之处在所难免，请读者与专家指正。

高职高专英语教材编写组
2005 年 1 月

CONTENTS

Unit One — **Learning English** 1
    Reading Selection 1
    Language Structure 11
        Words and Sentences (词和句子) 11
    Practice and Improvement 17

Teacher and student

Unit Two — **The Things around Us** 30
    Reading Selection 30
    Language Structure 37
        The Adverbial Clause (状语从句) 37
    Practice and Improvement 41

What a wonderful nature!

Unit Three — **Space Travel** 53
    Reading Selection 53
    Language Structure 62
        The Attributive Clause (定语从句) 62
    Practice and Improvement 66

Space Shuttle Atlantis

Unit Four — **Words and Their Stories** 80
    Reading Selection 80
    Language Structure 89
        The Noun Clause (名词从句) 89
    Practice and Improvement 94

The American Indians

Revision I	106
Unit Five **Twenty Questions**	115
Reading Selection	115
Language Structure	125
The Modal Verbs (情态动词)	125
Practice and Improvement	130

Playing language games

Unit Six **Fables about Mice**	143
Reading Selection	143
Language Structure	152
The Infinitive (不定式)	152
Practice and Improvement	157

Fables about mice

Unit Seven **Stories about Thomas Edison**	169
Reading Selection	169
Language Structure	178
The Participle (分词)	178
Practice and Improvement	183

The great inventor—Edison

Unit Eight **Life in the Countryside**	196
Reading Selection	196
Language Structure	205
The Gerund (动名词)	205
Practice and Improvement	210

Farm life in the U.S.

Revision II	223
Appendixes	231
Appendix I Irregular Verbs	231
Appendix II Presupposed Words and Phrases	234
Appendix III Glossary	242

Beautiful wild flowers

Unit One

LEARNING ENGLISH

Reading Selection

Text A

PRE-READING TASK

1. What language, do you think, is the most important in the information age?
2. Do you think it necessary to learn English? Why/Why not?
3. Do you agree that a person who doesn't know English is, in some sense, a modern illiterate (现代文盲)?

The Importance of English

There are thousands of languages in the world. Each language seems to be the most important to those who speak it as their native language.

The importance of a language can be judged in accordance with three aspects: the first is the number of its native speakers; the second is how widely the native speakers are spread over the world, the last is the cultural, economic and political influences of the people who speak it as their mother tongue.

There is no doubt that English is one of the world's most widely used languages. People use a language in one of the three ways: as a native language, as a second language, or as a foreign language. English is spoken as a native language by over three hundred million people: in America, Britain, Australia, New Zealand, Canada, South Africa and some Caribbean countries. As a second language, English is often necessary for official business: education, information and other activities in a lot of

1

countries such as India, Pakistan, Nigeria, Singapore, and the Philippines. Along with Chinese, French, Spanish and Russian, English is one of the working languages of the United Nations and is more frequently used than the others.

New students are having the Opening Ceremony.

New students are having military training.

(**In the new century, the students begin their new life at college.**)

English is the language of international transport. Most pilots in planes traveling from one country to another use it to contact airports; all ships sailing on the oceans use it to call for help by radio.

English is the language of the information age. It is said that about 60 percent of the world's radio and TV programs are broadcasted in English and that 70 percent of the world's mails are written in English. According to the statistics, over 90 percent of information is spread through Internet in English, and more than 80 percent of e-mails are sent to each other in English throughout the world.

English is the language of international exchange and cooperation. At international sports meets, at global trade fairs, at conferences of scientists from different countries, and at talks of writers and artists from the corners of the earth, English is the language most commonly used and most widely understood. The newest ideas in culture and education are exchanged in English, and the latest results in science and technology are published in English.

With the economic globalization and educational internationalization, English is getting more and more important; therefore we must study hard and try to have a good command of English. Without English, it seems difficult to get in touch with the outside world.

Text B

PRE-READING TASK

1. How long have you been learning English?
2. Have you met with any difficulty in your English study? How did you deal with it?
3. As a college student of the new century, what will you do in your English study?

The Study of English

It is quite a long time since I began to learn English. I am glad to say that I am getting on well with it. I know that English is very important to us. We can use English as a tool to learn advanced science and technology from other countries, so we can build our motherland into a prosperous country. We can use English as a medium to promote friendship between Chinese people and the people of the world, and in this way we can turn the earth into a peaceful globe.

The problem now is not why I should learn English but how I can master English as soon as possible. English is very useful, but it is quite difficult to learn. How hard I have been trying to get every sound right, to spell every word correctly, and to speak the little English I know. Our teachers have always required us to lay a solid foundation of everything we do, and in language study perhaps more than in anything else, well begun is half done.

The study of past years has taught me that we cannot learn English well if we don't watch out for its idiomatic usage. When I began to learn English, I took it for granted that English words had exact equivalents in Chinese. Therefore what I had to do was to memorize individual words and put them together according to the rules of grammar if I wanted to express my idea correctly. When I was taught to say "I see a book on the desk" and "I am going to see a friend," I thought I had learned everything about the word "see." I did not realize that we do not *see* but *read* a book until one day the teacher caught me out. My interest was aroused and since then I have always been on my guard against such blunders. I have learned to say to *join* the army but to *take part in* a discussion; I have learned to express to go to school *by bus* but *on foot*. Apart from that, I have paid attention to irregular verbs, such as *lie*, *lay*, *lain* and *lay*, *laid*, *laid*. I have also learned to absorb whole sentences without trying to translate them into Chinese. I fully understand that besides a good training in speaking, listening, reading, writing and translation, one has to pay close attention to English idioms in order to learn the language well and to use it freely.

I have made a little progress in English study, and however this is just a beginning. As a college student in the new century, I'm fully aware of my mission. I'm fully prepared for more hard work, or I would fall behind. There is still a long, long way to go, so I must learn more and practice more. Just as a proverb goes, "Practice makes perfect." Only through practice can I have a good command of English.

Word List

1. importance /imˈpɔːtns/ *n.* 重要(性); 重大
2. native /ˈneitiv/ *n.* 本地人, 土著 *a.* 本国的, 本族的; 土产的
3. widely /ˈwaidli/ *ad.* 广泛地, 普遍地
4. judge /dʒʌdʒ/ *v.* 判断, 裁判 *n.* 法官, 裁判员
5. accordance /əˈkɔːdəns/ *n.* 一致, 和谐
6. aspect /ˈæspekt/ *n.* 方面; 样子, 外表
7. cultural /ˈkʌltʃərəl/ *a.* 文化的
8. economic /iːkəˈnɔmik/ *a.* 经济(上)的, 经济学的
9. influence /ˈinfluəns/ *n. & v.* 影响, 感化
10. tongue /tʌŋ/ *n.* 舌头; 口语
11. master /ˈmɑːstə/ *v.* 掌握, 精通 *n.* 主人; 教师; 大师
12. activity /ækˈtiviti/ *n.* 活动, 行动
13. frequently /ˈfriːkwəntli/ *ad.* 常常, 经常
14. trade /treid/ *n.* 贸易, 交易, 买卖 *v.* 用……进行交换
15. transport /ˈtrænspɔːt/ *n.* 运输, 运输工具 /trænsˈpɔːt/ *v.* 运输, 输送
16. pilot /ˈpailət/ *n.* 飞行员, 领航员 *v.* 驾驶 (飞机等), 领航
17. broadcast /ˈbrɔːdkɑːst/ *v. & n.* 广播, 播音
18. program /ˈprougræm/ (UK programme /ˈprougræm/) *n. & v.* (安排) 节目, (编) 程序, (订) 规划
19. mail /meil/ *n.* 邮件, 邮政 *v.* 邮寄

20. statistics /stəˈtistiks/ n. 统计，统计表
21. internet /ˈintənet/ n. 因特网，国际互联网
22. e-mail /ˈiːmeil/ n. 电子邮件，电子信函
23. exchange /iksˈtʃeindʒ/ v. & n. 交流，交换
24. cooperation /kouɔpəˈreiʃən/ n. 合作，协作
25. global /ˈgloubl/ a. 全球的，世界的；球型的
26. fair /fɛə(r)/ n. 展览会，交易会 a. 公平的；(肤色)白皙的；(头发)金黄的
27. conference /ˈkɔnfərəns/ n. 会议，讨论会，协商会
28. artist /ˈɑːtist/ n. 艺术家，画家
29. corner /ˈkɔːnə/ n. 角落；(遥远的) 地区，偏僻处
30. percent /pəˈsent/ n. 百分比，百分数
31. globalization /ˌgloubəlaiˈzeiʃən/ n. 全球化
32. internationalization /ˈintəˌnæʃənəlaiˈzeiʃən/ n. 国际化
33. advanced /ədˈvɑːnst/ a. 先进的，高级的
34. technology /tekˈnɔlədʒi/ n. 技术，工艺(学)
35. prosperous /ˈprɔspərəs/ a. 繁荣的，昌盛的
36. medium /ˈmiːdiəm/ n. 媒介，媒体 a. 中等的，半生的
37. promote /prəˈmout/ v. 促进，发扬；提升，晋级
38. foundation /faunˈdeiʃən/ n. 基础，根本；地基；基金，基金会
39. idiomatic /ˌidiəˈmætik/ a. 惯用的，合乎语言习惯的
40. usage /ˈjuːsidʒ/ n. 用法，使用
41. memorize /ˈmeməraiz/ v. 记住，记忆
42. individual /ˌindiˈvidʒuəl/ n. & a. 个别(的)，个体(的)，单独(的)
43. realize /ˈriəlaiz/ v. 认识到，了解；实现；实行
44. arouse /əˈrauz/ v. 唤起，引起
45. blunder /ˈblʌndə(r)/ v. 做错 n. 错误，失误
46. irregular /iˈregjulə(r)/ a. 不规则的，无规律的
47. absorb /əbˈsɔːb/ v. 吸收，吸引
48. translation /trænsˈleiʃən/ n. 翻译，译文
49. idiom /ˈidiəm/ n. 成语，习语，土语
50. aware /əˈwɛə(r)/ a. 知道的，明白的，意识到的
51. mission /ˈmiʃən/ n. 使命，任务；代表团，使团
52. effectively /iˈfektivli/ ad. 有效地，有力地

Proper Names

1. New Zealand /njuːˈziːlənd/ n. 新西兰
2. Canada /ˈkænədə/ n. 加拿大

3. Nigeria /naiˈdʒiəriə/ n. 尼日利亚
4. Singapore /ˈsiŋəpɔː(r)/ n. 新加坡
5. the Philippines /filipiːnz/ n. 菲律宾；菲律宾群岛
6. Spanish /ˈspæniʃ/ n. & a. 西班牙语，西班牙(的)
7. Caribbean /kæriˈbiːən/ n. & a. 加勒比海(的)
8. South Africa 南非
9. Pakistan /pɑːkiˈstɑːn/ n. 巴基斯坦
10. the United Nations 联合国

Idioms and Expressions

1. one's native language 母语，本族语
2. in accordance with 根据，按照；与……一致
3. mother tongue 母语
4. along with 与……一起
5. get in touch with 与……接触
6. call for help 求救
7. from the corners of the earth 来自世界各地
8. have a good command of 精通，掌握
9. get on (well) with... 在……进行得(很)顺利
10. build...into 把……建成
11. turn...into 使……变为
12. as soon as possible 尽快
13. get...right 把……做对
14. lay a solid foundation of 在……打下坚实基础
15. take...for granted 认为……是理所当然的
16. catch...out 发现(某人的)错误
17. be on one's guard against 提防，谨防
18. word for word 字对字地，逐字地
19. be aware of 对……清楚/了解
20. be (fully) prepared for 为……做好(充分)准备

Word Derivation

1. importance—important—importantly
2. effect—effective—effectively
3. economy—economic—economically

4. idiom—idiomatic—idiomatically
5. science—scientific—scientifically
6. culture—cultural—culturally
7. globe—global—globalize—globalization
8. nation—national—international—internationalize—internationalization
9. operate—operation—cooperation
10. educate—education—educational—educationally

Notes to the Text

❶ The importance of a language can be judged in accordance with three aspects: the first is the number of its native speakers; the second is how widely the native speakers are spread over the world; the last is the cultural, economic and political influences of the people who speak it as their mother tongue. 一门语言的重要性可以根据三个方面进行判断：第一，将这门语言作为母语的人数；第二，将这门语言作为母语的人在世界的分布情况；最后，将这门语言作为母语的人的文化、经济和政治的影响。

句中，作者分别用 the first...; the second...; the last... 按照顺序分别叙述语言的重要性，条理清楚，一目了然。

❷ It is said that about 60 percent of the world's radio and TV programs are broadcasted in English and that 70 percent of the world's mails are written in English. 据说世界上大约百分之六十的无线电节目和电视节目是使用英语广播的，世界上百分之七十的信件是用英语写的。

句中，先行词 it 为形式主语，用 and 连接的两个 that 引导的名词从句为实际主语。60 percent 和 70 percent 是百分数，分别为百分之六十和百分之七十。

❸ Without English, it seems difficult to get in touch with the outside world. 没有英语，要和外界联系似乎很困难。

句中，先行词 it 为形式主语，实际主语是不定式 to get in touch with the outside world。

❹ It is quite a long time since I began to learn English. 自从我开始学习英语以来，已有很长时间了。

句中，began 为瞬间动词，不可接表示时间延续的状语，因此该句不可以用下面的句式表达：

I began to learn English for quite a long time. (×) 又如：

It has been three years since he joined the army. 他入伍已经三年了。

He has joined the army for three years. (×)

❺ When I began to learn English, I took it for granted that English words had exact equivalents in Chinese. 当我开始学英语时，我想当然地认为英语有和中文确切相对应的词汇。

句中，先行词 it 为形式宾语，实际宾语为 that 所引导的名词从句。

❻ Only through practice can I have a good command of English. 只有通过实践，我才能掌握英语。

副词 Only 放在句首强调状语时，句子中的主谓结构要用倒装语序。如：

Only after the bird flu spread did people know how dangerous it was. 只是在禽流感扩散后，人们才知道它有多么危险。

Exercises for Reading Comprehension

I. Answer the following questions.

1. How many languages are there in the world?
2. How can you judge the importance of a language?
3. English is one of the world's most widely used languages, isn't it?
4. Where is English spoken as a native language?
5. As a second language, English is spoken in many countries, isn't it? Can you give some examples?
6. How many working languages does the United Nations have? What are they?
7. Which working language is more frequently used than the others?
8. English has become the language of international transport, hasn't it?
9. Is it possible or impossible to have an international exchange and cooperation without English?
10. Do you think it important to study English? Why?
11. How long is it since you began to learn English?
12. Why must we have a good command of English?
13. What do the teachers require you to do in everything you do?
14. What have you learned from the study of past years?
15. Do you think one can learn a foreign language well only by memorizing individual words and grammar rules?
16. Are you interested in English idioms?
17. What's the difference between "join" and "take part in"? Can you give some examples?
18. Do you translate everything into Chinese while you are learning English?
19. Do you find English easy or difficult to learn?
20. Are you fully prepared for more hard work? Why?

II. Find the meaning of the words or expressions in Column (A) from those in Column (B).

(A)
1. memorize
2. contact
3. watch out for
4. absorb
5. one's native language
6. promote
7. in accordance with
8. from the corner of the earth
9. doubt
10. frequently

(B)
A. be not certain of
B. often, from time to time
C. get in touch with
D. from all parts of the world
E. help in the growth of
F. learn... by heart
G. take in or understand
H. pay close attention to
I. according to
J. one's mother tongue

III. Complete the following chart. If you are not sure, please consult a dictionary.

Country	Adjective	Person
Australia	Australian	an Australian
	American	
		a British man
	Canadian	
China		
	English	
		a Frenchman
India		
New Zealand		
Nigeria		
		a Pakistani
	Russian	
		a Singaporean
South Africa		
		a Spaniard

IV. Complete the sentences with the given expressions, and change the forms where necessary.

> along with   as soon as possible   build...into   call for help
> get on with   in accordance with   one's native language
> lay a solid foundation of   take...for granted   watch out for

1. Over 90 percent information is spread through Internet _____ statistics.
2. Michael was born in France, and French is _____.
3. The President of the United States, _____ some officials, is going to visit Japan next week.
4. He spent a lot of time in learning mathematics and _____ this subject.
5. The Chinese people are working hard so as to _____ their motherland _____ a strong and prosperous country.
6. If you want to have a good command of English, you must _____ its idiomatic usage.
7. Don't _____ it _____ that someone will help you when you are in need of help.
8. The ship _____ by radio before it sank.
9. How are you _____ your subjects?
10. He decided to study English hard and catch up with his classmates _____.

V. Complete the following passage by using appropriate words listed below. Be sure to use singular or plural forms for nouns, and appropriate forms for verbs.

> attention   correctly   effectively   exchange   grammar
> individual   language   memorize   native   thousand

What Is Language Study For?

Language study, it seems to some people, is for __(1)__ grammar rules and __(2)__ words. That's wrong. Language study, in my opinion, is for the __(3)__ of ideas, that is to say, for communication. Many students I have taught know hundreds of grammar rules and __(4)__ of English words, but they can't speak English correctly, that is, they can't use English __(5)__. They are afraid of making mistakes. We native speakers make mistakes and break __(6)__ rules, too. A famous English writer, Bernard Shaw wrote, "Foreigners often speak English too __(7)__." But the mistakes that native speakers make are different from those that Chinese students make. They are English mistakes in the English language. And if enough __(8)__ break a rule, it is no longer a rule. What used to be wrong becomes right. The people not only make history; they make __(9)__ as well. But they can only make their own language. They can't make another people's language. Therefore Chinese students of English should pay __(10)__ to grammar, but they should put communication first.

Language Structure

Words and Sentences（词和句子）

I. The Parts of Speech（词类）

序号	词类	缩写	例词
1	Noun（名词）	n.	mail, pilot, people, team, paper, glass, science
2	Pronoun（代词）	pron.	I, me, my, mine, myself, this, something, who, what
3	Verb（动词）	v.	memorize, spread, lie, lay, seem, do, can
4	Adjective（形容词）	a.	cultural, economic, individual, irregular, impossible
5	Adverb（副词）	ad.	frequently, effectively, perhaps, very, there, now, how, when, however, therefore, otherwise
6	Numeral（数词）	num.	one, ten, hundred, thousand, million, first, tenth
7	Article（冠词）	art.	a, an, the
8	Preposition（介词）	prep.	at, by, in, on, from, besides, except, through, throughout
9	Conjunction（连词）	conj.	because, as, and, nor, neither, but, or, so, for, whether
10	Interjection（感叹词）	Interj.	hello, oh, alas

词类是根据词义、句法作用和形式特征来划分的，前六种为实词（Notional Words），在句子中能独立担任成分；后四种为虚词（Form Words），不能在句子中独立担任成分。

同一个词在不同场合下可用作不同词类。如：

English seems to be the most important to those who speak it as their **native** language. (Adjective)

英语对那些作为母语的人来说似乎是最重要的。

Columbus called the local **natives** "Indians." (Noun)

哥伦布把当地的土著叫做印第安人。

There is no ***doubt*** that English is one of the world's most widely used languages. (Noun)
毫无疑问，英语是世界上使用最广的语言之一。

Some students ***doubt*** whether they can learn English well. (Verb)
有些学生怀疑自己是否能学好英语。

Without English, it is difficult to get in touch with the people of the ***outside*** world. (Adjective)
不懂英语，就难以与外界的人接触。

It is snowing hard, and it is terribly cold ***outside***. (Adverb)
雪下得很大，外面很冷。

II. The Members of a Sentence （句子成分）

句子由各个功能不同的部分构成，这些部分叫做句子成分。它们主要有七种：主语（Subject）、谓语（Predicate）、补语（Complement）、宾语（Object）、同位语（Appositive）、定语（Attribute）和状语（Adverbial）。

❶ 名词可以充当主语、宾语、补语、同位语等句子成分。如：

English is the language of international transport. (Subject)
英语是国际交通的语言。

I have learned the ***difference*** between "join" and "take part in." (Object)
我知道了如何区分"join"与"take part in"。

Edward is a ***freshman*** of our college. (Subject Complement)
爱德华是我们学院一年级新生。

Hard work has made Richard a top ***student***. (Object Complement)
勤奋好学使里查德成为一名优等生。

Ms. Green, an English ***professor***, will give us a talk on how to improve English. (Appositive)
一位英语教授格林女士将给我们作一个如何提高英语水平的讲座。

❷ 代词可以充当主语、宾语、补语、定语等句子成分。如：

I know English is one of the world's most widely used languages. (Subject)
我知道英语是世界上使用最广的语言之一。

The study of the past years has taught ***me*** that we cannot learn English well if we don't watch out for its idiomatic usage. (Object)
过去几年的学习经历告诉我如果我们不注意英语的习惯用法就不能学好英语。

That disk is ***yours***, and this one is ***mine***. (Subject Complement)
那个光盘是你的，而这个是我的。

I'm afraid that ***my*** English is not good enough to deal with the work. (Attribute)
恐怕我的英语程度还不足以处理这项工作。

❸ 动词可以充当谓语等句子成分。如：

The importance of a language ***can be judged*** in accordance with several aspects. (Predicate)

一门语言的重要性可以根据几个方面进行判断。

English ***has become*** the language of international exchange and cooperation. (Predicate)
英语已成为国际交流和合作的语言。

❹ 形容词可以充当定语、补语等句子成分。如：

Teachers have always required us to lay a ***solid*** foundation of everything we do. (Attribute)
老师总是要求我们对所做的一切打下坚实的基础。

I found English quite ***difficult*** to learn. (Object Compliment)
我发现英语学起来相当困难。

❺ 副词可以充当状语、补语，间或也可作定语。如：

English is the language ***most commonly*** used and ***most widely*** understood. (Adverbial)
英语是人们使用最普遍，接受最广泛的语言。

I'm afraid Mr. Smith is ***away*** at the moment. (Subject Compliment)
恐怕史密斯先生此刻不在。

The problem ***now*** is not why I should learn English but how I can master English as soon as possible. (Attribute)
现在的问题不是我为什么要学习英语，而是我怎样才能尽快地掌握英语。

The teachers ***here*** are very kind to us. (Attribute)
这里的老师对我们很亲切。

❻ 数词可以充当主语、宾语、补语、定语等句子成分。如：

The first is the number of the native speakers of the language. (Subject)
第一是使用这门语言作为本族语的人数。

How many do you want? I want ***four***. (Object)

Six and nine are ***fifteen***. (Subject Complement)

English is spoken as a native language by over ***three hundred million*** people. (Attribute)
以英语作为母语的有3亿多人。

III. The Basic Sentence Patterns（基本句型）

英语的基本句型主要有七种结构：

❶ 主——谓——补 （S—V—C）

English is the language of the information age.
英语是信息时代的语言。

❷ 主——谓 （S—V）

The new term begins.
新的学期开始了。

❸ 主——谓——状 （S—V—A）

Mr. Johnson works here.
约翰逊先生在此地工作。

❹ 主——谓——宾 （S—V—O）

He can speak a little French.
他会说一点法语。

❺ 主——谓——间宾——直宾 (S—V—O—O)
The teacher has given us some advice.
老师给我们提了一些建议。

❻ 主——谓——宾——补 (S—V—O—C)
I found English very interesting.
我发现英语很有趣。

❼ 主——谓——宾——状 (S—V—O—A)
He put his shoes upstairs.
他把鞋子放在楼上了。

[注] There be + 主 + （其它成分）这种句型实际上是第二种句型的变体，其中there 是引导词，be是谓语，主语一般是名词或名词词组，其它成分一般是状语或定语。

There are thousands of languages in the world.
世界上有数以千计的语言。
There is much work for us to do.
有很多工作要我们去做。

IV. The Types of Sentences（句子的类型）

根据句子包含的主谓结构，我们可以把句子分为简单句，并列句和复合句。

❶ 简单句 (Simple Sentences)

句子只含有一个主谓结构，而句子的各个成分都由单词或短语表示。如：

As a college student in the new century, I'm fully aware of my mission.
作为新世纪的大学生，我非常清楚自己的使命。

People use a language for one of the three ways: as a native language, as a second language or as a foreign language.
人们由于三种方式中的某种方式而使用一门语言：作为母语，作为第二语言，或者作为外语。

❷ 并列句 (Compound Sentences)

句子含有两个或更多互不依从的主谓结构，并列句的分句通常用分号或并列连词如 and（便是顺连），but（表示转折），or（表示选择），for，so（表示因果)等连接。如：

I have learned to say to join the army but to take part in a discussion; I have learned to express to go to school by bus but on foot.
我学会了说参军入伍和参加讨论，我学会了表达乘车上学和步行上学。

According to the statistics, over 90 percent of information is spread through Internet in English, *and* more than 80 percent of e-mails are sent to each other in English throughout the world.
据统计，全世界90%以上的信息是通过因特网用英语传播的，80%以上的电子邮件是用英语互相发送的。

English is very useful, ***but*** it is quite difficult to learn.
英语用途很大，但学起来可不容易。
I'm fully prepared for more hard work, ***or*** I would fall behind.
我已经为更艰巨的工作做好了充分准备，否则我就会掉队。
There is still a long, long way to go, ***so*** I must learn more and practice more.
路漫漫其修远兮，因此我必须多学习，勤实践。

[注] 并列句的分句也可用与并列连词意思相近的连接副词如 however, nevertheless, thus, hence, therefore, otherwise 或短语如 on the contrary, or else, as a result, in this way 等连接，但副词前一般要用分号，或加连词 and。如：

I have made a little progress in English study, ***and however*** this is just a beginning.
我虽然取得了一些进步，但这仅仅是开始。

With the economic globalization and educational internationalization, English is getting more and more important; ***therefore*** we must study hard and try to have a good command of English.
随着经济全球化和教育国际化，英语变得越来越重要，因此我们要努力学习并设法精通英语。

We can use English as a medium to promote friendship between Chinese people and the people of the world, and in this way we can turn the earth into a peaceful globe.
我们可以用英语作为媒介来增进中国人民和世界人民的友谊，这样我们就可以使地球成为一个祥和的星球。

❸ 复合句 (Complex Sentences)

复合句中包含两个或更多的主谓结构，其中某个(或更多的)主谓结构充当句子的某一(些)成分，如主语、宾语、补语、同位语、定语或状语。如：

Therefore ***what I had to do*** was to memorize individual words and put them together according to the rules of grammar if I wanted to express my idea correctly. (Subject Clause)
因此如果我想要正确地表达思想，我必须做的就是记忆单独的词语并根据语法规则把它们拼凑到一块。

I know ***that English is very important to us***. (Object Clause)
我知道英语对我们来说非常重要。

The second is ***how widely the native speakers are spread over the world***. (Complementary Clause)
其次是讲母语的人在世界上分布的广泛性。

There is no doubt ***that English is one of the world's most widely used languages***. (Appositive Clause)
毫无疑问英语是世界上使用最广泛的语言之一。

Each language seems to be the most important to those ***who speak it as their native language***. (Attributive Clause)
每门语言对于将其作为母语的人来说都是最重要的。

I did not realize that we do not "see" but "read" a book ***until one day the teacher***

caught me out. (Adverbial Clause)

直到有一天老师指出我的错误后，我才知道我们不是"see a book"而是"read a book"。

 Exercises for Language Structure

I. Check the following sentences according to the basic sentence patterns and correct the mistakes in them.

1. The hall large enough to hold one hundred people.
2. I like this American novel. Could I borrow?
3. He works.
4. She put the book.
5. The engineer last year invented a new device.

II. Rearrange each group of word into a simple sentence.

1. know the answer, both...and, Jane, Mary
2. read the book, seen the film, most of the people, either...or, have
3. should, English, computer science, not only...but also, we, master
4. the young girl, a poet, a singer, is, not...but
5. difficulties, failure, our steps, stop, can, neither...nor, forward

III. Rearrange each group of words into a compound sentence.

1. Mr. Smith, an engineer, in the workshop, and, is checking, is, he, the machine
2. the meal, the guests, but, already, yet, here, have come, ready, is, not
3. the goods, we, are, so, and, reasonable in price, shall place, a large order
4. otherwise, you, hurry up, will miss, the chance
5. for, for, of, us, English, to master, it, it, the language, necessary, the information age, is, is

IV. Rearrange each group of words into a complex sentence.

1. if, catch up with, will, he, he, hard, studies, his classmates
2. that, my suggestion, be carried out, at once, this plan, is
3. whether, they, they, are faced with, should continue, the problem, the work
4. that, it, he, English words, took, in Chinese, for granted, have equivalents
5. so that, Mary, the girl, she, talked to, alone, might not feel

Practice and Improvement

Reading Skills

Go through the following passages quickly, and after that, take note of the time, do the exercises, check the answers to the exercises and calculate words per minute.

Speed Reading A

Notes: Before reading the passage, try to get familiar with the following words and expressions.

1. vocabulary /vəˈkæbjuləri/ n. 词汇(量)
2. stunt /stʌnt/ v. & n. 阻碍，妨碍
3. paragraph /ˈpærəgrɑːf/ n. 段落
4. topic /ˈtɔpik/ n. 主题，话题
5. dim-witted /ˈdim-ˈwitid/ a. 笨的，傻的
6. electronic /ilekˈtrɔnik/ a. 电子的
7. reliable /riˈlaiəbl/ a. 可靠的，可信赖的
8. false /fɔːls/ a. 错误的，假的，虚伪的
9. explanatory /iksˈplænətəri/ a. 说明的，解释的
10. imaginable /iˈmædʒinəbl/ a. 可想像的，可能的
11. reward /riˈwɔːd/ v. 报答，酬劳 n. 奖金，报酬
12. definition /defiˈniʃən/ n. 定义，解说
13. isolation /aisəˈleiʃən/ n. 隔绝，孤立
14. context /ˈkɔntekst/ n. 上下文，文章的前后关系
15. likely /ˈlaikli/ a. & ad. 很可能(的)，有希望(的)
16. no wonder   难怪，不足为怪
17. look up   查词
18. hang around   聚在附近
19. come across   偶遇，偶然碰到
20. fit into   装进，放进……合适之处
21. feel at home   如在家中；没有拘束

Building Vocabulary as You Study

A poor vocabulary stunts your growth in several aspects. You miss the points of whole paragraphs, or sometimes even of lectures, because the topic sentence has a key word whose meaning you don't know or misunderstand. There are many different meanings that you can't express in your speech or writing because you don't have the necessary words. And worst of all, you decide you are dim-witted because you can't understand so many written and spoken ideas. However, you can really grasp those ideas easily if you know enough words.

So what do you do? The best advice is to use the dictionary. If you're using your dictionary just to finish the rest of your books, no wonder you have vocabulary problems. You should be using it to look up unfamiliar words as you read. Use the college dictionary on your desk and put an electronic dictionary in your pocket. Look up words actively and seriously. Of course, to find words to look up, you either have to read or hang around with people who have big vocabularies. Try both.

To get reliable help from your dictionary, you should first learn how to use it. For some reason, many people have false ideas of dictionaries. For example, they believe that the first meaning that is listed for a word is the "best" one. This is not true. The first meaning will often be the oldest meaning, so it could be the least common one. Therefore it is necessary to force yourself to read the explanatory notes at the beginning. It's not a lively reading imaginable, but it can be rewarding.

How do you learn words effectively? It is proved that it's better to learn words by coming across them and looking them up than by learning from a list with definitions. Vocabulary lists give you words in isolation, and that makes them hard to remember correctly. A word you find in a sentence within the context of a paragraph is more likely to fit into your head in the right place.

Once the meaning of a word has found a place in your mind, you need to make it feel at home by using the word. If you use it and people look at you with funny expression or put question marks in your writing, you know you haven't quite got it down. Look it up again, and use it again, and in this way, you will keep it in memory and can use it freely.

(418 words)

Time：_____

Comprehension

I. Choose the best answer according to the passage.

1. A poor vocabulary _____ your growth in several aspects.
   A. misses   B. helps   C. stops   D. makes
2. You may decide that you're _____ because you can't understand so many written and spoken ideas.
   A. clever   B. smart   C. intelligent   D. silly
3. If you want to find words to look up, the best way is _____.
   A. to look up words actively and seriously
   B. to use the college dictionary on your desk
   C. to put an electronic dictionary in your pocket
   D. to read or stay near people who have large vocabularies
4. If you want to learn words effectively, you had better _____.
   A. learn them from a list with definitions
   B. learn them by meeting them and looking them up
   C. learn them only by coming across them
   D. learn them only from your textbook
5. When the meaning of a word has fitted into your head in the right place, _____.
   A. you know that you haven't quite got it down
   B. you need to look it up again
   C. you could use it freely
   D. you should use it again and again

II. True or False:

( ) 6. If you don't know the key word in a topic sentence, you may miss or misunderstand the meaning of the paragraph.
( ) 7. When you have vocabulary problems, you can use your dictionary.
( ) 8. The writer says that it is very interesting to read the explanatory notes of dictionaries.
( ) 9. It is easier to remember new words correctly from vocabulary lists.
( )10. People who have big vocabularies may get along well with their studies.

Correct rate: _____ %
Reading speed: _____ wpm

Speed Reading B

Notes: Before reading the passage, try to get familiar with the following words and expressions.

1. **ideal** /aiˈdiəl/ n. & a. 理想(的)
2. **directly** /diˈrektli/ ad. 直接地；立即
3. **rely** /riˈlai/ v. 依靠，倚赖；信任
4. **audio-visual** /ˈɔːdiouˈviʒuːəl/ a. 视听的
5. **aid** /eid/ n. & v. 帮助，辅助
6. **CD = compact disc** /kəmˈpækt disk/ n. 光盘
7. **walkman** /ˈwɔːkmən/ n. 随身听
8. **ability** /əˈbiliti/ n. 能力，才干
9. **retell** /riːˈtel/ v. 复述，重讲
10. **dumb** /dʌm/ a. 哑的，无说话能力的
11. **mute** /mjuːt/ a. 哑的，无声的 n. 哑巴
12. **imitate** /ˈimiteit/ v. 模仿，仿效
13. **intonation** /intouˈneiʃən/ n. 语调，声调
14. **environment** /inˈvairənmənt/ n. 环境
15. **perseverance** /pəːsiˈviərəns/ n. 坚持
16. **rely on** 依靠，依赖
17. **pick up** 学会（语言）；捡起；加速；挑选
18. **insist on** 坚持

Learn to Speak Good English

How can we learn to speak good English? The ideal thing should be of course to live among the native speakers and learn directly from them. As this is impossible for most of us, a practical way is to learn to speak by relying on audio-visual aids, such as tapes, CDs, films and TV programs. If you have a radio, a walkman or a computer, it will be quite possible for you to learn to speak good English even without the help of a teacher. Of course you must have the right material and correct methods.

What is the best method to develop one's speaking ability? I think the best method is to listen to good English, that is, English which is spoken by native speakers and repeat after the speakers until you can retell the whole thing. This is in fact how the most people learn to speak. A child learns to speak by listening to its parents or nurse. A deaf child will certainly be dumb or mute. If you don't listen to good English, you will never be able to speak it. That is quite clear. But listening alone isn't enough. You have to listen to a piece of material again and again and try to imitate the native speaker's pronunciation and intonation, and if possible, try to retell it. A child picks up a language easily. That's because he lives in an environment where the language is spoken. But we are not living in an English-speaking environment and have no chance to hear a word or an expression repeated hundreds of times and our memories can't compare with that of a child. We can't expect to learn very fast unless we work very hard. Therefore we must have perseverance, listen to something with attention and try to retell what we have heard. If one can insist on doing this, he will finally be able to speak good English.

(326 words)

Time：_____

Comprehension

I. Choose the best answer according to the message.

1. Since it is impossible for most of us to live among native speakers and learn directly from them, a practical way is to learn to speak _____.
   A. from your teachers   B. from good books
   C. by relying on audio-visual aids   D. by imitating our parents

2. Most people in our country learn to speak English by _____.
   A. reading stories
   B. retelling stories
   C. listening to native speakers directly
   D. listening and repeating good English material

3. A child learns his mother tongue easily because _____.
   A. he works very hard   B. he listens to something with attention
   C. he lives in the language environment   D. he is very clever

4. We can't expect to learn fast _____ we don't study hard.
   A. unless   B. if   C. as   D. because

5. If we can insist on practicing spoken English, we will be able to speak good English _____.
   A. at the end   B. in the end   C. on time   D. in no time

II. True or False：

( ) 6. Most of us can learn to speak good English by imitating native speakers directly.

( ) 7. The writer says that we can't learn to speak good English if we don't live among native speakers.

( ) 8. In this passage, "good English" means English that is spoken by our teachers.

( ) 9. We can learn to speak good English by listening alone.

( )10. The writer says that perseverance is needed in learning to speak good English.

Correct rate _____ %
Reading speed _____ wpm

Cloze Procedure

A Letter to Your Middle School English Teacher

September 20, 2003

Dear Ms.Wang,

I'm very glad to receive your letter of August 28, from which I learned that you have been to Beijing for a meeting and have returned home __(1)__ . I'm sorry I haven't written to you for quite a long time, __(2)__ we have been busy with military training（军训）.

First I'd like to express my heartfelt thanks to you. I'll never forget your instructions(教导). You always require us to __(3)__ a solid foundation of everything we do. You are really my good teacher and helpful friend. Under your guidance, I have made __(4)__ great progress in my studies and now I become a college student.

The English teacher here is kind and patient with me. From his lecture, I learned that English is the language of the information age and it is very important to us, __(5)__ I am ashamed to say that I'm not good __(6)__ English. Sometimes a question seems very simple, but I can't do it correctly. I realize that I'm very weak at grammar because I paid little attention __(7)__ it in the past. Do you think it is necessary that I should do some grammar exercises?

As a college student in the new century, I am fully __(8)__ of my mission, that is, to build our motherland into a strong and prosperous country, and __(9)__ I'm fully prepared for more hard work. Just as a proverb goes, "Where there is a will, there is a way." I think ___(10)___ I study hard and practice more, I will soon catch up with my classmates and have a good command of English.

I know you are busy with your work, so don't trouble to answer this letter. Please give my best wishes to other teachers.

I'm looking forward to seeing you soon.

Yours sincerely
Zhang Hua

Notes:

1. military /ˈmilitəri/ a. 军事的
2. instruction /inˈstrʌkʃən/ n. 教育，指示
3. guidance /ˈɡaidəns/ n. 指导，教导
4. look forward to 盼望，期望

Fill in the blanks with the best answer:

1. A. safe   B. safely   C. safety   D. unsafe
2. A. and   B. but   C. for   D. or
3. A. lie   B. lay   C. lain   D. laid
4. A. few   B. a few   C. little   D. a little
5. A. but   B. however   C. so   D. therefore
6. A. in   B. on   C. at   D. for
7. A. at   B. in   C. for   D. to
8. A. know   B. understand   C. aware   D. realize
9. A. however   B. otherwise   C. so   D. therefore
10. A. if   B. unless   C. though   D. because

Speaking Skills

I. **Warm-up Exercise:** *Read the poem aloud.*

Reading

O for a book and shady nook   持书隐蔽之处，
Either indoor or out,   无论室内户外，

With the green leaves over my head
    Or the street cries all about,
Where I may read all at my ease
    Both the new and old,
For a jolly good book whereon to look
    Is better to me than gold.

绿叶轻拂头顶,
还是闹市喧街,
我可安闲读书,
知识融古通今,
好书一本在手,
胜过万两黄金。

II. Conversation

Practice the dialogue, and then write a dialogue under the title "Greeting a Person You Know Well" or "Introducing a Friend to Your Classmate" and practice it with your partner.

Dialogue 1

Wang Hong is a sophomore, and she meets her former schoolmate, Zhang Hua, a freshman at the school gate.

Wang Hong: Hello. Is that you, Zhang Hua?

Zhang Hua: Oh, hello, Wang Hong, this is a pleasant surprise. I didn't expect to meet you here.

Wang Hong: It's very nice to meet you here. Congratulations on your entrance into this college.

Zhang Hua: Thank you. Well, it's nice to see you again. You do look well.

Wang Hong: Oh, I'm fine, thank you. How are you getting along recently?

Zhang Hua: Very well indeed. And from now on we shall live and study together.

Wang Hong: Let's help each other and care for each other. Oh, you must be feeling tired after a long journey. Let me take you to the students' apartment and have a rest.

Zhang Hua: Thank you very much.

Wang Hong: Let's go.

Dialogue 2

On their way to the students' apartment, they meet Mr. James Bradley, Wang Hong's English teacher. He comes from Canada.

Wang Hong: Zhang Hua, I'd like you to meet Mr. Bradley.

Zhang Hua: Oh, yes.

Wang Hong: Good morning, Mr. Bradley.

Mr. Bradley: Good morning.

Wang Hong: Mr. Bradley, may I introduce Zhang Hua to you? He is my former schoolmate, but now he is a freshman of this college.

Mr. Bradley: It's nice to see you here.

Wang Hong: This is Mr. Bradley, my English teacher, and he is from Canada.

Zhang Hua: I'm delighted to see you, too.
Mr. Bradley: What are you going to study here, Zhang Hua?
Zhang Hua: Oh, I'm going to major in International Trade.
Mr. Bradley: Nice to have met you. Good-bye.
Wang and Zhang: Nice to have met you, too. See you later.

Notes:

1. sophomore /ˈsɔfəmɔː(r)/ n. 大学二年级生
2. freshman /ˈfreʃmən/ n. 新生，大学一年级生
3. congratulation /kənˌgrætjuˈleiʃən/ n. 祝贺，恭喜
4. entrance /ˈentrəns/ n. 进入；入口
5. apartment /əˈpɑːtmənt/ n. 公寓，单元住宅
6. former /ˈfɔːmə(r)/ a. 以前的，从前的
7. major in 主修，专攻

Listening Skills

I. **Directions**: *Listen to the following sentences. Tick the right words the speaker says.*

1. A. fair B. fare
2. A. their B. there
3. A. right B. write
4. A. hear B. here
5. A. red B. read
6. A. mail B. male
7. A. alone B. along
8. A. words B. world's
9. A. wrong B. long
10. A. food B. foot

II. **Directions**: *In this section, you will hear 10 short conversations. At the end of each conversation, a question will be asked about what was said. The conversation and question will be spoken only one time. After each question, there will be a pause. During the pause, you must read the four choices marked A, B, C and D, and decide which the best answer is, and then choose the corresponding letter.*

1. A. Britain. B. Japan. C. China. D. America.
2. A. Six. B. Thirteen. C. Fourteen. D. Sixteen.
3. A. Two. B. Three. C. Four. D. Five.

4. A. She likes it.　　B. It's too hot.　　C. It's too cold.　　D. She dislikes it.
5. A. 13 dollars.　　B. 30 dollars.　　C. 20 dollars.　　D. 21 dollars.
6. A. The woman has no dictionary.
   B. The woman is using her dictionary.
   C. The woman can get one from her desk.
   D. the woman can't use her dictionary.
7. A. 7:30.　　B. 7:20.　　C. 6:45.　　D. 7:00.
8. A. In his bag.　　B. In his office.　　C. He has no radio.　　D. At his home.
9. A. At the bank.　　　　　　　　　B. In the shop.
   C. At the post office.　　　　　　D. At the railway station.
10. A. Drink.　　B. Meal.　　C. Weather.　　D. Fruit.

III. Directions: *In this section, you will hear a passage of about 90 words three times. There are about 20 words missing. First, you will hear the whole passage from the beginning to the end just to get a general idea about it. Then, in the second reading, write down the missing words during the pauses. You can check what you have written when the passage is read to you once again without the pauses.*

How can we learn __(1)__ good English? The ideal thing should be __(2)__ to live among __(3)__ and learn directly from them. As this is impossible for most of us, __(4)__ is to learn to speak by relying __(5)__, such as tapes, CDs, films and __(6)__. If you have a radio, a walkman or __(7)__, it will be quite possible for you to learn to speak good English even __(8)__ the help of a teacher. Of course you must have the __(9)__ and __(10)__.

Translation Skills

I. Translate the following into English.
1. 精通英语对我们来说很有必要。（to have a good command of）
2. 作为新世纪的大学生，我非常清楚自己的使命。（to be fully aware of）
3. 我们要学习先进的科学技术，把中国建成一个繁荣昌盛的国家。（to build...into）
4. 我们要注意英语的习惯用法。（to watch out for）
5. 正如一句谚语所说："熟能生巧"。（just as）

II. Translate the following into Chinese.
1. He has a good memory, and he can memorize quite a lot of English idioms.
2. Perhaps it is possible for you to master English in the shortest possible time, but it is impossible for me to do so.
3. The people of the world are our friends, so we'll promote the friendship between the Chinese people and the people of the world.

4. You must pay attention to the difference between regular verbs and irregular verbs, or you will make mistakes.

5. His pronunciation was correct; he spelt the new word correctly.

Writing Skills

I. Join each pair of the sentences according to the model.

Model A: *I have made a little progress in English study. This is just a beginning.*
   I have made a little progress in English study, but this is just a beginning.
   I have made a little progress in English study; however, this is just a beginning.
   I have made a little progress in English study, and however, this is just a beginning.

1. I find English is very interesting. I'm not good at it.
2. He knows a little French. He can't read newspapers in French.
3. I have made a little progress in my English study. There is still a long, long way to go.
4. We love peace. We are not afraid of war.
5. I paid attention to English grammar. I didn't pay attention to its idiomatic usage.

Model B: *There is still a long, long way to go. I must learn more and practice more.*
   There is still a long, long way to go, so I must learn more and practice more.
   There is still a long, long way to go; therefore I must learn more and practice more.
   There is still a long, long way to go, and therefore I must learn more and practice more.

1. We can't expect to learn English very fast. We must have perseverance.
2. I know you are busy with your work. It is not necessary to answer my letter.
3. He insisted on learning English for five years. He had a good command of it.
4. He often imitates the pronunciation and intonation of native speakers. He can speak good English.
5. English is difficult to learn. I'm fully prepared for more hard work.

II. Practical Writing

启事（Notice）是一种公告性的应用文，要求行文简洁扼要，为机关或个人向群众说明某事，或要求群众做某事的一种公告。启事常贴在公告栏中或公共场所。涉及范围较广或内容紧要的启事往往刊登在报刊上。

1. 招领启事

```
        FOUND
```

FOUND

September 20, 2004

  I happened to find a briefcase in my taxi, inside of which there is a credit card and some other things. Loser is expected to come to our taxi company to claim it.

Finder,
James Brown
Safety Taxi Company
168 Seaside Street, Liverpool

2. 遗失启事

```
        LOST
```

LOST

September 10, 2004

  I was careless and lost a ring of keys in the reading room of the library yesterday evening. Will the finder please send it to the International Trade Department office or call me up to fetch it back.

Profound thanks from

Loser,
Zhang Hua

Address: Room 216, Students' Apartment 4
Tel. No. 5566216

Notes:

1. **notice** /ˈnoutis/ n. 启事，通知，布告　v. 注意到
2. **briefcase** /ˈbriːfkeis/ n. 公文包
3. **credit** /ˈkredit/ n. 信用，信誉；荣誉，赞扬；学分　v. 记入贷方
4. **profound** /prəˈfaund/ a. 深刻地，渊博的
5. **Lost and Found** 拾物招领处

Exercise

Write a Found Notice and a Lost Notice according to the materials given. You can model your writing on the above samples.

按照上面的格式分别写一张招领启事和遗失启事：

1. 招领启事

招领启事

本人在运动场拾得钱包一个，内有现金等物，希望失者前来我班教室认领。

拾物人　王　虹
国际贸易系二年级三班
2004年10月22日

2. 遗失启事

遗失启事

　　因本人不慎，昨天在公共汽车上遗失公文包一个。请拾者将公文包送到公共汽车公司拾物招领处（Lost and Found）或打电话通知本人取回。深表谢意。

遗失人　詹姆斯·弗兰克
2004年10月22日

地址：西街128号
电话号码：554780

A Proverb

That is a good book which is opened with expectation and ended with profit.

——L. M. Alcott

好书开卷引人入胜，终卷使人受益。

——阿尔考特

Unit Two

THE THINGS AROUND US

Reading Selection

Text A

PRE-READING TASK

1. Do you know what clouds are made of?
2. What is fog or mist?
3. How many colors is sunlight made of?

Clouds, Fog, Rain and Rainbows

When clouds float in front of the sun, they make shadows because they keep sunlight from shining on the ground beneath them. Though sometimes clouds look like cotton and sometimes they look like gray smoke, they are really made up of millions of tiny raindrops or bits of ice. They are such small and light drops that they float in the air just like little balloons. All these raindrops or ice drops that float in a bunch make a cloud. Even when the whole sky looks gray with these clouds, the sun is still there above the gray raindrops.

Sometimes the clouds are so low that they touch the ground, wrap them-

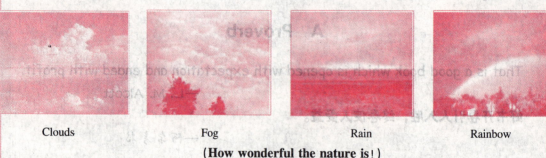

Clouds   Fog   Rain   Rainbow

(How wonderful the nature is!)

selves around the trees and float above the water. We call that fog, or mist.

Where the tiny drops of water that make clouds or fog are very close together, they join and make bigger drops. They are so heavy that they can't float in the air. As a result, they fall to the earth, and that is rain.

On sunny days the sky looks as blue as the sea. Sunlight is made of many colors and some of these colors are scattered through the air much better than others. On clear days you can see the blue color which shines from all over the sky.

Sometimes when the sun shines through millions of raindrops which hang in the air, we see all the colors of the sun's light—red, orange, yellow, green, blue, indigo and violet—in a beautiful arch across the sky. We call that a rainbow. Perhaps you have seen little rainbows when sunlight shines into your soap bubbles.

What a marvelous world we have! Since the world is full of wonderful things, we must keep our eyes open so that we may learn more things around us.

Text B

PRE-READING TASK

1. Do you know what snow is?
2. What's the difference between sleet and hail?
3. Why must we have more careful observation of things around us?

Snow, Sleet, Hail and Ice

In some parts of the world it always stays warm, but in other places winter is the time of cold and snow and frozen things.

There is always water in the air. When the air is very cold, snowflakes fall instead of rain. Millions and millions of snowflakes come down, and no two are exactly alike to each other.

Snow will not form unless the air is very cold. Nor will sleet, hail or ice. Sometimes the raindrops freeze after they have started to fall. If they freeze just a little bit, they are sleet. If they freeze into hard balls, we call that hail. Sometimes hailstones have snow in them, too.

Snow is frozen; hail and sleet are frozen, and so is just plain ice.

Have you ever touched a piece of ice? It is cold and hard and slippery.

If ice is very thin, you can see through it, just as you can see through glass. If it is thick, it is very firm and strong. Even though you skate on it, the ice will not break. But no matter how hard it is, it is made of water. As long as you put ice in a warm place, it will soon melt. And you can see that it is only frozen water.

How wonderful the things around us are! We must observe them carefully in order that we can take good advantage of nature.

Word List

1. rainbow /ˈreinbou/ n. 虹
2. float /flout/ v. 漂浮, 浮动; 飘扬
3. shadow /ˈʃædou/ n. 影子, 阴影; 阴暗
4. sunlight /ˈsʌnlait/ n. 日光, 阳光
5. beneath /biˈniːθ/ prep. 在……之下
6. gray /grei/ n. & a. 灰色（的）
7. fog [fɔg] n. 雾, 尘雾
8. mist /mist/ n. 薄雾
9. tiny /ˈtaini/ a. 极小的
10. raindrop /ˈreindrɔp/ n. 雨滴, 雨点
11. balloon /bəˈluːn/ n. 气球
12. bunch /bʌntʃ/ n. 捆, 束, 团
13. wrap /ræp/ v. 缠绕, 包裹, 遮蔽
14. result /riˈzʌlt/ n. 结果, 后果 v. 导致, 引起
15. scatter /ˈskætə/ v. 撒, 散布; 驱散
16. indigo /ˈindigou/ n. & a. 靛青色（的）
17. violet /ˈvaiəlit/ n. & a. 紫色（的）, 紫罗兰（色的）
18. arch /ɑːtʃ/ n. 弧, 拱; 拱状物
19. across /əˈkrɔs/ prep. 横过; 越过
20. soap /soup/ n. 肥皂

21. bubble /ˈbʌbl/ n. 水泡，泡沫
22. marvelous /ˈmɑːvələs/ a. 奇妙的
23. sleet /sliːt/ n. 雪雨，雨夹雪
24. hail /heil/ n. 冰雹 v. 向……欢呼
25. freeze (froze, frozen) /friːz/ v. (使)结冰；凝固，冻僵
26. snowflake /ˈsnəufleik/ n. 雪花，雪片
27. alike /əˈlaik/ a. 相似的，类似的
28. exactly /igˈzæktli/ ad. 准确地；正好
29. unless /ʌnˈles/ conj. 如果不，除非
30. hailstone /ˈheilstəun/ n. 冰雹块
31. plain /plein/ a. 普通的，平坦的 n. 平原，平地
32. slippery /ˈslipəri/ a. 滑的
33. firm /fəːm/ a. 坚固的；严格的 n. 商号，公司
34. melt /melt/ v. 融化，溶解
35. observe /əbˈzəːv/ v. 观察；遵守
36. advantage /ədˈvɑːntidʒ/ n. 益处

Idioms and Expressions

1. look like   看起来像……
2. be made of   由……组成，由……制成
3. millions of   数以百万计的，无数的
4. in a bunch   一团，一束
5. as a result   所以，因此
6. keep one's eyes open   睁大眼睛，注意观察
7. instead of   代替，而不是
8. be alike (to) 与……相似(类似)
9. see through   看穿，识破
10. take advantage of   利用

Word Derivation

1. sun—sunny—sunlight
2. rain—rainy—raindrop—rainbow
3. snow—snowy—snowflake—snowfall
4. ice—icy

5. cloud—cloudy
6. slip—slippery
7. hail—hailstone
8. like—alike—likely
9. exact—exactly
10. plain—plainly

Notes to the Text

❶ ... because they keep sunlight from shining on the ground beneath them. ……因为云彩遮住了阳光，使之不能照射到下面的大地。

句中 keep...from+动名词，意为"使……不"，"使免于"。如：

The heavy rain kept us from going out.

❷ All these raindrops or ice drops that float in a bunch make a cloud. 所有这些成团漂浮的雨滴或冰粒形成了云彩。

句中 that 是关系代词，引导定语从句。课文中类似的结构还有：

On clear days you can see the blue color which shines from all over the sky.

❸ In some parts of the world it always stays warm. 在世界某些地方，天气总是温暖的。

句中 stay 为联系动词，意为"保持"。如：

The weather stayed fine for three days.

❹ What a marvelous world we have! 我们拥有一个多么奇妙的世界！

句中 what 是感叹词，引出感叹句，并在句子中修饰名词。如：

What a colorful rainbow it is!

❺ Snow will not form unless the air is very cold. Nor will sleet, hail or ice. 如果空气不是很冷，雪就不会形成。雪雨、冰雹或冰块也不会形成。

用否定词 nor，neither 等开头的句子，一般要用倒装语序。如：

He is not wrong, and nor are you.

He has never seen the film before. Neither have I.

❻ Snow is frozen; hail and sleet are frozen, and so is just plain ice. 雪是凝固的水，冰雹和雪雨是凝固的水，普通的冰块也是凝固的水。

So 放在句首，代替上文中的形容词、名词或动词时，一般要用倒装语序。如：

My brother can swim, and so can my sister.

Clouds are made of millions of water drops. So are rainbows.

❼ But no matter how hard it is, it is water. 但不管冰有多硬，它总是水。

No matter +who，what，which，how，when 等连接代词或副词，可引导让步状语从句。如：

No matter what he said, we didn't trust his words.

No matter how difficult the task is, we'll finish it in time.

❽ How wonderful the things around us are! 我们周围的事物是多么奇妙！

句中 **how** 是感叹词，引出感叹句，并在句子中修饰形容词、副词或动词。如：

How seriously he studies!

How she loves her motherland!

Exercises for Reading Comprehension

I. Answer the following questions.

1. What do clouds make when they float in front of the sun?
2. Sometimes clouds look like cotton and sometimes they look like gray smoke, don't they?
3. What are clouds made of?
4. What's the difference between clouds and fog?
5. What do we call bigger drops of water when they fall to the earth?
6. When does the sky look as blue as the sea?
7. Sunlight is made of many colors, isn't it?
8. Have you seen little rainbows when sunlight shines into your soap bubbles?
9. How many colors is sunlight made of?
10. What should we do if we want to learn more things around us?
11. Where does it always stay warm?
12. Is there any water in the air?
13. When do snowflakes fall instead of rain?
14. The snowflakes are alike to each other, aren't they?
15. What's the difference between sleet and hail?
16. Is ice cold, hard and slippery?
17. Can you see through a piece of ice if it is very thick?
18. Under what condition will ice melt?
19. If you skate on the thick ice, it will soon break, won't it?
20. Why must we learn the things around us?

II. Find words in the texts which mean approximately or the same as the following, using the given letters as a clue.

1. part of a circle — a_____
2. stay up in the air or on top of a liquid — f_____
3. very small — t_____
4. be so cold that it turns to ice — f_____
5. almost the same in appearance — a_____

6. falling snow with rain   s_____
7. if not   u_____
8. tiny balls of air or water   b_____
9. hard and strong   f_____
10. become liquid under high temperature   m_____

III. Complete the sentences with the given expressions, and change the forms where necessary.

look like	be made of	millions of	in a bunch
as a result	instead of	be alike to	see through
keep one's eyes open		take advantage of	

1. The manager decided _____ the favorable market situation to sell more products.
2. They plan to make furniture with plastics _____ wood.
3. The photograph doesn't _____ her at all.
4. The twin sisters _____ each other.
5. Don't play trick on me. I _____ your little game.
6. The shop assistant tied the flowers _____ and gave them to the customer.
7. He worked hard at mathematics. _____, he succeeded in passing the exam.
8. In fact, clouds are made of _____ tiny drops of water.
9. The paper is made from wood, and the furniture _____ wood.
10. The students _____ while they watched the teacher making the experiment.

IV. Complete the following passage by using appropriate words listed below. Be sure to use singular or plural forms for nouns.

cloud	fog	hailstone	ice	mist
rain	sleet	snow	snowflake	water

There is always (1)_____ in the air. (2)_____ are made of millions of tiny drops of water. When they touch the ground, they become (3)_____ or (4)_____. If the tiny drops of water join together and make bigger drops, they become so heavy that they fall to the earth, and that is (5)_____. Sometimes when the air is very cold, the raindrops freeze. As a result, (6)_____ fall instead of rain. If the raindrops freeze just a little bit, they are (7)_____. In fact sleet is the falling (8)_____ with rain. And if the raindrops freeze into hard little balls, they are (9)_____. Snow, hail, and sleet are frozen water, and so is plain (10)_____.

Language Structure

The Adverbial Clause （状语从句）

在主从复合句中作状语的从句，叫做状语从句。状语从句可放在句尾，也可放在句首。放在句首时，通常用逗号和主句分开。常见的状语从句有下列几种：

I. 时间状语从句（Adverbial Clause of Time）：时间状语从句常用 *when*, *whenever*, *as*, *as soon as*, *before*, *after*, *since*, *until*, *till* 等连词引导。如：

When the air is very cold, snowflakes fall instead of rain.
大气层很冷时，下雪而不下雨。
Rivers flow on *until* they reach the ocean.
江河继续奔流，直至流进海洋。
We have to clean the waste water *before* it flows into the river.
在废水注入江河之前，我们必须将其净化。
As soon as it hit the ground, the raindrop lost its round shape.
雨点一落到地面，就失去了其圆形。

II. 原因状语从句（Adverbial Clause of Cause）：原因状语从句常用 *because*, *since*, *as*, *that*, *now that* 等连词引导。如：

When clouds float in front of the sun, they make shadows *because* they keep sunlight from shining on the ground beneath them.
云彩在太阳前面漂浮时，就形成了阴影，因为云彩挡住了阳光，使之不能照射到下面的大地。
Since the world is full of wonderful things, we must keep our eyes open.
既然世界上充满了奇妙的事物，我们就必须注意观察。
I'm glad *that* you have made great progress in your English study.
我很高兴，你们在英语学习方面取得了很大的进步。

III. 目的状语从句（Adverbial Clause of Purpose）：目的状语从句常用 *that*, *so that*, *in order that* 等连词引导。如：

We must keep our eyes open *so that* we may learn more things around us.
我们必须注意观察，以便可以了解周围更多的事物。
We must learn things around us *in order that* we can take good advantage of nature.
为了更好地利用自然，我们必须了解周围的事物。

IV. 结果状语从句（Adverbial Clause of Result）：结果状语从句常用 *so that*，*so...that*，*such...that* 等连词引导。如：

Air holds up birds and planes *so that* they can fly in the sky.
空气托住了鸟和飞机，因此它们能在空中飞翔。

They are *such* small and light drops *that* they float in the air just like little balloons.
它们是又小又轻的水滴，因此就像小气球一样漂浮在空中。

Sometimes the clouds are *so* low *that* they touch the ground and wrap themselves around the trees and float over the water.
有时云彩很低，以致接触大地，遮蔽树木，并在水面漂浮。

V. 地点状语从句（Adverbial Clause of Place）：地点状语从句常用 *where*，*wherever* 等连接副词引导。如：

Where the tiny drops of water that make clouds or fog are very close together, they join and make bigger drops.
在形成云彩或雾的微细水滴紧挨在一起的地方，它们就结合并形成较大的水滴。

He is always ready to help others *wherever* there is a chance.
不管在什么地方，只要有机会，他总是随时准备帮助别人。

VI. 让步状语从句（Adverbial Clause of Concession）：让步状语从句常用 *though*，*although*，*even if*，*even though*，*as*，*whatever*，*no matter what/how*，*whether* 等连词引导。如：

Though sometimes clouds look like cotton and sometimes they look like gray smoke, they are really made of millions of tiny raindrops or bits of ice.
虽然有时云彩看起来像棉花，有时看起来像灰烟，但实质上它们是由无数极小的雨点或冰粒组成的。

Even though you skate on it, the ice will not break.
即使你在冰上滑行，它也不会破碎。

No matter how hard it is, the ice is water.
不管冰有多硬，它毕竟是水。

Whether it is rainy or sunny, he always gets to his office on time.
不管天晴还是下雨，他总是按时上班。

VII. 条件状语从句（Adverbial Clause of Condition）：条件状语从句常用 *if*，*unless*，*suppose*，*as long as*，*in case* 等连词引导。如：

If the ice is thick, it is very firm and strong.
如果冰块厚，就牢固结实。

Snow will not form *unless* the air is very cold.
除非空气很冷，否则不会形成雪。

As long as you put ice in a warm place, it will soon melt.

只要你把冰块置于温暖的地方，它就会很快融化。

VIII. 比较状语从句（Adverbial Clause of Comparison）：比较状语从句常用 *as...as*，*not so*（*as*）*...as*, *than* 等连词引导。如：

On sunny days the sky looks **as** blue **as** the sea (*is*).
晴天时，天空像大海一样一望如碧。
Sunlight is made of many colors and some of the colors are scattered through the air better **than** others (*are*).
太阳光五颜六色，其中有几种颜色比别的颜色更容易通过大气层。

IX. 方式状语从句（Adverbial Clause of Manner）：方式状语从句通常用 *as*，*just as*，*as if*，*as though* 等连词引导。如：

If it is very thin, you can see through the ice, ***just as*** you can see though glass.
如果冰块很薄，你可以看透冰块，就像你能看透玻璃一样。
He behaved ***as if*** nothing had happened.
他装做若无其事的样子。

Exercises for Language Structure

I. Fill in the blanks with *so, so that, such* or *such a/an*.

1. They become _____ heavy drops that they can't float in the air.
2. It was _____ hot day that they went swimming.
3. It was _____ cold weather that I had to stay at home.
4. Football is _____ interesting game that people all over the world like to watch football matches.
5. He spoke _____ fast that no one could follow him.
6. The story has been made into a film _____ many people may see it.
7. He got up early _____ he caught the early bus.
8. He'll get up early _____ he can get to his office in time.
9. The ice is _____ thick that we can skate on it.
10. We learn English hard _____ we can exchange ideas with foreigners.

II. Fill in the blanks with conjunctions *as*, *when*, *whenever*, *while*, *before*, *after*, *since*, *till*, *until* or *as soon as*; each conjunction is allowed to use only once.

1. Mr. Smith had learned a little Chinese _____ he came to China.
2. _____ she had finished her homework, Nancy watched TV for a while and then went to bed.

3. Great changes have taken place in China _____ China entered into WTO.

4. Not _____ he finished his work did Mr. Ford return home.

5. I'll wait for you here _____ you come back.

6. Raindrops lose their shape _____ they hit the ground.

7. On National Day, the villagers sang _____ they danced up to midnight.

8. _____ I was a child, I was determined to become an engineer.

9. Yesterday evening I was doing my homework _____ Jane was reviewing her lessons.

10. He was fully prepared for the situation, and _____ there was a chance, he would seize it.

III. Choose the best answer.

1. He is sure to attend the meeting _____ he is ill.
   A. as   B. if   C. as long as   D. unless

2. We must do _____ the teacher tells us.
   A. as   B. as if   C. since   D. because

3. He studied in a high school _____ he entered the college.
   A. when   B. while   C. before   D. after

4. _____ he was busy, he still found some time to read.
   A. But   B. Though   C. However   D. Nevertheless

5. _____ we can have a better understanding of the nature, we must make a careful observation of things around us.
   A. In order to   B. So as to   C. In order that   D. So that

6. He waited for me _____ I went back home.
   A. until   B. when   C. before   D. after

7. An ocean is _____ bigger and broader _____ a sea.
   A. much...as   B. more...as   C. much...than   D. more...than

8. _____ we have finished our work, we may sit down and take a rest.
   A. For now   B. By now   C. Now that   D. Since that

9. _____ he does his work, I don't mind when he arrives at the office.
   A. So far as   B. As long as   C. As soon as   D. As well as

10. The problem isn't _____ easy _____ you imagine.
    A. such...as   B. such...that   C. so...as   D. so...that

IV. Find out which of the underlined parts in each sentence is not correct in written English.

1. You can tell him the news when he will call on you next week.
         A   B   C   D

2. If you will go shopping tomorrow, please bring me a cake of soap.
      A   B   C   D
3. Whatever you go on the earth, you find plants and animals living together.
   A   B   C   D
4. They are so interesting stories that I think they should be put on the reading list.
             A   B   C   D
5. The cost of college education has risen so rapidly in the past several years as it is
       A   B   C

   beyond the reach of some families.
         D
6. When you are lost in the deep woods, no matter how way you turn, the forest looks
              A   B   C   D

   the same.
7. Not till the sun rose high in the sky did he get up and then go to work in a hurry.
   A   B   C   D
8. You had better take an umbrella with you in any case it rains.
       A   B   C   D
9. The lecture was such dull that some students lost interest and fell asleep.
                  A   B   C   D
10. The child was too tired that he went to bed immediately after supper.
                 A   B   C   D

Practice and Improvement

Reading Skills

Go through the following passages quickly, and after that, take note of the time, do the exercises, check the answers to the exercises and calculate words per minute.

Speed Reading A

Notes: Before reading the passage, try to get familiar with the following words and expressions.

1. thunder /ˈθʌndə(r)/ n. 雷，雷声 v. 打雷
2. lightning /ˈlaitniŋ/ n. 闪电
3. breathe /briːð/ v. 呼吸；吸口气

41

4. breeze /briːz/ n. 微风
5. destroy /diˈstrɔi/ v. 破坏，摧毁
6. electricity /ilekˈtrisiti/ n. 电；电学
7. wire /ˈwaiə/ n. 金属线
8. flash /flæʃ/ n. & v. 闪光，闪现
9. swell /swel/ v. 膨胀，肿胀
10. cause /kɔːz/ n. 原因，起因 v. 引起
11. pull up 拔起；阻止，使停止
12. a flash of 一道，一线

Air, Wind, Thunder and Lightning

All around the earth there is air. We breathe air, and so do other plants and animals. The sun shines through it, and the clouds float in it. Air holds up birds and planes so that they can fly. Air also holds up tiny raindrops.

When the air moves slowly, it is a breeze. When it moves faster, it is wind. That is what wind is.

If the wind blows very hard, there is a storm. Sometimes it is so strong that it can pull up trees and destroy houses. And sometimes thunder and lightning come with a storm. Do you know what lightning is? It is electricity in the sky. But electricity in the sky hasn't any wires to go through, so it has to jump from one place to another. A flash of lightning is electricity which jumps from cloud to cloud or from a cloud to the ground.

Lightning heats the air, passes through it and makes it swell up. This causes the big noise that is thunder.

(176 words)

Time: _____

Comprehension

I. Choose the best answer according to the passage.

1. _____ breathe air.
   A. Only men   B. Only plants
   C. Only animals   D. Men, plants and animals

2. Air can not hold up _____.

A. birds　　　　　　　　　B. planes
C. tiny raindrops　　　　　D. big raindrops

3. When the air moves very slowly, there is _____.

　　A. wind　　　B. a breeze　　C. storm　　D. nothing

4. The lightning in the sky _____.

　　A. jumps from one place to another　　B. go through wires
　　C. jumps with the wind　　　　　　　　D. comes with a breeze

5. Thunder is a big noise caused by _____.

　　A. wind　　　B. lightning　　C. storm　　D. planes

II. True or False：

(　) 6. The sun shines through clouds.
(　) 7. Planes can fly because air holds them up.
(　) 8. Wind has nothing to do with the air.
(　) 9. Lightning is the electricity in the sky.
(　)10. Lightning can jump from cloud to cloud or from a cloud to the ground without any wires.

Correct rate: _____%
Reading speed: _____ wpm

Speed Reading B

Notes：Before reading the passage, try to get familiar with the following words and expressions.

1. ocean　　/ˈouʃən/　n. 海洋，大洋
2. seep　　 /siːp/　v. 渗进，渗入
3. system　 /ˈsistəm/　n. 系统，制度
4. source　 /sɔːs/　n. 水源，来源
5. spring　 /spriŋ/　n. 泉，源泉
6. brook　　/bruk/　n. 溪流，小溪
7. pollution /pəˈluːʃən/　n. 污染
8. fresh　　/freʃ/　adj. 新鲜的；淡的
9. however /hauˈevə/　ad. 可是，然而；无论如何，不管怎样
10. flow　　/flou/　v. 流动，川流不息
11. find one's way to/into　进入
12. work with　同……一起工作；对……起作用

Water

Water is the "life blood" of our earth. Animals can't live without water, and neither can plants. Where there is plenty of water, the plants grow well. Water is in every living thing. It runs through mountains and valleys. It forms lakes and oceans. An ocean is much bigger than a lake. Water is everywhere.

Nature has a great water system. When water seeps into the ground, it becomes the source of springs. Rain water also finds its way to brooks and rivers. Rivers flow on until they reach the ocean. At the mouth of the rivers, fresh water joins the salt water of the ocean.

Here at the mouth of the river there is much important plant and animal life. However, we have to clean the waste water before it flows into the rivers. Man has to work with nature—not against it.

(176 words)
Time:_____

Comprehension

I. Choose the best answer according to the passage.

1. Water is like _____ to the life of our earth.
   A. clouds   B. wind   C. rain   D. blood
2. _____ is in every living thing.
   A. Blood   B. Water   C. Heat   D. Air
3. The mouth of a river is near _____.
   A. the ocean   B. the brook   C. the mountains D. the bank
4. The rivers bring _____ water to the ocean.
   A. salt   B. clean   C. fresh   D. waste
5. Fresh water does not have _____ in it.
   A. salt   B. life   C. pollution   D. fish

II. True or False:

( ) 6. Rivers are part of the great water system.
( ) 7. When rain water seeps into the ground, it flows into the ocean directly.
( ) 8. Pollution is a serious problem we have to deal with.
( ) 9. The water in brooks and rivers comes from the rain.

(　) 10. There is little plant and animal life at the mouth of the river.

Correct rate:＿＿＿％
Reading speed:＿＿＿wpm

Cloze Procedure

The Story of a Raindrop

One summer day a rain drop fell from a cloud. Many other raindrops fell at the same time, but our story is about just one raindrop.

The raindrop fell to the ground on the side of a hill. __(1)__ it hit the ground, it lost its round shape. The water in the raindrop ran down the hill into a little brook. The raindrop traveled in the brook for many miles. The brook carried it to a river. The raindrop in the river traveled past many cities and villages. At last the river carried the raindrop to the ocean. There the water of the raindrop joined the salt water of the ocean, which looked as blue __(2)__ the sky.

The sun shone brightly on the ocean, __(3)__ it made the water on the surface of the ocean very warm. __(4)__ the water became warm, some of it changed to water vapor. The water vapor left the ocean and went up into the air. No one could see it leave the ocean __(5)__ water vapor can not be seen. Soon the entire raindrop was in the air. __(6)__ the raindrop changed to water vapor and went up into the air, it did not carry any salt with it. It left the salt into the ocean.

The warm air with the vapor from the raindrop in it moved about. One day __(7)__ the warm air moved toward the north, it met some cold air, which pushed the warm air high above the ground. The warm air was cooled when it was pushed up. Then the water vapor of the raindrop changed into very tiny drops of water. The tiny drops joined millions of tiny drops high above the ground. They made a big cloud. __(8)__ the tiny drops in the cloud were close together, they came into bigger and bigger drops. At last, the drops were __(9)__ big that they were too heavy to float in the air, and they fell to the earth.

This time the water of the raindrop fell in one of the streets of the town. It ran along the street __(10)__ it found its way to a river, where the water of our raindrop started another journey to the ocean again.

Notes：

1. **shape** /ʃeip/ n. 形状 v. 形成
2. **mile** /mail/ n. 英里（= 1.609千米）
3. **surface** /ˈsəːfis/ n. 表面，外观
4. **journey** /ˈdʒəːni/ n. 旅程，旅行

Fill in the blanks with the best answer.

1. A. As soon as   B. As long as   C. Before   D. Until
2. A. that   B. than   C. like   D. as
3. A. so   B. such   C. that   D. so that
4. A. Before   B. After   C. Until   D. While
5. A. that   B. so that   C. because   D. though
6. A. Before   B. After   C. When   D. As soon as
7. A. as soon as   B. as   C. since   D. because
8. A. Unless   B. If   C. Though   D. Even if
9. A. so   B. such   C. too   D. enough
10. A. before   B. after   C. when   D. until

Speaking Skills

I. Warm-up Exercises: *Read the poem aloud.*

The Wind

By Christina Rosette (1830~1894)

Who has seen the wind?   有谁见过风？
Neither I nor you;   不是我也不是你；
But when the leaves hang trembling, 一旦树摇叶婆娑，
The wind is passing thro'.   顿觉飘然风乍起。
Who has seen the wind?   有谁见过风？
Neither you nor I;   不是你也不是我；
But when the trees bow down their heads, 但当树木低头时，
The wind is passing by.   便是一阵风吹过。

—克里斯蒂娜·罗塞蒂 (1830~1894)

II. Conversation

Practice the dialogues with your partner.

Dialogue 1 Talking about Weather

A: Where do you come from, Cooper?

B: I come from Britain.

A: It's very hot today. Do you mind the heat?

B: Well, it's all right. I'd say it's much better than Britain. It's so humid there.

A: Yes, it's rather hot here in this season.

B: What's the temperature today?

A: About 32 degrees centigrade or 83 degrees Fahrenheit.

B: Oh, that's pretty high. What is the maximum temperature you get here?

A: About 38 degrees, I'd say. It's exceptionally hot this year though. It's been a constant 34 to 35 degrees these past few weeks.

B: What is the minimum temperature in the winter?

A: Oh, it's freezing cold, around ten degrees below zero.

B: I see. What's the weather forecast for tomorrow?

A: Cloudy in the morning, overcast in the afternoon.

B: How long do you think this hot weather will last?

A: Not too long, for it is mid-autumn now. What kind of weather do you have at this time of the year?

B: It's not this hot. The highest temperature there is about 30 degrees, and there's more rain. But I have got used to the weather here.

Dialogue 2 Talking about Climate

A: Where are you from?

B: I come from Yueyang of Hunan Province. It's on the east bank of the Dongting Lake.

A: What's the climate like in your hometown?

B: Oh, the four seasons are very clear. It's very hot in summer but very cold in winter.

A: Which season do you like best?

B: Autumn because I am fond of its charming scenery. It's neither hot nor cold. The sun often shines and the weather is fine.

A: Why don't you like spring?

B: Because it keeps an unbroken spell of wet weather.

A: How about the other seasons?

B: The weather is too hot in summer and too cold in winter. Our climate is not very pleasant, but it's certainly good for rice to grow, so our hometown is a natural granary of our country.

Notes:

1. humid /ˈhjuːmid/ a. 潮湿的，湿润的
2. temperature /ˈtemprətʃə/ n. 温度，气温
3. degree /diˈɡriː/ n. 度，程度
4. centigrade /ˈsentiɡreid/ a. 摄氏的，百分度的
5. maximum /ˈmæksiməm/ a. 最高的，最大极限的 n. 最大量，最大限度，极大
6. exceptionally /ikˈsepʃənli/ ad. 特别地，例外地
7. constant /ˈkɔnstənt/ a. 持续的
8. minimum /ˈminiməm/ a. 最低的，最小的 n. 最低值，最小限度
9. forecast /ˈfɔːkɑːst/ n. & v. 预测，预报
10. overcast /ˈouvəˈkɑːst/ a. 阴天的，阴暗的 n. 覆盖，阴天 v. (使)阴暗
11. last /lɑːst/ v. 持续，维持
12. charming /ˈtʃɑːmiŋ/ a. 妩媚的，迷人的
13. scenery /ˈsiːnəri/ n. 风景，景色
14. spell /spel/ n. 一段时间；轮班；符咒；魅力 v. 拼写；拼字；轮值；招致
15. Fahrenheit /ˈfærənhait/ a. 华氏温度计的 n. 华氏温度计
16. get used to 逐渐适应，逐渐习惯
17. the Dongting Lake 洞庭湖(中国第二大湖，位于湖南、湖北两省之间)

Listening Skills

I. Directions: *Listen to the following sentences. Tick the right words the speaker says.*

1. A. weather   B. whether
2. A. son   B. sun
3. A. plane   B. plain
4. A. sea   B. see
5. A. breeze   B. breathe
6. A. heat   B. hit
7. A. glass   B. grass
8. A. seeps   B. ships
9. A. flash   B. fresh
10. A. down   B. town

II. Directions: *In this section, you will hear 10 short conversations. At the end of each conversation, a question will be asked about what was said. The conversation and question will be spoken only one time. After each question, there will be a pause. During the pause, you must read the four choices marked A, B, C and D, and* *decide which the best answer is, and then choose the corresponding letter.*

1. A. England.   B. America.   C. Australia.   D. Canada.
2. A. 7:30.   B. 8:30.   C. 9:00.   D. 9:30.
3. A. She baked the cake herself.   B. She wants the man to bake the cake.
   C. Tom made the cake for her.   D. Tom bought the cake for her.
4. A. In the hospital.   B. Home in bed.   C. At work.   D. In Bill's home.
5. A. A dance.   B. A lecture.   C. The Student Center.   D. A meeting.
6. A. He found something missing while packing.
   B. He's got everything to leave.
   C. He can't find his camera.
   D. He'll pack one more thing into the suitcase.
7. A. She thought that the job would be difficult.
   B. The experiment was the same as usual.
   C. She was unable to continue the experiment.
   D. The job was not like what she had expected.
8. A. Monday morning.   B. Monday afternoon.
   C. Wednesday morning.   D. Thursday afternoon.
9. A. He has been told to call back.   B. He is talking on the phone.
   C. He is not in at the moment.   D. He is going out this afternoon.
10. A. She's almost recovered.   B. She enjoys working in the fields.
    C. She'll be home tomorrow.   D. She still has pains in her back.

III. Directions: *In this section, you will hear a passage of about 90 words three times. There are about 20 words missing. First, you will hear the whole passage from the beginning to the end just to get a general idea about it. Then, in the second reading, write down the missing words during the pauses. You can check what you have written when the passage is read to you once again without the pauses.*

If the wind __(1)__ very hard, there is a storm. Sometimes it is __(2)__ that it can __(3)__ trees and __(4)__ houses. And sometimes __(5)__ and lightning come with a storm. Do you know what lightning is? It is __(6)__ in the sky. But electricity in the sky hasn't any wires __(7)__, so it has to __(8)__ from one place to another. __(9)__ is electricity which jumps from cloud to cloud or from a cloud __(10)__.

Translation Skills

I. Translate the following into English.

1. 他看起来像一位学问渊博的教授。(look like)

2. 既然世界上充满了奇妙的东西，我们就应该注意观察。（keep one's eyes open）

3. 今天晚上，我打算看电视，而不是看电影。（instead of）

4. 阳光是由赤、橙、黄、绿、青、蓝、紫七种颜色组成的。（be made of）

5. 这两位孪生兄弟彼此非常相像。（be alike to）

II. Translate the following into Chinese.

1. *As long as* we study hard, we can achieve good results.

2. I'll tell Jane the news *as soon as* I see her.

3. *As far as* I know, he doesn't know the truth at present.

4. *Just as* the earth moves around the sun, the moon moves around the earth.

5. Though this building is not *as* high *as* that one, it's more beautiful than that building.

Writing Skills

I. Rewrite each of the sentences after the model.

Model A: *Snow is frozen. Plain ice is frozen, too.*

Snow is frozen, and so is plain ice.

Snow is frozen; so is plain ice.

Snow is frozen. So is plain ice.

1. A bird flies. A plane flies, too.

2. Clouds are made of millions of tiny drops of water. Fog is also made of millions of tiny drops of water.

3. Snowflakes are cold. Hailstones are cold, too.

4. A plant needs water. An animal also needs water.

5. On sunny days, the sky looks blue. On sunny days, the sea looks blue, too.

Model B: *Snow will not form unless the air is very cold. Ice will not form, either.*

Snow will not form unless the air is very cold, and nor/neither will ice.

Snow will not form unless the air is very cold; nor/neither will ice.

Snow will not form unless the air is very cold. Nor/Neither will ice.

1. People can't live without water. Animals can't live without water, either.

2. The train didn't leave until twelve. The bus didn't leave until twelve, either.

3. Kate will not go out if it rains. I won't go out, either.

4. Dr. Harris doesn't smoke. His wife doesn't smoke, either.

5. Mr. Bradley isn't going to say anything at the meeting. I am not going to say anything at the meeting, either.

II. Practical Writing

单据（Bill）是一种凭证，起着证据的作用。单据种类繁多，包括借条、收据、领条、欠条等等。单据是查验的根据，不能随便更改。

1. 借条　　　　　　　I. O. U.

I. O. U.

October 15, 2003

To Mr. Edward Green:
　　I. O. U USD1000 (One thousand US dollars only) to be paid within one year from this date with interest at 5% per annum.

Jones Bradley

2. 收据　　　　　REPAYMENT RECEIPT

REPAYMENT RECEIPT

October 15, 2004

Received from Mr. Jones Bradley USD1050 (One thousand and fifty US dollars only) in full repayment of the loan lent to him on october 15, 2003, plus interest.

Edward Green

Notes:

1. I. O. U = I owe you　欠条
2. USD = U.S. dollars　美元
   STG = British sterling pounds　英镑
3. per annum = per year　每年

Exercise

Write an I.O.U. and a Repayment Receipt according to the materials given. You can model your writing on the above samples.

按照上面的格式分别写一张借条和收据：

1. 借条

借　条

今借到凯特·麦肯娜（Kate McKenna）女士STG500（伍佰英镑整），言明一年内归还，年息6厘，此据。

詹尼·罗丝（Jenny Ross）
2003年10月18日

2. 收据

收　据

今收到詹尼·罗丝女士2003年10月18日的还款STG530（伍佰叁拾英镑整），包括利息，此据。

凯特·麦肯娜
2004年10月18日

A Proverb

Nature never deceives us; it is always us who deceives us.

——Rousseau

大自然永远不会欺骗我们，欺骗我们的往往是我们自己。

——卢梭

Unit Three

SPACE TRAVEL

Reading Selection

Text A

PRE-READING TASK

1. Have you heard about Jules Verne—a famous French science fiction writer?
2. What are his most famous books?
3. Can you talk about something in relation to his books?

Some strange Journeys

Jules Verne was a Frenchman who was born in 1828. He was neither an inventor nor a scientist, but he read so many scientific books that he had a very strong imagination. He loved adventure though he did not have many great adventures himself. He wrote a number of exciting books about the things which he thought that scientists and inventors would one day be able to do. At that time, his science fictions seemed like fairy tales.

Many of Jules Verne's attempts to look into the future, however, were surprisingly accurate. For example, a book was called **From the Earth to the Moon** in which three men and a dog made a trip around the moon. They did this in a hollow ship that had been fired from the gun. After they went round the moon, they returned to the earth. The spaceship splashed down into the sea not far from the place where the first real moon travelers landed in July 1969, about a hundred years later.

Jules Verne's most famous book is **Twenty Thousand Leagues under the Sea**. A league is an old word which means about three miles. In those days

China launches its manned spaceship, Divine Ship V.

Chinese astronaut Yang Liwei returns to the earth.

(On October 15, 2003, China succeeded in launching its first manned space craft.)

submarines had not been invented, but he described an underwater ship, which was very like a modern submarine. The captain of the ship is called Captain Nemo, which means "no man." He and his crew have such surprising adventure that they find many strange things at the bottom of the ocean. This book has been made into a film, which you perhaps have seen.

In all his books Jules Verne used both his scientific knowledge and his strong imagination to describe the future inventions. Sometimes he was wrong, but often the accuracy of his descriptions was surprisingly correct, which enlightened the future inventors as well as writers. This is the reason why Jules Verne is regarded as "the pioneer of science fictions."

Jules Verne died in 1905 at the age of 77. Many years later, explorers really made their trip to the moon, one part of which was named after Jules Verne.

Text B

PRE-READING TASK

1. Do you know something about space travel?
2. Who was the first space traveler?
   A. *A scientist.*   B. *A doctor.*   C. *An astronaut.*   D. *An animal.*
3. Do you want to go into outer space some day?

The First Space Travelers

As is known to all, dogs and monkeys are intelligent animals, and they played an important role in space travel. Before astronauts flew into outer space, dogs and monkeys had been sent into space so that doctors and scientists could collect some data that astronauts needed to know in their space trip.

The first traveler who was sent out from our world into outer space was named Laika, a small Russian dog. She went out to space in a tiny rocket ship. Russian doctors listened to the radio to hear sounds from her ship. By listening to the way Laika flew through space in her small ship, doctors learned something that would be useful for astronauts' space travel.

The first American space travelers were monkeys whose names were Sam and Miss Sam. Doctors gave Sam and Miss Sam checkups before they were sent out into space. When they came back, they each had another checkup right away. Both Sam and Miss Sam seemed to feel fine after their trip.

After Sam and Miss Sam returned, Ham, another monkey who had been to "space school," was sent out into space again. He was such a smart monkey that he knew how to turn things on and off by himself when lights flashed on in his spaceship. He did so well in space that his trip was very successful. His spaceship splashed down into the sea, where Ham stayed in his cabin until it was lifted onto a ship.

On the day when he returned to the earth, Ham was interviewed by some reporters. And soon newspapers all over the world had pictures of his coming out of the tiny spaceship. He was standing with what looked like a proud smile on his face. And the man with whom Ham was shaking hands was his doctor.

In 1969, American astronauts made an exploration of the moon, and now, of course, men and women travel far out in space. However, it was animals like Laika, Ham, Sam and Miss Sam who first helped us learn how space travel could be made safe for people.

1. inventor /in'ventə(r)/ n. 发明家，创造者
2. invention /in'venʃən/ n. 发明，创造

3. scientific /saiən'tifik/ a. 科学的
4. imagination /iˌmædʒi'neiʃən/ n. 想像力，幻想
5. adventure /əd'ventʃə/ n. 冒险，惊险活动
6. fiction /'fikʃən/ n. 小说；虚构
7. fairy /'fɛəri/ n. 妖精，仙女 a. 仙境的，幻想中的
8. tale /teil/ n. 故事，传说；谎话，谣言
9. attempt /ə'tempt/ n. & v. 尝试，企图
10. surprisingly /sə'praiziŋli/ ad. 出乎意外地，令人惊奇地
11. accurate /'ækjurit/ a. 正确的，精确的
12. accuracy /'ækjurəsi/ n. 正确，精确
13. hollow /'hɔlou/ a. 空的，空心的
14. return /ri'tə:n/ n. & v. 返回，归还
15. splash /splæʃ/ n. & v. 溅，泼
16. traveler /'trævələ(r)/ n. 旅行者，旅客
17. land /lænd/ n. 土地，大陆 v. 登陆，着陆
18. shuttle /'ʃʌtl/ n. 梭，梭状物 v. 穿梭
19. league /li:g/ n. 里格(长度名，在英美约为3英里)；同盟，联盟；协会，社团
20. submarine /'sʌbməri:n/ n. 潜艇；海底动物 a. 水下的，海生的
21. captain /'kæptin/ n. 船长，机长；首领，队长
22. describe /di'skraib/ v. 记述，描写
23. description /di'skripʃən/ n. 记述，描写；叙事文
24. underwater /'ʌndəwɔ:tə(r)/ a. 水下的，水中的
25. crew /kru:/ n. (全体)乘务员；船员，水手
26. bottom /'bɔtəm/ n. 底，底部；基础，根底
27. enlighten /in'laitən/ v. 启发，启示，开导
28. future /'fju:tʃə(r)/ n. & a. 将来(的)，未来(的)
29. regard /ri'gɑ:d/ n. & v. 关心，注意；重视，尊敬；致意，问候
30. explorer /iks'plɔ:rə(r)/ n. 探险者；探测员
31. intelligent /in'telidʒənt/ a. 聪明的，有才智的；[计]智能的
32. role /roul/ n. 作用；角色
33. astronaut /'æstrənɔ:t/ n. 宇航员，航天员
34. outer /'autə(r)/ a. 外部的，外层的
35. collect /kə'lekt/ v. 收集，聚集
36. datum /'deitəm/ n. 数据，信息   data /deitə/ (datum的复数形式)
37. Russian /'rʌʃən/ n. 俄语，俄国人 a. 俄国的，俄国人的
38. rocket /'rɔkit/ n. 火箭 v. 急速上升
39. checkup /'tʃekʌp/ n. 检查，身体检查；审查，鉴定
40. smart /smɑ:t/ a. 精明的，灵巧的，巧妙的
41. successful /sək'sesful/ a. 成功的，圆满的

42. cabin /ˈkæbin/ n. 船舱，小屋
43. interview /ˈintəvjuː/ n. & v. 采访；会见；面试
44. reporter /riˈpɔːtə(r)/ n. 记者，通讯员
45. proud /praud/ a. 骄傲的，自豪的；妄自尊大的
46. shake (shook, shaken) /ʃeik/ v. & n. 摇动，振动
47. exploration /ekspləˈreiʃən/ n. 探险，探测

Idioms and Expressions

1. neither...nor   既不……也不
2. a number of   一批，若干
3. fairy tale   神话，童话
4. look into   展望；调查；看……的内部或深处
5. splash down   （宇宙飞行器在水面上）溅落
6. space shuttle   航天飞机
7. at the bottom of   在……的底部
8. both...and   既……又，两者都
9. as well as   也，又；以及
10. be regarded as   看待，当做
11. at the age of   在……年龄
12. make a trip to   到……旅行
13. name...after   以……命名
14. play a role in   在……发挥作用；扮演……角色
15. outer space   外层空间
16. send out   送出，发出
17. rocket ship   火箭飞行器，火箭宇宙飞船
18. have a checkup   进行体格检查
19. right away   马上，即刻
20. turn on   打开（电器、自来水、煤气等）
21. turn off   关上（电器、自来水、煤气等）
22. shake hands with   与……握手

Word Derivation

1. imagine—imagination—imaginative
2. invent—inventor—invention—inventive
3. explore—explorer—exploration—explorative

4. describe—description—descriptive
5. science—scientist—scientific—scientifically
6. surprise—surprising—surprisingly
7. accuracy—accurate—accurately
8. pride—proud—proudly
9. succeed—success—successful—successfully
10. intelligence—intelligent—intelligently

Notes to the Text

❶ Jules Verne 儒勒·凡尔纳（1828~1905）是著名的法国作家，开科幻小说之先河。他的科幻小说包括《气球旅行五星期》(1863)、《从地球到月球》（1865)、《海底两万里》(1870)、《环游地球80天》（1873）等等。在其一系列科幻小说中，他对以后许多的科学发明做出了令人惊奇的预言。

❷ He was neither an inventor nor a scientist, but he read so many scientific books that he had a very strong imagination. 他既不是发明家，也不是科学家，但他阅读过许多科学书籍以致具有丰富的想像力。

① 句中，neither...nor 是表示否定的连词短语，用来连接两个并列的句子成分。如：
Neither he nor I am going to make a speech at the meeting.
He can speak neither French nor German.

② 在引导结果状语从句时，名词前面一般用 such 修饰，但名词前有 many 或 much 限制时，则用 so 而不能用 such。如：
He told us so many fairy tales that all of us were excited.
Mr. Bradley has so much wisdom that we all rely on him when we make decisions.

❸ Many of Jules Verne's attempts to look into the future, however, were surprisingly accurate. 然而，儒勒·凡尔纳进行了许多探索未来的尝试，其精确程度令人吃惊。
however 是表示转折的连接副词，在句子中位置比较活跃，可以置于句首、句尾或句子当中。

❹ In all his books, Jules Verne used both his scientific knowledge and his strong imagination to describe the future inventions. 儒勒·凡尔纳在他的书中，既使用了科学知识又使用了丰富的想像力来描述未来的发明。
句中，both...and 是表示肯定的连词短语，用来连接两个并列的句子成分。如：
Both clouds and fog are made of millions of tiny drops of water.

❺ By listening to the way Laika flew through space in her small ship, doctors learned something that would be useful for astronauts' space travel.
通过测听莱卡在她的小宇宙飞船中航行这一方法，医生们了解到对宇航员太空旅行有用的一些情况。
句中，listening to the way 是动名词短语作介词by的宾语，way后是定语从句。

❻ He was such a smart monkey that he knew how to turn things on and off by himself when lights flashed on in his spaceship.

他是一个灵巧的猴子，学会了在宇宙飞船灯亮之后怎么操纵开关。

句中knew后接不定式做宾语时，往往在不定式前面加连接代词或连接副词。此外 advise, decide, discuss, find out, forget, learn, remember, show, tell, teach 等动词后加不定式做宾语时，不定式前也常常加连接代词或连接副词。例如：

Can you advise us how to improve our oral English?

Please tell me what to do next.

❼ He was standing with what looked like a proud smile on his face.

他站着，脸上带有一种看起来像是骄傲微笑的神色。

句中连接代词 what 引导名词从句，作介词 with 的宾语。

❽ However it was animals like Laika, Ham, Sam and Miss Sam who first helped us learn how space travel could be made safe for people.

但正是像莱卡、哈姆、山姆和山姆小姐那些动物起初帮助我们了解了宇宙飞行怎样对人们来说才是安全的。

① 句中 it was...that/who... 为强调句式，可以用来强调句子的主语、宾语和状语。如：

I bought a dictionary in the bookstore yesterday afternoon.

It was I who/that bought a dictionary in the bookstore yesterday afternoon.

It was a dictionary that I bought in the bookstore yesterday afternoon.

It was in the bookstore that I bought a dictionary yesterday afternoon.

It was yesterday afternoon that I bought a dictionary in the bookstore.

② 句中连接副词 how 引导名词从句作 learn 的宾语。

Exercises for Reading Comprehension

I. Answer the following questions.

1. Was Jules Verne a scientist or a writer?
2. What kind of books did he like to read?
3. He had many adventures, didn't he?
4. Can you describe his books in two words?
5. Who traveled in the hollow ship around the moon?
6. Where did the ship fall to the earth?
7. What happened near the place a hundred years after?
8. Which is Jules Verne's most famous book?
9. Where do many of the adventures in the book take place?
10. Jules Verne's descriptions of the future were always right, weren't they?
11. Who were the first travelers that were sent out from our world to outer space?
12. What did the Russian doctors listen to?

13. Why was Laika sent out from our world into outer space?
14. Who were the first American space travelers?
15. Who gave Sam and Miss Sam checkups before they were sent out into space?
16. Where had Ham been?
17. How did Ham do in space?
18. Where did Ham's spaceship splash down?
19. Whom was Ham shaking hands with?
20. Who helped us learn how space travel could be made safe for people?

II. Find the meaning of the words or expressions in Column (A) from those in Column (B).

(A)	(B)
1. inventor	A. used in science
2. scientific	B. learning or information
3. imagination	C. with nothing inside it or empty
4. adventure	D. the ability to see things in the mind
5. accurate	E. someone who invents things
6. hollow	F. say what a person or thing is like
7. knowledge	G. without any mistakes
8. describe	H. something invented by an inventor
9. explorer	I. an exciting or dangerous happening
10. invention	J. a person who travels through a strange place to learn about it

III. Complete the sentences with the given expressions, and change the forms where necessary.

at the age of	at the bottom of	be regarded as	fairy tale
have a checkup	look into	play a role in	splash down
turn on	turn off		

1. After the spaceship made a three-day trip to the moon, it returned to the earth and _____ into the sea.
2. Can you _____ your radio? It's late at night and I can't go to sleep.
3. Jules Verne _____ the pioneer of science fictions.
4. When I was a child, Grandma told me a lot of _____.

5. Every student must _____ before he enters a college.
6. The famous actor _____ the film which was shown last week.
7. _____ the future, we are full of confidence.
8. There are some peach trees _____ the hill.
9. He _____ the light because it was dark in the room.
10. Jules Verne was born in 1828 and died in 1905, _____ 77.

IV. Fill in the blanks with the words listed below, and be sure to use appropriate verb forms and appropriate singular and plural forms for nouns.

> accuracy, accurate, accurately;   explore, explorer, exploration
> invent, inventor, invention;   imagine, imagination, imaginative
> science, scientist, scientific

1. The study of natural things is called _____, for example, physics and chemistry belong to science, and someone who studies science or works with science is a _____, who often uses _____ instruments in his work.
2. When a scientist checks something, he tries very hard to be _____, and he tries not to make mistakes because _____ is very important in science, that is to say, he must make his researches _____.
3. In 1969, man first _____, or made an _____ of, the moon, and the _____ were from the United States.
4. When an _____ makes something new, or _____ something, he often doesn't know all the different ways in which his _____ will be used.
5. A person who writes a science fiction must have a strong _____, for example, Jules Verne was an _____ writer, who _____ that three men and a dog made a trip to the moon in one of his science fictions *From the Earth to the Moon*.

V. Complete the following passage by using appropriate words listed below, and be sure to use singular or plural forms for nouns.

> astronaut   cabin   exploration   fiction   knowledge
> imagination   inventor   rocket ship   spaceship   space shuttle

Jules Verne was a French writer of science (1) , and he used both scientific (2) and strong (3) to describe what would happen in the future, which enlightened the future scientists and   (4) . Russia was the first country to send out a __(5)__ with a dog into outer space. In 1969, American __(6)__ made a trip to the moon. According to the Chang'e Project (嫦娥计划), China also sent a manned __(7)__, Divine Ship V, around the earth on October 15, 2003 with an astronaut inside its __(8)__. Of course man has met some failures in space travel, such as the explosion (爆炸) of Challenger (挑战者号) Space Shuttle in 1986, and Columbia __(9)__ in 2003, but man will never stop making his __(10)__ of outer space, however.

Language Structure

The Attributive Clause (定语从句)

在主从复合句中充当定语的从句，叫做定语从句。这种从句置于被修饰或限制的名词或代词之后，因此被修饰或限制的名词或代词就叫做先行词 (antecedent)，定语从句可用关系代词或关系副词与主句相连。

I. 关系代词 (Relative Pronouns)：关系代词引导定语从句修饰或限制先行词，同时又在从句中充当一定的成分。如：主语、宾语、定语、补语等等。

Who (指人，主格)，whom (指人，宾格)，whose (指人或物，所有格)，which (指物)，that (指人或物) 如：

The first traveler *who* was sent out from our world into space was named Laika, a small Russian dog.
从我们地球送往太空的第一个旅行者叫做莱卡，一条俄国小狗。

This is the doctor *whom* you want to see.
这就是你想见的医生。

The monkey *whose* name was Ham had been to "space school."
这个名叫哈姆的猴子曾进过"宇航学校"。

From the window, we saw a high mountain *whose* top (or: the top of *which*) was covered with snow.
从窗户中，我们看到一座积雪封顶的高山。

He wrote a number of exciting science fictions about the things *which* he thought that scientists and inventors would one day be able to do.
他写了一些激动人心的科幻小说，书中涉及了他认为有朝一日科学家和发明家能做到的事情。

They made a trip around the moon in a hollow ship *that* had been fired from a gun.
他们乘坐一艘用火炮发射的空心飞船进行了环月球旅行。

[注] ❶ 关系代词在定语从句中做宾语时往往可以省略。如：

Doctors learned some of the things (**that**) astronauts needed to know so that they could fly in space.

医生们了解了宇航员去太空旅行需要知道的一些事情。

The man (**whom**) you talked to just now is a famous scientist.

刚才与你交谈的人是个著名的科学家。

❷ 修饰定语从句的关系代词在介词后面时，关系代词不能省略，而且只能用 whom，which，不能用 that。如：

The monkey with **whom** the doctor was shaking hands was named Ham.

正与医生握手的那只猴子叫做哈姆。

The rocket ship in **which** Laika was sent out into space was tiny.

莱卡乘坐前往太空旅行的火箭飞船很小。

❸ 在形容词最高级、序数词或 all，no，much，only，any，anything，everything 等词或被它们修饰的名词后面，不论关系代词充当主语还是宾语或补语，如指物，一般常用 that。

Harry Porter is one of the most interesting science fictions **that** I have ever read.

《哈利·波特》是我曾读过的最有趣的科幻小说之一。

After Sam and Miss Sam returned, the first thing **that** doctors wanted to do was to give them a checkup.

山姆和山姆小姐返航后，医生们想做的第一件事就是对他们进行一次体格检查。

He refused all the plans **that** were given to him.

他拒绝了所有交给他的计划。

Is there anything **that** can be done now?

现在有什么事情可以做吗？

II. 关系副词 (**Relative Adverbs**)：关系副词引导定语从句修饰先行词，同时又在定语从句中充当状语，常见的关系副词有 when，where 和 why 等。

❶ when 指时间，在定语从句中充当时间状语。如：

On the day **when** he returned to the earth, Ham was interviewed by some reporters.

哈姆返回地球的那一天，受到了一些记者的采访。

❷ where 指地点，在定语从句中充当地点状语。如：

The spaceship splashed down into the sea not far from the place **where** the first real moon travelers landed in July 1969, about a hundred years later.

宇宙飞船溅落在大海中，这与大约100年后，1969年7月首次真正月球旅行者的着陆地点相距不远。

❹ why 指原因，在定语从句中充当原因状语。如：

This is the reason **why** Jules Verne is regarded as "the pioneer of science fictions."

这就是人们认为儒勒·凡尔纳是"科幻小说先驱"的原因。

III. 限制性定语从句 (Restrictive Attributive Clause):

限制性定语从句是先行词意义上不可缺少的定语，如果省略，主句的意思就不完整或者完全失去意义；它和主句的关系十分密切，书写时不用逗号隔开。如：

Jules Verne was a French writer **who** *had a strong imagination.*
儒勒·凡尔纳是个具有丰富想像力的法国作家。

On the moon, there is no wind **that** *blows the dust about.*
在月球上，没有扬起灰尘的风。

The time **when** *the spaceship was sent out finally come.*
宇宙飞船发射的时刻终于来临了。

IV. 非限制性定语从句 (Non-restrictive Attributive Clause):

非限制性定语从句和主句的关系不十分密切，只是对主句中某个词、短语或整个句子进一步加以补充说明。它在形式上虽然不失为定语从句，但究其含义来看，却相当于并列句、并列成分或明确成分，与主句之间的关系松懈，如果省略，也不致影响主句的完整性，因此与主句之间一般用逗号分开，朗读时也有停顿，并且一般不用 that 引导，但可用关系代词 as 引导。非限制性定语从句主要分为下列两类：

1) 起延续叙述作用：

This book has been made into a film, **which** *you perhaps have seen.*
这本书已被拍成了影片，你也许已经看过了。

Many years later, explorers really made their trip to the moon, *one part of* **which** *was named after Jules Verne.*
多年以后，探险者真正进行了月球旅行，并将月球的某地以儒勒·凡尔纳的名字命名。

2) 起明确注释作用：

The captain of the ship is called Captain Nemo, **which** *means "no man."*
船长名叫内摩，其意为"并无此人"。（说明短语）

As *is known to all*, dogs and monkeys are intelligent animals.
众所周知，狗和猴子是很聪明的动物。（说明全句）

Exercises for Language Structure

I. Fill in the blanks with relative pronouns *who*, *whom*, *whose*, *which*, *that*, or *as*.

1. The students _____ don't study hard will not pass the examination.
2. The man is our chemistry teacher, _____ you saw in the lab just now.
3. This is the boy _____ sister is a famous singer.
4. The man with _____ our teacher shook hands just now is our president.
5. The spaceship in _____ we sit is circling the moon.
6. The farmer and the cows _____ you saw just now have gone to the grassland.

7. _____ has been proved, the earth travels around the sun.
8. Prof. Smith will give us a talk next week, _____ is exactly what we want.
9. The sun shines through millions of raindrops _____ hang in the air.
10. Mathematics, _____ its name suggests, is the study or science of numbers.

II. Fill in the blanks with relative adverbs *when*, *where*, *why*.

1. July 23, 1969 was the day _____ man first landed on the moon.
2. The time _____ Chinese astronauts will land on the moon will soon come.
3. Can you tell me the reason _____ you have turned down my proposal?
4. From space the astronauts looked down at the earth _____ their relatives live.
5. Last Sunday, I visited the factory _____ my parents work.
6. Ham's spaceship splashed down into the sea, _____ it was lifted onto a ship.
7. We'll put off the meeting till next week, _____ we'll not be so busy.
8. The shop _____ I bought an English-Chinese dictionary is near a theater.
9. They didn't tell us the reason _____ their products are so popular in market.
10. During those days _____ I was ill, my sister often came to see me.

III. Choose the best answer.

1. Elephants have good memories, _____ makes them easy to train.
   A. which   B. that   C. as   D. why
2. Miss Green _____ you met at the gate just now will teach us English.
   A. who   B. whom   C. whose   D. which
3. Many years later, astronauts really explored the moon; one part of _____ was named Jules Verne.
   A. when   B. where   C. which   D. that
4. Charlie, _____ father is a famous scientist, is a good friend of mine.
   A. who   B. whom   C. whose   D. which
5. Mr. Brown will give a talk on computer science this afternoon, _____ we all eager to know.
   A. that   B. which   C. where   D. when
6. The reason _____ he is absent today is that he is ill.
   A. when   B. where   C. why   D. how
7. At present Dr. Brown is the only one of the doctors who _____ able to cure SARS in the hospital.
   A. am   B. are   C. is   D. were
8. Ms. Ross is one of the judges who _____ going to look into the case.
   A. am   B. are   C. is   D. was
9. He talked about the teachers and the school _____ he had visited.
   A. who   B. which   C. where   D. that

10. Here is the knife with which you can cut the apple.
    A. who   B. whom   C. which   D. that

IV. Find out which of the underlined parts in each sentence is not correct in written English.

1. All what you have to do is to listen to the teacher carefully.
       A   B   C   D
2. I passed him a large glass of water, that he drank immediately.
      A   B   C   D
3. There are some students their questions are difficult for me to answer.
              A   B   C   D
4. The letter which I received it yesterday was from one of my former classmates.
              A   B   C   D
5. Nobody knows the reason what he is so angry.
      A   B   C   D
6. The children hailed the panda and the tamer who had given them a wonderful
                  A   B   C   D
   performance.
7. The room in that we live is much bigger and wider than yours.
              A   B   C   D
8. The place where I reached last Sunday is a forest park.
      A   B   C   D
9. I met him at the end of the street, where there is a bookstore there.
              A   B   D
10. She is one of my classmates who helps me with my physics and mathematics.
           A   B   C   D

Practice and Improvement

Reading Skills

Go through the following passages quickly, and after that, take note of the time, do the exercises, check the answers to the exercises and calculate words per minute.

Speed Reading A

Notes: Before reading the passage, try to get familiar with the following words and expressions.

1. telescope /ˈteliskoup/ n. 望远镜
2. nonsense /ˈnɔnsens/ n. 废话，胡说
3. flat /flæt/ a. 平坦的，浅的
4. discover /disˈkʌvə(r)/ v. 发现
5. recent /ˈriːsənt/ a. 近来，最近
6. compare /kəmˈpɛə/ v. 比较，比作
7. kilogram /ˈkiləgræm/ n. 千克
8. gram /græm/ n. 克
9. in the daytime 在白天
10. in the night 在夜晚

Some Facts about the Moon

When we look at the moon through a telescope, we can see lines and circles. People used to say that this was the man's face and that there was a man in the moon. Perhaps you have seen pictures like this in fairy tale books for children. The moon has eyes, a nose and a mouth and is smiling, which is nonsense, of course. There is no man on the moon. The lines and circles that we have seen are mountains, valleys and deep holes. There are also plains, where the ground is quite flat.

We know many facts about the moon now. Scientists have studied the moon through telescope for many years, and they have discovered many facts. In recent years, spaceships with astronauts inside have reached the moon.

What do we learn about the moon? First of all, if we compare the moon with the earth, we find that the moon is much smaller. It is about one quarter of the size of the earth. The moon circles round the earth just as the earth circles round the sun.

Day and night on the moon are very long. One day on the moon is as long as two weeks on the earth, and so is one night. In the daytime the moon is very hot: 120°C, but in the night it is very cold: -156°C. The moon is much hotter in the daytime and much colder in the night than the earth. The moon has no light of its own. Moonlight is only sunlight that shines on the moon.

There is another surprising thing. On the moon things are not so heavy as they are on the earth. Something that weighs one kilogram on the earth weighs 160 grams on the moon. Did you know that?

(300 words)

Time: _____

Comprehension

I. Choose the best answer according to the passage.

1. The line and circles on the moon are _____.
   A. mountains   B. valleys   C. deep holes   D. A, B and C
2. The earth is _____ the moon.
   A. bigger than   B. smaller than   C. as big as   D. the same in size as
3. The moon travels round the earth just as _____.
   A. the moon travels around the sun   B. the sun travels around the moon
   C. the earth travels around the sun   D. the sun travels around the earth
4. In the daytime the moon is _____ the earth.
   A. more hotter than   B. much hotter than
   C. more colder than   D. much colder than
5. On the moon, things are _____ they are on the earth.
   A. heavier than   B. as heavy as
   C. the same in weight as   D. not so heavy as

II. True or False:

(　) 6. In the past, people often said that lines and circles on the moon were the man's face.

(　) 7. The moon is so hot in the daytime that it sends out the light of its own.

(　) 8. The scientists still know little about the moon.

(　) 9. The earth is four times as big as the moon.

(　) 10. On the moon, nights are longer than days.

Correct rate: _____ %

Reading speed: _____ wpm

Speed Reading B

Notes: Before reading the passage, try to get familiar with the following words and expressions.

1. pretend /pri'tend/ v. 假装；假设
2. fare /fɛə(r)/ n. 车旅费；机票，船票
3. aboard /ə'bɔːd/ ad. & prep. 在船上，在飞机上
4. increase /in'kriːs/ v. /'inkriːs/ n. 增加，增长，增大
5. speed /spiːd/ n. 速度 v. 加速
6. count /kaunt/ v. 数；计算
7. roar /rɔː/ n. & v. 吼叫，怒吼
8. engine /'endʒin/ n. 引擎，发动机
9. eagerly /'iːgəli/ ad. 热切地，渴望地
10. lonely /'lounli/ a. 孤独的，寂寞的
11. lunar /'luːnə(r)/ a. 月球的；阴历的
12. orbit /'ɔːbit/ n. （天体的）轨道 v. 沿轨道运行，把……送入轨道
13. eager /'iːgə(r)/ a. 热切的，渴望的
14. ladder /'lædə(r)/ n. 梯子
15. step /step/ v. 走，举步 n. 脚步；梯阶；步骤
16. powder /'paudə(r)/ n. 粉末
17. silence /'sailəns/ n. 寂静，沉默
18. silently /'sailəntli/ ad. 寂静地，沉默地
19. dust /dʌst/ n. 灰尘，尘土
20. rock /rɔk/ n. 岩石
21. go on a journey 旅行
22. lift off 起飞，发射
23. move about 走来走去，四下活动
24. in sight 看得见
25. in silence 无声地，沉默地

Journey to the Moon

Perhaps one day in the future anyone will be able to take a trip to the moon, which is just like going on a train or bus journey. What an adventure that will be!

Let us pretend that you and I are going to the moon. When we have paid our fare, we climb aboard the spaceship just as we go aboard a plane. Both you and I have to lie down at first because the rocket will increase speed very quickly.

The captain counts: "Seven, six, five, four, three, two, one—lift off!" There is a sudden roar when the engines are turned on. The great rocket begins to rise, slowly at first, then faster and faster. We are glad that we are lying down because there is something to be holding us. Neither you nor I can move a bit.

This lasts for about twenty minutes. Then we reach our highest speed that is about 4,000 kilometers an hour. We are on our way to the moon. Now we can stand and move about.

(Astronauts in the Space Shuttle)

Eagerly we go to the windows for our first look at space. What a surprise! The sky is not blue but dark now. We can see stars all around us. What is that big shining ball? It is our earth, which looks like a very big moon. We look down at the earth where all our friends are living, and we feel a little lonely.

The moon is also in sight but it is getting bigger all the time. Three days later, the spaceship in which we sit is circling in the lunar orbit. At last it sinks slowly down until it is standing on the moon.

We are eager to go outside, but first we must put on our special clothes. Then we climb down the ladder and step onto the moon. Our feet sink into the ground a little and we see that we are walking on a kind of powder. The moon is covered with dust. There is no air on the moon, so there is no wind that blows the dust about.

We walk along silently. Then we see a piece of rock, and we jump over it. We find that we have jumped several feet into the sky. We walk around the holes in the ground and we walk up some of the hills, but we soon become tired of that. Everywhere looks the same. There are no trees, flowers, grass, birds or animals. The moon is a dead place. We are glad that we shall soon return to our earth.

(435 words)

Time: _____

Comprehension

I. Choose the best answer according to the passage.

1. We can take a trip to the moon by _____.
   A. train B. bus C. spaceship D. plane
2. The moon is in complete silence because there is no _____.
   A. air B. wind C. dust D. sound
3. The trip to the moon lasts about _____.
   A. twenty minutes B. seven hours C. three days D. a week
4. After we walk along the moon, we _____.
   A. think the trip is very surprising B. think the trip is very exciting
   C. become tired of the trip D. are glad that we have taken the trip
5. _____ can live on the moon.
   A. Only plants B. Only animals
   C. Both animals and plants D. Neither animals nor plants

II. True or False:

( ) 6. The writer has really made a trip to the moon.
( ) 7. According to the passage, the big shining ball in the sky is the sun.
( ) 8. When we have climbed aboard the spaceship, we must lie down until we reach the moon.
( ) 9. After we leave the earth, the sky looks dark.
( ) 10. We feel a little lonely because we have left our friends who live on the earth.

Correct rate: _____%
Reading speed: _____ wpm

Cloze Procedure

Landing on the Moon

On July 20, 1969, about a half billion people in 49 countries kept their eyes fixed on the television screens. Three American astronauts (1) would fly to the moon were waiting in a spaceship, Apollo 11, sitting on top of a rocket (2) was 36 storey high.

All those (3) were watching TV knew that the landing of men on the moon would be a great success. They also knew that something might go wrong at any time.

The time (4) the spaceship was sent out came at last, "Seven, six, five, four, three, two, one—lift off!"

76 hours after they left the earth, they were orbiting the moon. When they looked down at the earth (5) their friends lived, it looked like a big shining ball. A short time later, two of the astronauts who prepared to land on the moon left their spaceship in a lunar landing craft. While millions of people back on the earth watched TV, the first astronaut climbed out of the landing craft and stepped down. As his left foot touched the surface of the moon, he said, "That's one small step for a man; one great leap for mankind."

Twenty minutes later, the second astronauts followed the first astronaut, with (6) he walked on the moon. The first thing (7) was done by them was to explore the place around and nearby. Then they took pictures and collected sixty pounds of moon rocks to take back to the earth with them. They also set up a television camera with (8) the whole world could watch the landing on the moon.

While they were exploring the moon, the third astronaut who waited for the other two men to return was flying the spaceship in the lunar orbit. They spent twenty hours and thirty-seven minutes on the lunar visit. Then they went aboard their lunar landing craft and lift off. After returning to their spaceship, all three astronauts flew back to the earth. On July 24, at the time (9) Apollo 11 returned to the earth, people all over hailed the three astronauts (10) trip to the moon was thought of as the wonder of space travel.

Notes:

1. **billion** /ˈbiljən/ *num.* 十亿
2. **storey** /ˈstɔːri/ *n.* （层）楼
3. **craft** /krɑːft/ *n.* 船，飞行器；工艺，手艺
4. **leap** /liːp/ *n. & v.* 跳跃，跃进
5. **mankind** /mænˈkaind/ *n.* 人类
6. **Apollo 11** 阿波罗11号
7. **lunar landing craft** 登月舱

Fill in the blanks with the best answer.

( ) 1. A. who   B. whom   C. whose   D. which
( ) 2. A. where   B. when   C. who   D. which
( ) 3. A. who   B. whom   C. which   D. whose
( ) 4. A. where   B. when   C. why   D. that
( ) 5. A. where   B. when   C. which   D. that
( ) 6. A. who   B. whom   C. whose   D. which
( ) 7. A. who   B. when   C. which   D. that
( ) 8. A. who   B. whom   C. which   D. that
( ) 9. A. who   B. when   C. which   D. that
( ) 10. A. who   B. whom   C. whose   D. that

Speaking Skills

I. Warm-up Exercises: *Read the poem aloud.*

Dreams （梦想）

By Langston Hughes （1902~1967）

Hold fast to dreams　　　　　　　　紧紧抓住梦想，
　　For if dreams die　　　　　　　　　因为梦想若是死亡，
Life is a broken-winged bird　　　　生命就像断翅的鸟儿，
　　That cannot fly.　　　　　　　　　再也不能翱翔。

Hold fast to dreams　　　　　　　　紧紧抓住梦想，
　　For when dreams go　　　　　　　因为梦想一旦消亡，
Life is a barren field　　　　　　　　生命就像荒芜的田野，
　　Frozen with snow.　　　　　　　　从此冰封雪藏。

——兰斯顿·休斯（1902~1967）

II. Conversation

Practice the dialogues with your partner.

Dialogue 1　Going to the Movies

A: What are you going to do this evening?

B: Since it is Saturday, I'm going to see a film.

A: Good idea! What will be shown tonight?

B: *The Empire Strikes Back.*

A: Oh, I've heard that it is another terrific science fiction film after the *Star Wars*.

B: Yes, this film displays a society which lives in a galaxy far, far away with beautiful music and attractive scenes. It's really a joy to see it. Are you going with us?

A: I'd like to. I'm not a Star Wars fanatic, but I do enjoy the *Star Wars* movies. By the way, when will the film start?

B: At 7:30. Let's meet at the school gate at half past six.

A: Ok, good-bye.

B: See you later.

Dialogue 2　Talking about a TV Play

A: Hi, Nancy. Nice to see you!

B: Hi, Bob. Nice to see you, too! What did you do yesterday evening?

A: I watched a TV play.

B: Can you tell me what it is about?

A: Oh, it's about a huge monster who comes from outer space and lives under the sea. He wants to destroy our human beings and rule the earth.

B: My God, it sounds terrible.

A: However, a group of scientists are organized to fight with him and finally drive him out of the earth.

B: Great! By the way, what do you think of the TV play?

A: Really wonderful. Although I'm not a science fiction film fanatic, I like it very much. And there will be another science fiction TV play on channel 8 this evening. Are you going to join me?

B: Sorry, I have a lot of homework to do this evening. Perhaps this weekend.

A: Okay, I'll call for you on Saturday evening.

Notes:

1. empire　/ˈempaɪə(r)/ *n.* 帝国，帝权
2. terrific　/təˈrɪfɪk/ *a.* (口语) 极佳的；令人恐怖的
3. display　/dɪˈspleɪ/ *v. & n.* 展示，展览；陈列
4. galaxy　/ˈɡæləksi/ *n.* 星系；银河

5. attractive /əˈtræktɪv/ a. 吸引人的，有魅力的
6. scene /siːn/ n. 场面，景色，情景，布景
7. fanatic /fəˈnætɪk/ n. 狂热者，入迷者； a. 狂热的，入迷的
8. monster /ˈmɒnstə(r)/ n. 怪物，妖怪
9. The Empire Strikes Back 《帝国反击》(美国科幻影片)
10. Star Wars 《星球大战》(美国科幻影片)

Listening Skills

I. Directions: Listen to the following sentences. Tick the right words the speaker says.

1. A. planes   B. plains
2. A. fare   B. fair
3. A. lip   B. leap
4. A. ship   B. sheep
5. A. pride   B. proud
6. A. light   B. night
7. A. glass   B. grass
8. A. long   B. wrong
9. A. science   B. silence
10. A. holes   B. holds

II. Directions: In this section, you will hear 10 short conversations. At the end of each conversation, a question will be asked about what was said. The conversation and question will be spoken only one time. After each question, there will be a pause. During the pause, you must read the four choices marked A, B, C and D, and decide which the best answer is, and then choose the corresponding letter.

1. A. To buy a car.   B. To buy a ticket.
   C. To visit friends.   D. To hear a musical program.
2. A. America.   B. England.
   C. Switzerland.   D. Sweden.
3. A. They will have lunch at the restaurant.   B. They will have their lunch in the park.
   C. They don't want to have lunch.   D. They want to have lunch at the restaurant
4. A. The performance was bad.   B. The performance was good.
   C. He'd like to see it again.   D. He didn't go to the performance.
5. A. Typed more than ten papers.   B. Typed all his paper.
   C. Typed part of his paper.   D. Typed ten papers.
6. A. 8:40.   B. 7:40.   C. 7:20.   D. 7:46.

7. A. He teaches.　　　　　　　　　B. He gives legal advice.
   C. He studies.　　　　　　　　　 D. He teaches law.
8. A. There is no shoemaker nearby.　B. She just had her shoes repaired.
   C. She is a new comer herself.　　D. Her shoes were repaired two days ago.
9. A. In a post office.　　　　　　　B. In a department store.
   C. At the airport.　　　　　　　　D. At the train station.
10. A. Ten dollars.　　　　　　　　　B. Eleven dollars.
    C. Thirteen dollars.　　　　　　 D. Sixteen dollars.

III. Directions：In this section, you will hear a passage of about 90 words three times. There are about 20 words missing. First, you will hear the whole passage from the beginning to the end just to get a general idea about it. Then, in the second reading, write down the missing words during the pauses. You can check what you have written when the passage is read to you once again without the pauses.

When we look at the moon __(1)__ we can see __(2)__. People used to say that this was __(3)__ and that there was a man in the moon. __(4)__ you have seen pictures like this in __(5)__ for children. The moon has eyes, a nose and a mouth and is smiling, which is __(6)__, of course. There is no man __(7)__. The lines and circles that we have seen are __(8)__, valleys and __(9)__. There are also __(10)__, where the ground is quite flat.

Translation Skills

I. Translate the following into English.
1. 人们探测月球的尝试终于成功了。
2. 内摩船长和船员经历了许多惊人的冒险活动，以致在海底发现了许多怪物。
3. 工业在国民经济发展中发挥着重要作用。
4. 火箭飞船返回地球时，溅落于大海之中。
5. 正是在他的科幻小说中，儒勒·凡尔纳描述了许多将来的发明。

II. Translate the following into Chinese.
1. The first American space traveler who had been to "space school" was a smart monkey.
2. The famous scientist, whose son is my classmate, will give us a report on science next week.
3. This is the most exciting football game that I have ever watched.
4. As is well-known, air pollution does great harm to plants and animals.
5. Do you know the reason why dogs are the favorite animals of people?

Writing Skills

I. Rewrite each of the sentences after the model.

Model A: *Jules Verne used his scientific knowledge to describe future inventions.*
Jules Verne used his strong imagination to describe future inventions, too.
Jules Verne used both his scientific knowledge and his strong imagination to describe future inventions.

1. Sam seemed to feel fine after his trip.
   Miss Sam seemed to feel fine after her trip, too.
2. The doctors gave Sam a checkup after his trip right away.
   The doctors gave Miss Sam a checkup after her trip right away, too.
3. Air can hold up birds.
   Air can hold up planes, too.
4. Clouds are made of millions of tiny drops of water.
   Fog is made of millions of tiny drops of water, too.
5. Snow is frozen water.
   Ice is frozen water, too.

Model B: *He was not an inventor. He was not a scientist, either.*
He was neither an inventor nor a scientist.

1. Snow will not form unless the air is very cold.
   Ice will not form unless the air is very cold, either.
2. There is no air on the moon.
   There is no water on the moon, either.
3. Mr. Green doesn't teach physics.
   Mr. Green doesn't teach chemistry, either.
4. I don't smoke.
   My brother doesn't smoke, either.
5. John doesn't go to school by bus.
   John doesn't go to school on foot, either.

II. Practical Writing

便条（Notes） 是一种简易形式的书信，一般用于熟人之间，常写在纸条上，没有写条人和收条人的地址，也没有结束语等。其特点是文字简短，格式简单，开门见山。内容包括临时性的通知、询问、留言和要求等。便条一般是临时留言或委托他人转交，所涉及的一般是近期内发生的事情。

便条的格式包括：便条日期、称呼、正文、署名等项。日期写在便条的右上角，一般写上月、日，也可写上星期几，上午或下午；称呼用语可以随便一些；正文用词尽量通俗一些，简明扼要，讲清事情就行；署名可用 Yours，Yours sincerely 等等，如果是十分熟悉的人，也可只写姓名。

1. 请假条

Asking for Sick Leave

Asking for Sick Leave

Nov. 20

Dear Mr. Jones,

　　I am very sorry I will be unable to go to office because of illness. Enclosed please find a certificate from the doctor who said that I must stay in bed for a few days. As soon as I feel better, I'll come back to resume my work.

Yours sincerely
Li Ming

2. 留言条

Transmitting a Telephone Message

Transmitting a Telephone Message

6:30 p.m. Tuesday

Dear George,

　　Mr. Harris of Galaxy Trade Company rang up this afternoon, saying that he will come to discuss the problem of delivery with you at 9:30 a.m. tomorrow. Ring him back if it is not convenient for you.

Watson

Notes:

1. enclose /in'klouz/ v. 放入封套；装入
2. certificate /sə'tifikit/ n. 证明；证书
3. resume /ri'zju:m/ v. 再继续；重新开始
4. transmit /trænz'mit/ v. 传达，转送；传导；发射
5. a.m. （缩）上午，午前
6. delivery /di'livəri/ n. 交货，递交
7. p.m. （缩）下午，晚上，午后
8. convenient /kən'vi:njənt/ a. 便利的，方便的
9. Galaxy Trade Company 天河贸易公司

Exercise

Writer two Notes according to the materials given. You can model your writings on the above samples.

按照上面的格式分别写一张请假条和留言条：

1. 请假条

请假条

布莱德利教授：

　　我因病不能前往听课，谨表歉意。随函附上证明一张，医生嘱我卧床休息数日。一旦病情好转，我即回班学习。

您的学生
张华
11月22日

2. 留言条

留言条

爱德华：

　　天河贸易公司的哈里斯先生下午打电话来要你明天上午10时去他的办公室讨论产品的设计问题。如果不便，请打电话告知。

鲁尼
11月22日下午5:30

A Proverb

Imagination is more important than knowledge to science.

——Einstein

对科学来说，想像力比知识更重要。

——爱因斯坦

Unit Four

WORDS AND THEIR STORIES

Reading Selection

Text A

PRE-READING TASK

1. *Do you often use "okay" when you speak English?*
2. *What does "okay" mean?*
3. *Can you tell us the origin of the word, that is, where it came from?*

Okay

The word "okay" is known to and used by millions of people all over the world. Still, language experts do not agree on where it came from.

Some explain that it came from the Indian people. When Europeans first came to the Americas, they heard hundreds of different languages, many of which were well developed.

It is said that one tribe especially had a well-developed language. This was the Chocktaw tribe. They were farmers and fishermen who lived in the rich Mississippi Valley in what is now the state of Alabama. When problems appeared, Chocktaw leaders discussed them with their wise chief. They sat in a circle and listened to the wisdom of the chief.

When he heard the different proposals, he often raised and lowered his head in agreement, saying, "Okay," which means "it is so."

The Indian languages have given many words to English. Twenty-four of the American states—almost half—have Indian names. And the names of many rivers, mountains, cities and towns are Indian.

However, many people dispute the idea that "okay" came from Indi-

The chief of an Indian tribe 印第安部落酋长

The American Indians 美洲印第安人

ans. Some say that President Andrew Jackson first used "okay." Others say that a poor railroad clerk made up this word. His name was Obadiah Kelly. It was believed that he put his initials, O. K., on each package people gave him to ship by train.

So it goes; each story sounds reasonable and official, but we don't know whether it is true or not. Perhaps the most believable explanation is that the word "okay" was invented by a political organization in the 1800's. At that time, Martin Van Buren was running for President. A group of people organized a club to support him. They called their political organization the "okay club." The letters "o" and "k" were taken from the name of Van Buren's hometown, Old Kinderhook, New York.

In spite of the fact that people have different opinions about where it came from, they do agree that the word "okay" is pure American and it has spread to almost every country on earth.

There is something about the word that interests people of every language. Yet here in America it is used mostly in speech, not in serious writing. Serious writers would rather use "agree," "confirm" and so on than use "okay."

In recent time, "okay" has been given an official place in the English language.

Text B

PRE-READING TASK

1. Have you heard of Christopher Columbus and the great discovery of geography?

2. Do you know why the native people of North America and South America were called Indians?

3. Did Columbus know where he had been before he died?

Indian

About 480 years ago, a man stood alone on the coast of Spain. He looked towards the west and said to himself, "The earth can't be flat, if I sail westward, sooner or later, I shall see the land, India perhaps, and the queen will have a new and short route to the rich country."

Christopher Columbus sold his idea to Queen Isabella of Spain. She gave him some sailors and three ships. And Columbus sailed westward for many weeks, through rough seas.

At last, he saw land: a group of islands called the West Indies. Columbus was sure that it was India, and he called the natives "Indos."

Stories of what Columbus found quickly spread across Europe. His word "Indos" became "Indians" to the English language. And all the native people of the West Indies and Central America became known as "Indians."

Christopher Columbus made four trips to the New World. Yet, when he died in Spain, he still had no idea where he had been. He died with the belief that he had sailed to India.

It was soon learned that Columbus had made a mistake, but the word "Indian" was well established in Europe. When the first settlers arrived in what is now the seashore of the United States in the early 1600's, they called the natives Indians. Today the word is used to describe the descendants of the first peoples of North America and South America.

Not only language experts but also scholars have long known that the American Indians were not really Indians at all. And one scholar proposed a name—Amerinds. He made up this name by joining American and Indians. This word is now very popular among other scholars, but the general public has heard little of it.

1. okay /ˈəuˈkei/ *a. & ad.* 对；好；可以 *n. & v.* 同意，认可

2. expert /ˈekspɜːt/ n. 专家，能手　a. 熟练的；有专长的
3. develop /diˈveləp/ v. 发展；使成长，生长；显现出
4. tribe /traib/ n. 部落；宗族
5. appear /əˈpiə(r)/ v. 出现；出版，发表；看来(好像)
6. chief /tʃiːf/ n. 首领；长官；主任　a. 首席的，主要的
7. wise /waiz/ a. 明智的，英明的；博学的
8. wisdom /ˈwizdəm/ n. 才智；英明；学问
9. proposal /prəˈpouzl/ n. 提议，建议；计划
10. lower /ˈlouə/ v. 放下；降低；减弱
11. agreement /əˈɡriːmənt/ n. 同意，一致；协定，协议
12. dispute /disˈpjuːt/ v. 争论，辩驳
13. president /ˈprezidənt/ n. 总统；校长；董事长；总裁
14. railroad /ˈreilroud/ n. (UK railway) 铁路
15. clerk /klɜː(r)k/ n. (UK /klɑːk/) 职员，办事员，管理员，店员
16. initial /iˈniʃəl/ n. 首字母；姓名(或组织名称)的开头字母　a. 最初的，开始的
17. package /ˈpækidʒ/ n. 包，包裹；包装用物
18. reasonable /ˈriːznəbl/ a. 合理的，有道理的
19. official /əˈfiʃəl/ a. 正式的；有根据的；官方的　n. 官员；公务员
20. believable /biˈliːvəbl/ a. 可相信的，可信任的
21. explanation /ekspləˈneiʃən/ n. 解释，说明；辩解
22. political /pəˈlitikəl/ a. 政治的，政治上的
23. organization /ɔːɡənaiˈzeiʃən/ n. 组织，团体，机构
24. club /klʌb/ n. 俱乐部，社；棍棒
25. opinion /əˈpinjən/ n. 意见，看法；评价；鉴定
26. pure /pjuə(r)/ a. 纯粹的，纯正的，纯洁的
27. spread (spread, spread) /spred/ v. 伸展；传播；扩散；撒
28. popular /ˈpɔpjulə(r)/ a. 流行的，通俗的，受欢迎的
29. confirm /kənˈfɜːm/ v. 批准，确认，进一步证实
30. coast /koust/ n. 海岸，海滨地区
31. Spain /spein/ n. 西班牙
32. westward /ˈwestwəd/ a. & ad. 向西（的）
33. sailor /ˈseilə(r)/ n. 水手，海员
34. sail /seil/ v. 航海；翱翔　n. 帆，篷
35. rough /rʌf/ a. 汹涌的；粗暴的；粗糙的
36. island /ˈailənd/ n. 岛，岛屿
37. central /ˈsentrəl/ a. 中心的，中央的；主要的
38. belief /biˈliːf/ n. 信任，信仰，信心
39. establish /isˈtæbliʃ/ v. 建立；证实；制定
40. settler /ˈsetlə(r)/ n. 移民，移居者；殖民者，开拓者

41. seashore /ˈsiːʃɔː(r)/ n. 海岸，海滨
42. descendant /dɪˈsendənt/ n. 子孙，后裔
43. scholar /ˈskɒlə(r)/ n. 学者
44. propose /prəˈpəuz/ v. 提议，建议；提名，推荐；计划
45. general /ˈdʒenərəl/ a. 一般的，综合的 n. 一般；概要；将军
46. Amerind /ˈæmərɪnd/ n. & a. 美洲印第安人（的）
47. public /ˈpʌblɪk/ n. 公众 a. 公共的，公众的；公立的

Proper Names

1. the Chocktaw tribe　印第安人乔克托部落
2. the Mississippi Valley　密西西比河流域
3. Alabama　阿拉巴马（美国州名）
4. President Andrew Jackson（1767~1845）　安德鲁·杰克逊总统（美国第七任总统，1829~1837）
5. Obadiah Kelly　奥巴代亚·凯利（人名）
6. Martin Van Buren（1782~1865）　马丁·范布伦（美国第八任总统，1837~1841）
7. Old Kinderhook　欧德·金德霍克（地名）
8. Christopher Columbus（1451~1506）　克里斯托弗·哥伦布（意大利航海家，于1492年发现美洲）
9. Queen Isabella（1451~1506）　伊莎贝拉女王（统一西班牙，开拓海外殖民地的君主）
10. the West Indies　西印度群岛
11. Central America　中美洲
12. North America　北美洲
13. South America　南美洲
14. the New World　西半球，美洲大陆
15. the Old World　东半球，尤其指欧洲

Idioms and Expressions

1. agree on　对……意见一致
2. in agreement　同意，与……一致
3. make up　编造，虚构；弥补，化妆
4. run for　竞选
5. in spite of...　虽然……但是
6. would rather...than　宁愿……不愿，与其……倒不如
7. sooner or later　迟早，早晚

8. and so on　　等等
9. sell one's idea to　　向……兜售其主意
10. not only...but also　　不仅……而且
11. be popular among　　在……流行或受欢迎
12. general public　　公众，大众

Word Derivation

1. believe—belief—believable
2. agree—agreement—agreeable
3. reason—reasonable
4. develop—development
5. establish—establishment
6. organize—organization
7. explain—explanation
8. descend—descendant
9. propose—proposal
10. wise—wisdom

Notes to the Text

❶ It is said that one tribe especially had a well developed language. 据说有一个部落的语言特别发达。

It is said... 据说，句中 it 为形式主语，真正的主语为 that 引导的名词从句。类似的结构还有：

It is reported... 据报道……　　It is announced... 据宣布……
It is expected... 人们期望……　　It is well-known... 众所周知……等等。如：
It was believed that he put his initials, O.K., on each package people gave him to ship by train.
人们认为他把自己姓名的首字母 O.K. 写在人们交给他用火车托运的包裹上。

❷ They were farmer and fishermen who lived in the rich Mississippi Valley in what is now the state of Alabama.

他们住在当今阿拉巴马州富饶的密西西比流域，以耕作、捕鱼为生。
句中 what 所引导的名词从句作介词 in 的宾语。

❸ So it goes; each story sounds reasonable and official.
如此这般，每个故事听起来都合情合理，有根有据。
句中 sound 是联系动词，意思是听起来，形容词 reasonable 和 official 作补语，类似用法的联系动词还有 appear, look, seem, feel, smell, taste 等等。如：

He appears strong, but in fact he is weak.

The fruit smells terrible, but tastes delicious.

❹ In spite of the fact that people have different opinions about where it came from, they do agree that the word "okay" is pure American and it has spread to almost every country on earth.

尽管人们对"okay"这个词的出处持有不同意见，但有一点是一致的，即该词是纯粹的美语，并已传播到世界上几乎每一个国家。

①句中短语介词 In spite of 后接名词 fact，后面再接 that 引导的同位语从句。

②句中助动词 do 用来加强语气，当 do 用于肯定句或祈使句时，意为"的确"、"一定"等等。如：

I do think you should help him with his English.

我的确认为你应该帮助他学习英语。

Do come next Sunday when you have time.

下个星期天如有时间，一定要来哟。

❺ Serious writers would rather use "agree", "confirm" and so on than use "okay".

严肃的作家宁愿使用"同意"、"确认"等字眼，而不愿使用"okay"。

Would rather 意为"宁愿"，后接不带 to 的动词不定式，表示否定时，副词 not 应置于 rather 之后；would rather...than 意为"宁愿……不愿"，"与其……倒不如"。如：

I would rather watch TV this evening.

我今晚宁愿看电视。

I would rather not go to the movies this evening.

我今晚不愿看电影。

I would rather watch TV than go to the movies this evening.

今晚，我宁愿看电视，不愿看电影。

❻ When the first settlers arrived in what is now the seashore of the United States in the early 1600's, they called the natives Indians.

17世纪初期，当首批移民到达现在美国沿海地区时，他们把当地的土著叫做印第安人。

in the early 1600's 17世纪初期，1600's 也可写作 1600s （读作sixteen hundreds）。如：

in the late 1900's   20世纪末叶

in the 1990's   20世纪90年代

in the early   2000's 21世纪初叶

❼ Not only language experts but also scholars have long known that the American Indians were not really Indians at all.

不仅语言学家而且学者们也早就知道美洲的印第安人实际上根本不是印度人。

①句中 not only...but also 是并列连词，意为"不仅……而且"，表示递进关系。如：

Air can hold up not only birds but also planes.

He is not only fond of handwriting, but also good at it.

②at all 常用于否定句或条件状语从句，以加强语气。如：

He appears a scholar, but he doesn't know the subject at all.

他看起来像个学者，但对这门学科可说是一无所知。

Do it well if you do it at all. 要做就要把它做好。

Exercises for Reading Comprehension

I. Answer the following questions.

1. By whom is the word "okay" used?
2. Language experts have different opinions about where it came from, don't they?
3. How many different languages did the European settlers hear when they first came to America?
4. Which tribe especially had a well-developed language?
5. How did the Chocktaw leaders deal with the problems when they appeared?
6. How did the chief do when he heard the different proposals?
7. Who put his initials O.K. on each package people gave him to ship by train?
8. What did a group of people organize to support Martin Van Buren to run for President?
9. Is "okay" used mostly in speech or in serious writing?
10. When has "okay" been given an official place in the English language?
11. Why did Columbus want to sail westward?
12. Whom did Columbus sell his idea to?
13. At last he saw India, didn't he?
14. Why did he call the natives "Indos"?
15. What did the natives of the West Indies and Central America become known as?
16. How many trips did Columbus make to the New World?
17. Did Columbus know where he had been when he died in Spain?
18. Who is the word "Indian" used to describe today?
19. Only language experts have long known that the American Indians were not really Indians, haven't they?
20. How did a scholar make up the word, "Amerinds"?

II. Find words in the texts which mean approximately the same as the following, using the given letters as a clue.

1. seashore   c_____
2. make up   i_____
3. a person with great knowledge   s_____
4. a person with special knowledge or training   e_____
5. American Indian   A_____
6. suggest   p_____

7. trust b _____
8. clever and intelligent w _____
9. disagree about d _____
10. what you believe or think about o _____

III. Complete the sentences with the given expressions, and change the forms where necessary.

agree on	and so on	be popular among	general public
in spite of	make up	run for	sell one's idea to
sooner or later		would rather...than	

1. _____ his shortcomings, he also has some strong points.
2. After Iraqi War, President Bush began to pay attention to economy so that he could win the support of the _____.
3. Our products are the best seller of this year, and they _____ the children and adults.
4. Did you know who _____ the word "hello"?
5. If you study hard, you'll catch up with your classmates _____.
6. He tried every means _____ me, but I turned it down finally.
7. China has made a great leap in some fields, such as machine building, information technology _____.
8. In 1992, a group of people established an organization to support Bill Clinton _____ President of the United States.
9. Finally, the two parties made half way to each other and _____ the terms of payment.
10. I _____ watch football games _____ play football myself.

IV. Complete the following passage by using the appropriate words listed below, and be sure to use appropriate verb forms and appropriate singular or plural forms for nouns.

| believe | belief | believable | sail | sailor |
| arrive | expert | opinion | rough | sound |

The word "hello" is probably used more often than any other one in the English language. The first thing you hear when you pick up the telephone is "hello."

The language __(1)__ have different __(2)__ about where the word came from. There are all kinds of __(3)__. The most __(4)__ explanation is that it came from the French language, "ho" and "la", which means "Oh, there!" Perhaps this word __(5)__ in England in 1065.

"Ho, la" slowly became something that __(6)__ like "hallow" in the 1300's. Two hundred years later, "hallow" became "halloo." This word was often used by __(7)__ when they met each other after __(8)__ a long time at __(9)__ seas.

As time went on, "halloo" changed into "hullo." It was how people said when they met each other in America during the 1800's.

It was __(10)__ that the American inventor, Edison, was the first person to use "hello" in the late 1800's soon after the invention of the telephone. As we know, Edison was a man of few words, who wasted no time. As soon as he picked up the telephone, he did not ask if anyone was there. He was sure that someone was there and said "hello."

From then on, the word "hullo" has become "hello," as it is heard today.

Language Structure

The Noun Clause (名词从句)

在主从复合句中起名词作用的从句，叫做名词从句。名词从句包括主语从句、补语从句、宾语从句和同位语从句。

I. 主语从句（The Subject Clause）

起主语作用的名词从句，叫做主语从句。引导主语从句的连接词语有：
连词 that，whether；连接代词 who，whom，whose，what，which；连接副词 how，when，where，why 等。如：

Whether he will attend the meeting is not certain.
他是否参加这个会议还不一定。

What we need is more time.
我们所需要的是更多的时间。

Where this word came from is not known exactly.
该词出自何处人们知道得尚不确切。

主语从句放在句首，句子往往显得笨重，因此句首常用"It"作形式主语，而把主语从句放在句末，这样可以使句子结构更为紧凑。如：

It was soon learned **that** Columbus had made a mistake.

人们不久就知道哥伦布搞错了。

It is not known exactly **how** long elephants can live but it is generally believed **that** they are long-lived animals.

大象能活多久，人们知道得还不够确切，但普遍认为大象是寿命较长的动物。

II. 补语从句（The Supplementary Clause）

起补语作用的名词从句叫做补语从句，引导补语从句的连接词语有：

连词*that*，*because*，*whether*，*as if / as though*（好像，仿佛）；连接代词*who*，*whom*，*whose*，*what*，*which*；连接副词*how*，*when*，*where*，*why*等。如：

The reason why Asian elephants are easily trained is **that** they have good memories.

亚洲大象易于训练的原因在于它们记忆力强。

This was **because** Columbus didn't know where he had been.

这是因为哥伦布不知道他到过的是什么地方。

It looks **as if** it is going to rain.

看起来像要下雨的样子。

China is no longer **what** it used to be.

中国不再是过去的老样子了。

This is **why** the word has spread to almost every country on earth.

这就是该词传播到地球上几乎每一个国家的原因。

III. 宾语从句（The Object Clause）

起宾语作用的名词从句叫做宾语从句。引导宾语从句的连接词语有：

连词 *that*，*whether*，*if*（=whether，仅用于宾语从句）；连接代词 *who*，*whom*，*whose*，*what*，*which*；连接副词*how*，*when*，*where*，*why*等。如：

We don't know **whether** it is true or not.

我们不知道这件事是真是假。

I wonder **if / whether** you will give us a talk on words and their stories next week.

我想知道您在下星期是否给我们作关于词语掌故的讲座。

Some explain **that** this word came from the Indian people.

有人解释说该词出自印第安人。

Can you tell me **whose** bike this is?

你能告诉我这是谁的自行车吗？

Please let me know **when and where** we can find such things.

请告诉我何时何地能找到这些东西。

[注] 与宾语从句有关的几个问题：

❶ 在 believe，guess，know，say，suppose，think 等动词后，连词 that 可以省略。如：

I guess (**that**) he will be back soon.

我想他很快就会返回的。

We know (*that*) foreign languages are very important in international trade.
我们知道外语在国际贸易中是非常有用的。

❷ 在带宾语补足语的句子中，往往用 it 作形式宾语，而将宾语从句置于句末做实际宾语，表达具体内容。如：
We think it necessary *that* we should learn words and their stories well.
我们认为掌握词语掌故是非常必要的。
He felt it his duty *that* he should explain it clearly.
他觉得有责任把这件事解释清楚。

❸ 有些介词，如 about, in, of, on 等，它们后面也可以接宾语从句。如：
When they were inspected by their leaders, the soldiers were worried about *what* they looked.
当士兵们面临上司视察时，非常担心自己的军容。
Stories of *what Columbus found* quickly spread across Europe.
有关哥伦布新发现的消息很快传偏了欧洲。
Still language experts do not agree on *where it came from*.
关于该词出自何处，语言学家们仍然莫衷一是。

IV. 同位语从句 (The Appositive Clause)

起同位语作用的名词从句叫做同位语从句。引导同位语从句的连接词语有：
连词 *that*, *whether*；连接代词和连接副词。同位语从句一般跟在像 belief, fact, hope, idea, message, news, promise 这类名词之后，用以说明名词所表达的具体内容。如：
He died with the belief *that* he had sailed to India.
他死时仍然认为他曾航行去过印度。
When he died in Spain, he still had no idea *where* he had been.
他死于西班牙时，仍然不知道他曾去的地方是哪里。
In spite of the fact *that* people have different opinions about where it came from, they do agree on that the word "okay" is pure American.
尽管人们对"okay"一词的出处意见纷纭，但对于该词是纯粹的美国话却是意见一致的。

Exercises for Language Structure

I. Fill in the blanks with conjunctions *as if, as though, because, if, whether* **or** *that*.

1. I don't know _____ it is sunny or rainy tomorrow.
2. He looked _____ he had known the secret.

4. The reason why he was late for class this morning was _____ he missed the bus.
5. It is necessary _____ we should grasp some words and their stories if we want to learn English well.
6. I wonder _____ you can finish your work in time.
7. It was reported _____ a traffic accident happened on the street yesterday.
8. He expressed his hope _____ he would become an astronaut some day.
9. She told me the news _____ many people died of SARS in that area.
10. She always gets good results in exams. That is _____ she has formed good study habits.

II. Fill in the blanks with conjunctive pronouns who, whom, whose, which, what **or conjunctive adverbs** how, when, where, why.
1. The teacher is quite satisfied with _____ the students have done.
2. Do you know _____ the train will arrive at the railroad station?
3. _____ he said was quite different from what he did.
4. I want to find out _____ has taken my book away.
5. Can you tell me _____ far it is from the earth to the moon?
6. The boss asked the clerk _____ he was always late for work.
7. There were so many beautiful dresses that the lady didn't know _____ one she should choose.
8. The language experts haven't agreed on _____ this word comes from.
9. It is not known _____ pen this is.
10. I have no idea _____ I can return home.

III. Choose the best answer.
1. _____ that not all officials are honest.
    A. In my opinion   B. My believing is
    C. It seems to me   D. I think in my mind
2. _____ is quite clear.
    A. Where is war   B. Why is war
    C. What is war   D. What war is
3. Can you tell me _____ ?
    A. where does he live   B. where has he lived
    C. where he does live   D. where he lives
4. The reason why he didn't go to work on time was _____ he got up late this morning.
    A. why   B. because   C. that   D. which
5. If we look at the room carefully, we can see _____ .
    A. that dirty it is   B. what dirty is it
    C. how dirty it is   D. very dirty is it

6. They found at last _____ they had been looking for.
   A. that   B. what   C. where   D. which
7. John has a new car. I want to know when _____ it.
   A. he got   B. did he get C. he gets   D. he will get
8. The sky is full of dark clouds. I wonder _____.
   A. when it rains   B. if it rains
   C. when will it rain   D. if it will rain
9. _____ we shall go to the movies or not is not decided.
   A. When   B. Where   C. Whether   D. How
10. He always plays and wastes his time. That is _____ he didn't pass the exam.
    A. because   B. why   C. that   D. when

IV. **Find out which of the underlined parts in each sentence is not correct in written English.**

1. If he will attend the meeting doesn't matter too much.
   A   B   C   D
2. I wonder when will they make a trip to the moon.
     A   B   C   D
3. I want to know if she gets here the day after tomorrow.
     A   B   C   D
4. Please tell me if Prof. Brown will give us a report or not.
          A   B   C   D
5. The reason why Mary didn't come here yesterday was because she was ill.
              A   B   C   D
6. We think this important that we should learn English well.
            A   B   C   D
7. Have you heard the news what the animals are sent to the moon next month?
   A   B   C   D
8. It was said which a railroad clerk, whose name was Obadiah Kelly, made up the
   A   B   C   D
   word O. K.
9. As is known to all that sunlight is made of seven colors.
   A   B   C   D
10. Many people dispute the idea what "okay" came from the American Indians.
    A   B   C   D

93

Practice and Improvement

Reading Skills

Go through the following passages quickly, and after that, take note of the time, do the exercises, check the answers to the exercises and calculate words per minute.

Speed Reading A

Notes: Before reading the passage, try to get familiar with the following words and expressions.

1. expression /iksˈpreʃən/ n. 词组；表达
2. phrase /freiz/ n. 短语，词组
3. daily /ˈdeili/ a. 日常的 n. 日报
4. sour /ˈsauə(r)/ a. 酸的；刺耳的；讨厌的
5. obey /əˈbei/ v. 服从，顺从
6. unpleasant /ʌnˈpleznt/ a. 令人不快的，讨厌的
7. familiar /fəˈmiljə(r)/ a. 熟悉的，常见的 n. 密友，熟客
8. inspect /inˈspekt/ v. 检查，视察
9. equipment /iˈkuipmənt/ n. 装备，设备
10. shiny /ˈʃaini/ a. 闪亮的，刺眼的
11. inspection /inˈspekʃən/ n. 检查，视察
12. band /bænd/ n. 乐队；带；镶边
13. at least 至少
14. be familiar to 为……所熟悉

To Face the Music

Like every language, American English is full of special expressions and phrases that come from the daily life of the people, and develop in their own way. Do you know what the expression "to face the music" means?

When someone says, "Well, I guess I'll have to go to face the music," it doesn't mean that he's planning to go to a concert. It is something far less pleasant, just as you are called in by your boss to explain why you did this and did that, and why you did not do this or that. Sour music indeed, but you have to face it. At sometime or another, every one of us has had to face the music, especially as children. We can all remember Father's angry voice, "I want to talk to you." It is only because we did not obey him. What an unpleasant thing it was!

The expression "to face the music" is familiar to every American, young or old. It is at least one hundred years old. However, where this expression came from is not known exactly. One explanation about this expression goes back to the army. When the men were inspected by their leaders, the soldiers were worried about what they looked. Was their equipment clean and shiny enough to pass the inspection? Still the men had to go out and face the music of the band and the inspection. What else could they do?

(244 words)

Time:_____

Comprehension

I. Choose the best answer according to the passage.

1. The expression "to face the music" means _____.
   A. to go to a concert
   B. to face something unpleasant
   C. to talk to somebody
   D. to pass an inspection

2. _____ Americans know the expression quite well.
   A. Few
   B. Some
   C. Each
   D. Almost all

3. When father said, "I want to talk to you," it means that father _____.
   A. had something to talk to his child
   B. had an unpleasant thing
   C. was worried about his child
   D. was angry with his child

4. It is said that the expression came from _____.
   A. the army at least one hundred years ago
   B. a boss who inspected his clerks
   C. a soldier who did not obey his leaders
   D. a band which performed music in a concert

5. If the soldier did not keep their equipment clean and shiny, they had to _____.
   A. stand before their leader
   B. pass the inspection
   C. face the band
   D. face the music

II. True or False:

( ) 6. Every language has many expressions and phrases that come from the daily life of the people, and develop in their own way.

( ) 7. People are happy when they have to face the music.

( ) 8. The boss will have to face the music when he asked his men to explain why they did this or that.

( ) 9. If you didn't obey your father, he would have a friendly talk with you.

( )10. About one hundred years ago, the expression "to face the music" came into English.

Correct rate: _____ %
Reading speed: _____ wpm

Speed Reading B

Notes: Before reading the passage, try to get familiar with the following words and expressions.

1. Yankee /ˈjæŋki/ n. & a. 美国佬(的)
2. Scottish /ˈskɔtiʃ/ a. 苏格兰(人)的
3. trader /treidə(r)/ n. 商人
4. Holland /ˈhɔlənd/ n. 荷兰   Hollander n. 荷兰人
5. cheese /tʃiːz/ n. 奶酪，干酪
6. settle /ˈsetl/ v. 定居，安家；解决；决定
7. nickname /ˈnikneim/ n. 诨名，绰号
8. civil /ˈsivl/ a. 国内的；文明的；公民的
9. southern /ˈsʌðən/ a. 南方的，南部的
10. ally /ˈælai, əˈlai/ n. 同盟国 v. 与……结盟
11. New England 新英格兰(美国东北部地区)
12. play a joke on 对……开玩笑
13. the American Civil War 美国内战
14. take on 具有；接纳；呈现；承担；流行；穿上；雇用
15. be familiar with 对……熟悉

Yankee

The word "Yankee" is about 300 years old. It was first used for the settlers in New England. But what did this word mean? How did it get into the English language?

There are twenty stories which explain where "Yankee" came from, but experts say that only two of these stories are believable.

A number of people believe that it came from a Scottish word, which means smart and clever. Even today, anyone who is a small trader is called a "Yankee trader." But most of the experts agree that "Yankee" came from Holland.

Many years ago, the Hollanders who made cheese were called "Jan Kee" by the Germans. Some of the Hollanders came to America in the early 1600's. They settled near the New England settlers. The Holland settlers were great farmers. They played a joke on the New England settlers who tried to build farms on the mountain rocks. And so, the Holland settlers gave their own nickname to the New England settlers. The Englishmen quickly picked up the nickname and the New England settlers became Yankees.

During the American Civil War, "Yankee" took on a wider meaning. The soldiers in the northern states were called Yankees by the men of the southern army.

During World War One, the word was made shorter to "Yank." The people of the Allied Nations are familiar with the song, "The Yanks Are Coming," which brought tears and joy to them.

Today, "Yankee" is known throughout the world as another name for an American.

(253 words)

Time: _____

Comprehension

I. Choose the best answer according to the passage.

1. It is said that the word "Yankee" came from a Scottish word, which means _____.
   A. lazy and foolish B. smart and clever
   C. handsome   D. well-learned
2. The Holland settlers played a joke on the New England settlers _____ they were building farms on the mountain rocks.
   A. though   B. because   C. while   D. until
3. _____ were called Yankees during the American Civil War.
   A. The Holland settlers   B. The New England settlers

C. The soldiers of the northern army   D. the men of the southern army

4. "The Yanks Are Coming" was a song, _____ brought tears and joy to the people of the Allied Nations.

   A. that   B. which   C. it   D. this

5. "Yankee" *took on* a wider meaning during the American Civil War. In this sentence "took on" means _____.

   A. appeared   B. put on   C. became popular   D. began to have

II. True or False:

( ) 6. About three hundred years ago, the word "Yankee" came into English.

( ) 7. The New England settlers were called Yankees by the Holland settlers.

( ) 8. Language experts believed all the twenty stories about where the word "Yankee" came from.

( ) 9. The song, "The Yanks Are Coming", was well-known to the people of the Allied Nations during the Second World War.

( ) 10. The Holland settlers were not good farmers but smart traders.

Correct rate: _____ %
Reading speed: _____ wpm

Cloze Procedure

Christopher Columbus

Christopher Columbus was born in 1451 in Italy. When he grew up, he became a sailor and he also made maps. A long time ago, it was believed __(1)__ the heaven was round and the earth was flat. No one knew __(2)__ America was, and people at that time had no idea __(3)__ there was America or not.

Later on, Europeans traveled all the way around Africa to go to India. This voyage was long, slow and dangerous. So Columbus wanted to find a safe and short route to India. His belief was __(4)__ the world was round and that he could go to India by sailing west across the Atlantic Ocean.

Columbus went to Spain and sold his idea to Queen Isabella. The Queen believed __(5)__ he said and gave him sailors and three ships.

Columbus, with his men, sailed westward though he did not know __(6)__ the journey was. For many days the crew could not see land. __(7)__ they could arrive in India or not remained unknown, and they began to wonder __(8)__ Columbus decision was right. They said, "Turn back to

Spain, Columbus." But (9) they said could not change his mind. Columbus said firmly, "I'll not turn back. We'll sail on until we reach India."

On October 12, 1492, the three ships reached an island of America. Columbus called the natives there Indians. The reason was (10) Columbus thought that the place he had reached was India. Now we call these people American Indians.

Today Columbus is regarded as a great man who found, or discovered America.

Fill in the blanks with the best answers.

1. A. that   B. which   C. where   D. what
2. A. that   B. which   C. where   D. what
3. A. that   B. when   C. whether   D. what
4. A. that   B. why   C. because   D. whether
5. A. that   B. which   C. where   D. what
6. A. what   B. how   C. what long D. how long
7. A. Whether   B. When   C. Where   D. What
8. A. if   B. unless   C. though   D. that
9. A. whoever   B. whenever   C. however   D. whatever
10. A. because   B. that   C. for   D. why

Speaking Skills

I. Warm-up Exercises: *Read the poem aloud.*

A Lyrical Ballad（抒情诗）

By William Wordsworth (1775~1850)

I traveled among unknown men	我曾在陌生人中间作客，
In lands beyond the sea;	在那遥远的海外；
Nor, England! Did I know till then	英格兰，那时我才懂得
What love I bore to thee.	我对你多么挚爱。
'Tis past, that melancholy dream!	终于过去了，那凄凉的梦境！
Nor will I quit thy shore	我再不离开你远游；
A second time; for still I seem	我心中对你的蜜意深情
To love thee more and more.	时间愈久愈淳厚。

——威廉·华兹华斯（1775~1850）

II. Conversation

Practice the dialogues with your partner, and then write a dialogue about advice and suggestions.

Dialogue 1 How to Improve English

A: Prof. Bradley, can you give us some advice on how to improve our English?

B: Okay. Do you remember that I gave you some lectures on the importance of English at the beginning of this term?

A: Yes, I do. We know that English is the language of the information age as well as the language of international exchange and cooperation.

B: Quite right. Besides vocabulary, grammar and idiomatic usage, I think it is necessary for you to grasp some words and their stories, which will help you to know the origin of these words, so you can have a better understanding of these words.

A: Yes, the texts in this unit are very interesting. We have learned a lot from this unit.

B: What's more, by doing this, you can know some cultural and historical background of English-speaking countries, which is helpful to your English study.

A: I think so. By the way, we'd like to invite you to give us a talk on the culture and history of the United States.

B: I'm very glad to receive your invitation, but I'm quite busy with my work at the moment. Perhaps I'll give you the talk next week.

A: Prof. Bradley, it's been very useful talking to you. Thank you very much.

B: You're welcome.

Dialogue 2 Talking about Words and Their Stories

A: Hi, Wang Hong.

B: Hi, Zhang Hua. How are you getting on with your English study?

A: Recently, we have learned some English words and stories. I find they are very interesting and want to know more of them. Do you have any suggestions?

B: Yes, learning words and their stories, on one hand, can help you grasp more words and expressions, and on the other hand, it can offer you some cultural and historical backgrounds of English-speaking countries. Thus you can have a better understanding of English.

A: It's true. I really feel it necessary for us to grasp words and their stories, but some of them are quite difficult. What do you advise me to do?

B: Why not ask Prof. Bradley to give you a talk on words and their stories?

A: A good idea. Let's go to invite him.

B: In fact, I have invited Prof. Bradley to give us a talk on American culture and history on behalf of the English Lovers' Association.

A: Really? When is he going to give us the talk?
B: At 2 o'clock next Tuesday afternoon. Are you going to attend it?
A: Sure. Please call for me on Tuesday.

Notes:

1. background /'bækgraund/ n. 背景，后台
2. behalf /bi'hɑːf/ n. 利益
3. association /əsousi'eiʃn/ n. 协会；联合；结交；联想
4. what's more 此外，另外
5. on one hand 一方面
6. on the other hand 另一方面
7. on behalf of 作为……代表，为了……的利益

Listening Skills

I. Directions: Listen to the following sentences. Tick the right words the speaker says.

1. A. wear   B. where
2. A. hear   B. here
3. A. whether   B. weather
4. A. sad   B. said
5. A. along   B. alone
6. A. made   B. mad
7. A. then   B. than
8. A. belief   B. believe
9. A. laugh   B. rough
10. A. route   B. road

II. Directions: In this section, you will hear 10 short conversations. At the end of each conversation, a question will be asked about what was said. The conversation and question will be spoken only one time. After each question, there will be a pause. During the pause, you must read the four choices marked A, B, C and D, and decide which the best answer is, and then choose the corresponding letter.

1. A. The man did not study.   B. The man is not nervous.
   C. The woman did not study.   D. The woman will not take the test.
2. A. She got up too late.   B. The bus was late.
   C. She forgot her class.   D. She took the wrong bus.
3. A. Yesterday.   B. Two days ago.   C. Three days ago.   D. Last week.
4. A. The man.   B. The woman.

C. A secretary.   D. The man's friend.
5. A. Do homework.   B. Write letters.
   C. Prepare for the exam.   D. Watch TV.
6. A. It's easy to choose.   B. It doesn't matter which color to choose.
   C. It's difficult to decide.   D. She doesn't like each color.
7. A. The woman is a fast walker.   B. The woman couldn't walk.
   C. The woman can't walk any farther. D. The woman walks slowly.
8. A. She preferred apple.   B. There wasn't anything else to eat.
   C. She was on a diet.   D. She liked to eat apple.
9. A. At the department store.   B. In the club.
   C. In the garden.   D. In the zoo.
10. A. Eat before seeing the movies.   B. See the movies before eating.
    C. Stay in the town for a while.   D. Go to the town before eating.

III. Directions: In this section, you will hear a passage of about 90 words three times. There are about 20 words missing. First, you will hear the whole passage from the beginning to the end just to get a general idea about it. Then, in the second reading, write down the missing words during the pauses. You can check what you have written when the passage is read to you once again without the pauses.

The expression "to face the music"   (1)   every American, young or old. It is   (2)   one hundred years old. But where   (3)   came from is not known exactly.   (4)   about this expression   (5)   the army. When the men   (6)   by their leaders, the soldiers were worried about   (7) . Was their equipment   (8)   enough to pass the inspection? Still the men had to go out and   (9)   of the band and the inspection.   (10)   could they do?

Translation Skills

I. Translate the following into English.
1. 他宁愿站着死不愿跪着生。（would rather...than）
2. 英语不仅是信息时代的语言，而且是国际交流和合作的语言。（not only...but also）
3. 别向我兜售你的主意了，我决不会同意的。（sell one's idea to）
4. 语言专家对该词的出处仍然莫衷一是。（agree on）
5. 他说的话听起来合情合理，有根有据。（sound）

II. Translate the following into Chinese.
1. It was reported that a traffic accident happened at the crossroad.
2. This is why the word has been given an official place in the English language.

3. I wonder when Prof. Bradley will give us a talk on the culture and history of the U.S.
4. When the sports meet will be held has not been decided.
5. Please give Tom a message about whether he can come to my office.

Writing Skills

I. Rewrite each of the sentences after the model.

Model A: *Serious writers prefer using "agree," "confirm" and so on to using the word "okay."*
Serious writers would rather use "agree," "confirm" and so on than use the word "okay."

1. I prefer watching TV to going to the movies this evening.
2. He prefers watching football games to playing football himself.
3. The space travelers prefer living on the earth to living on the moon.
4. The panda prefers eating bamboo leaves to eating fruits.
5. I prefer repairing the computer by myself to having it repaired.

Model B: *Language experts have long known that the American Indians were not really Indians at all, and so have the scholars.*
Not only language experts but also scholars have long known that the American Indians were not really Indians at all.

1. Clouds are made of millions of tiny drops of water, and so is fog.
2. Dogs are intelligent animals, and so are monkeys.
3. He has good command of English grammar, and he has a good command of English idioms, too.
4. Jules Verne used scientific knowledge to describe future inventions, and he also used strong imagination to describe future inventions.
5. English can be used as a tool to learn advanced science and technology, and it can also be used as a medium to promote friendship between the Chinese people and the people of the world.

II. Practical Writing

通知（Notice）是上级对下级，组织对成员部署工作、传达信息或召开会议所使用的一种文体。同级单位有什么事情要互相协商和讨论，也可以互发通知。

一般来说，通知本文上面正中的地方往往有 Notice 作为标志，正文的下面是发出通知的单位名称，出通知的人或单位可写在右下角，发出通知的日期一般写在左下角，这两项有时可以省略。

通知　　　**Notice about an English Talk**

Notice about an English Talk

All Are Warmly Welcome
Under the Auspices of
the English Learners' Association
a talk will be given
on culture and history of America
by visiting American Prof. Bradley
in multimedia classroom 320 of teaching building 2
on Tuesday, Nov.16, 2004
at 2 o'clock p.m.
The English Learners' Association

Nov. 12, 2004

Notes:

1. auspices /ˈɔːspisis/ n. (复) 主办，赞助
2. multimedia /ˌmʌltiˈmiːdjə/ n. 多媒体
3. under the auspices of　由……主办

Exercise

Write a Notice according to the materials given. You can model your writing on the above Notice.

根据所给的材料按照上面的格式写一张通知：

通　知

信息技术系主办讲座

主讲人：李云峰教授
题　目：Windows XP软件操作
地　点：实验楼202计算机实验室
时　间：2004年11月18日星期四晚7时
　　　　热烈欢迎大家出席

信息技术系
2004年11月15日

A Proverb

Reading makes a full man, conference a ready man, and writing an exact man.

—Francis Bacon

读书使人完美，谈话使人敏捷，写作使人准确。

——弗朗西斯·培根

REVISION I

Test Paper 1

(For Unit1~Unit 4)
(to be finished within 120 minutes)

Part I. Listening Comprehension (15%)

Section A. Directions: *Listen to the following sentences. Tick the right words the speaker says.* (5%)

1. A. word   B. world
2. A. sea   B. see
3. A. red   B. read
4. A. fool   B. full
5. A. feet   B. fit
6. A. food   B. foot
7. A. thin   B. thing
8. A. flash   B. fresh
9. A. long   B. wrong
10. A. belief   B. believe

Section B. Directions: *In this section, you will hear 10 short conversations. At the end of each conversation, a question will be asked about what was said. The conversation and question will be spoken only one time. After each question, there will be a pause. During the pause, you must read the four choices marked A, B, C and D, and decide which the best answer is, and then choose the corresponding letter.* (5%)

11. A. She started swimming.   B. She stopped reading.
    C. She lost weight.   D. She only ate bread last week.
12. A. The woman.   B. The man.   C. Joe.   D. Jim.
13. A. Bob can't help.   B. Bob will help.

C. Bob will not help. D. Bob will be asked for help.
14. A. 30 minutes ago. B. 60 minutes ago.
    C. 90 minutes ago. D. 120 minutes ago.
15. A. They will not eat in that restaurant. B. They will not eat at home.
    C. They will eat in that restaurant. D. They will eat at home.
16. A. She has cleaned the window. B. She has closed the window.
    C. She has broken the window. D. She has fixed the window.
17. A. She is also a customer. B. The vase has already been sold.
    C. The vase is not for sale. D. She can't tell the price.
18. A. 6:30. B. 7:30. C. 8:00. D. 8:30.
19. A. Go with Bill. B. Bill will see the man.
    C. Try to visit Bill. D. Bill will go to New York, too.
20. A. Susan. B. Sue. C. Susan and Sue. D. Helen.

Section C. Directions: *In this section, you will hear a passage of about 90 words three times. There are about 10 words missing. First, you will hear the whole passage from the beginning to the end just to get a general idea about it. Then, in the second reading, write down the missing words during the pauses. You can check what you have written when the passage is read to you once again without the pauses.* (5%)

A Weather Report

And now for the __(21)__ weather report. Right now the skies over the __(22)__ area are sunny and __(23)__. We are expecting warm dry __(24)__ to continue throughout the day with temperatures in the middle to upper 80's. Winds will __(25)__ slightly variable as high as __(26)__ miles per hour. We are going to have __(27)__ weather continuing over the next couple of __(28)__ so that means clear and somewhat cooler weather __(29)__. Tomorrow will be sunny again and quite warm. No rainfall is expected for at least three or __(30)__ days.

Part II. Grammar and Vocabulary (30%)

Section A. *Fill in the blanks with proper prepositions.* (10%)

31. Don't translate English into Chinese word _____ word.
32. The students improved their English _____ practice.
33. The clouds keep sunlight _____ shining on the ground beneath them.
34. Sometimes the clouds are so low that they float _____ the water.
35. Man has to work with nature, not _____ it.
36. When the spaceship returned to the earth, it splashed down _____ the sea.
37. Ham was standing up with what looked _____ a proud smile on his face.
38. When he heard different proposals, the chief often raised and lowered his head _____ agreement.
39. Language experts still do not agree _____ where the word came from.
40. Stories of what Columbus had found quickly spread _____ Europe.

Section B. *Write the words in the right column according to the meaning in the left column, using the given letters as a clue.* (10%)

41. take in sth. or hold the attention and interest of sb.	a_____
42. light or gentle wind	b_____
43. say what a person or thing is like	d_____
44. stay up in the air or on top of a liquid	f_____
45. covering or affecting the whole world	g_____
46. learn... by heart	m_____
47. what you believe or think about	o_____
48. sth. that is suggested	p_____
49. a person with great knowledge	s_____
50. a person who is making a journey	t_____

Section C. *Choose the best answer.* (10%)

51. He's giving an _____ of how the machine works.
 A. explain B. explaination C. explanation D. explaining
52. Her mother is a _____ businesswoman.
 A. succeed B. success C. successful D. succeeded

53. Hanson is our professor of _____.
    A. Germany   B. German   C. Germans   D. the Germans
54. What we heard is the _____ tick of the clock because something is wrong with it.
    A. regular   B. irregular   C. irregularly   D. irregularity
55. They went in the direction that _____ pointed to.
    A. native   B. natives   C. the natives   D. little natives
56. Would you please help me to _____ up these new books?
    A. wrap   B. send   C. post   D. bring
57. If you can't go, let Mary go _____.
    A. instead   B. instead of   C. in place   D. in turn
58. No, this is not my dictionary. It _____ Robert.
    A. belongs for   B. belongs to   C. is owing for   D. is owed to
59. John and his brother are so _____ that they could almost be twins.
    A. like   B. alike   C. same   D. similar
60. The boy _____ this jacket to that T-shirt.
    A. prefers   B. chooses   C. selects   D. likes
61. You don't have to tell him! He is fully _____ the danger.
    A. sure of   B. aware of   C. blind to   D. familiar to
62. We _____ the fine weather today to play football.
    A. took the place of   B. took the advantage of
    C. took place of   D. took advantage of
63. There are more native speakers of Chinese than English. _____ English is the most frequently used international language.
    A. And   B. But   C. Nevertheless   D. So
64. It is because he is too nervous _____ he can not find the answer.
    A. so   B. that   C. so that   D. therefore
65. I'm interested in _____ you have told me.
    A. which   B. all that   C. all what   D. that
66. He talked about Thailand _____ he had been there himself.
    A. as if   B. as from   C. as for   D. as to
67. Take the umbrella with you _____ it rains.
    A. in case   B. in case of   C. lest   D. for fear that
68. If we look at the room carefully, we can see _____ it is.
    A. that dirty   B. how dirty   C. what dirty   D. very dirty
69. _____ we shall hold the conference or not is not decided.
    A. When   B. Where   C. Whether   D. How
70. The place _____ I visited yesterday is a beautiful city.
    A. when   B. where   C. what   D. that

Part III. Reading Comprehension (30%)

Directions: There are 3 passages in this part. Each passage is followed by some questions. For each of them there are four choices marked A, B, C and D. You should decide on the best choice.

(I)

Before a liquid changes into a gas, it must be heated. We see this happening when a kettle boils on a fire. Before a gas can change into a liquid, it must lose heat. This is the principle (原理) on which a refrigerator (冰箱) works.

All refrigerators, therefore, contain a liquid refrigerant (冷冻剂) which can turn easily into a gas and back again into a liquid. A refrigerator stores food, and so it is much better if the liquid is clean and safe and has no strong smell. For this reason, most refrigerants are chemicals which contain the gas fluorine (氟), which has all the necessary qualities.

At the bottom of a refrigerator there is an electric pump. This pump forces the liquid through a pipe to the top of the refrigerator. Here the pipe branches into many channels around the freezer box. The liquid spreads itself out through these channels and becomes a gas. But in order to change into a gas, it must be heated; and so it takes heat from the freezer. So the freezer becomes the coldest part of the refrigerator, where water turns to ice and food is frozen.

Any warm air in the refrigerator rises towards the freezer and helps to change the liquid refrigerant into a gas. The gas flows round to the bottom again, where the pump compresses (压缩) it. When this gas is compressed, it loses heat; and turns back into a liquid. The heat escapes from the refrigerator into the air outside. The liquid refrigerant now starts its journey again and soon reaches the freezer. There, it draws in more heat and again becomes a gas. And so the process goes on and on.

71. Why is a refrigerator cold inside?

    A. Because it gives its heat to the refrigerant.

    B. Because this is the principle on which a refrigerator works.

    C. Because fluorine gas is always very cold.

    D. Because the refrigerator stops the air outside from coming inside.

72. How can a gas be given a liquid form?

    A. By burning it.   B. By heating it.

    C. By pumping it through a pipe.   D. By compressing it.

73. What is the most necessary quality of a food refrigerant?

    A. It must be safe chemical to use in the house.

    B. It must be clean.

    C. It must readily turn from gas to liquid and from liquid to gas.

    D. It must not have a strong smell.

74. How does the refrigerant become a gas?

    A. It does this very easily by itself.

    B. It draws heat from the freezer and its contents.

    C. it draws heat from the warm air outside the refrigerator.

    D. It draws the heat escaping from the refrigerator.

75. What is the use of the electric pump in the refrigerator?

    A. To let the heat in the refrigerator escape into the air.

    B. To force the liquid refrigerant to the top of the refrigerator.

    C. To compress the gas into a liquid.

    D. Both B and C.

(II)

English is a language particularly rich in synonyms, i. e., different words which stand for the same thing. This is partly because of the convention, particularly in written English, that one should avoid repeating the same word over and over again. So instead of repeating "enough," one may use "sufficient." No two words are exactly the same, however. It is usually possible to find some differences between them or some context in which one is appropriate but not the other. Such differences can take several forms. It may be a difference in regional variety. "Autumn" and "fall," for example, both refer to the same season, but one is used in British English, the other in American English. Similarly, "snack" and "baggin" both refer to a light meal, but the former is standard English and the latter is a regional variety from the north of England. There may be stylistic differences. "Salt" and "sodium chloride" are synonymous, but the former is an everyday expression, and the latter is technical. There may also be differences in the emotional connotations (内涵) of words. "Youths" and "youngsters" are synonymous, but youths sounds less pleasant than youngsters. The emotional associations which a word brings to mind will often differ from person to person, so are to some degree unpredictable. Thus calling someone a "republican" may suggest he has praise worthy qualities to those in England who wish to abolish the monarchy, but connote (含有) objectionable characteristics to those who support it.

76. Synonyms are _____.
    A. exactly the same words
    B. different words of different meanings
    C. different words representing the same thing
    D. completely different words

77. The partial reason for using synonyms in English is _____.
    A. the people   B. the convention   C. the economy   D. the literature

78. The difference between "autumn" and "fall" was in _____.
    A. stylistic difference   B. emotional difference
    C. regional difference   D. personal preference

79. According to the passage, which of the following is NOT the possible difference between synonyms?
    A. regional variety   B. personal habits
    C. emotional connotations   D. stylistic difference

80. According to this passage, which of the following statements is NOT true?
    A. "Autumn" is a formal expression of "fall."
    B. "Youngsters" sound more pleasant than "youths."
    C. "Sodium chloride" is the technical term for "salt."
    D. "Snack" is standard English for a light meal.

(III)

Scientists used to say the moon was extremely dry—a virtual (事实上的) desert in the sky. Now they think they've discovered water on the lunar surface!

It's not ready-to-drink liquid water, says Paul D. Spudis, a geologist (地质学家) at the Lunar and Planetary Institute in Huston. "We think we have found ice," he says, and lots of it—mixed with rocks and dirt in a 7,700-square-kilometer area at the moon's South Pole. That's the area about twice the size of Rhode Island. If Spudis is right, he and other scientists envision future space traveler's stopping off at a lunar "filling station." They could melt ice to drink and could also refuel their rockets. (The hydrogen and oxygen in water are also components of rocket fuel.)

Spudis helped make the discovery while analyzing radar signals sent back by "Clementine," a small space craft that orbited the moon in 1994. The signals, which reflected toward Earth after bouncing off the moon, indicate which areas are rocky and which areas may be icy, Spudis explains.

To check if this wet-and-wild discovery is true, NASA will launch another moon-orbiting spacecraft. "We have a long way to go before people live on the moon, " Spudis says. But this discovery "is an indication that it might be possible."

81. What does "on the lunar surface" mean in the first paragraph?
    A. On the surface of the desert.
    B. On the surface of the moon.
    C. On the extremely dry surface.
    D. On the surface of a planet.

82. Which of the following is NOT true according to the passage?
    A. Water on the moon is the form of ice.
    B. Now scientists have melted the moon ice to drink.
    C. Moon ice is mixed with rocks and dirt.
    D. Water on the moon is made up of hydrogen and oxygen.

83. How was water discovered on the moon?
    A. Radar signal analysis suggested there is ice on the moon.
    B. Spudis discovered water while observing the moon.
    C. Clementine analyzed the signals and drew the conclusion.
    D. Clementine landed on the moon and made the discovery.

84. What is the significance of the discovery?

A. It makes people believe they can soon live on the moon.

B. It causes NASA to send another moon-orbiting spacecraft.

C. It indicates that people might live on the moon in the future.

D. It enables people to use a new source of energy.

85. The passage was written in a style of _____.

    A. an interview   B. a short story   C. a travel guide   D. science news

Part IV. Translation (10%)

Direction: In this part, there are five sentences which you should translate into Chinese. These sentences are all taken from the reading passages you have just read in the Test Paper.

86. Before a gas can change into a liquid, it must lose heat. This is the principle (原理) on which a refrigerator (冰箱) works.

87. English is a language particularly rich in synonyms, that is, different words which stand for the same thing.

88. "Salt" and "sodium chloride" are synonymous, but the former is an everyday expression, and the latter is technical.

89. Scientists used to say the moon was extremely dry—a virtual (事实上的) desert in the sky.

90. We have a long way to go before people live on the moon. But this discovery is an indication that it might be possible.

Part V. Practical Writing (15%)

写一张通知，通告全体艺术设计系的学生去听留美归来的王教授的讲座"计算机辅助设计"。

时间：2003年12月3日（星期三）晚7点

地点：教学楼第二多媒体教室

Unit Five

TWENTY QUESTIONS

Reading Selection

Text A

PRE-READING TASK

1. Have you heard "Twenty Questions" in the BBC English by radio programmes?
2. Have you played this language game with your classmates? If so, can you explain the rules for the language game?
3. Would you like to play this game with a robot with artificial intelligence on line? If so, you can click http://www.20q.net/ to start the game.

The Rules for Twenty Questions

At a Summer School in England for Europeans who are advancing their English, a group of adult students have been invited to take part in

Ms. Green is guiding the adult students how to play "Twenty Questions" on line.

The girl student is playing language games in the computer lab.

(Playing "Twenty Questions" is a good way to improve English.)

"Twenty Questions," a global experimental language game. Ms. Green is explaining the rules on how to play the language game.

Ms.Green: You all know something about the language game, I'm sure. Some of you may have heard it in the BBC English by radio programmes, or some of you may have contacted the website through the Internet to play the game with the artificial intelligence robot. The address of the web site is http://www.20q.net/.

Anne: No, I haven't. Will you tell me how to play this game on line, Ms. Green?

Ms.Green: Take it easy, Anne. Let's play it this afternoon, shall we?

Anne: Okay.

Ms.Green: So first, I had better say a few words about it. I'm going to think of something, and you will try to work out what I've thought of. You are allowed to ask twenty questions. If you find the answer in twenty questions, or in a smaller number, you win; if you don't, I win. You are only allowed to ask twenty questions that I can answer by "Yes" or "No." In addition to the yes-no questions, you can also ask questions with an "or" in the middle, for example, "Is it wet or dry?" and I shall give you a piece of information. Now I shall tell you what I'm thinking of. The object is *animal*, *vegetable*, or *mineral*.

Pedro: I have heard of this game before, but I'm not quite sure about the rules. *Animal* is used in this game to indicate a kind of living things, isn't it?

Ms.Green: Quite right. It stands for any kind of living things except plants, such as grass and trees. *Animal*, that is to say, includes insects, birds, fishes, snakes as well as cats, dogs and so on. It includes men, of course.

Harry: May I ask you a question, Ms. Green? What do feathers belong to?

Ms.Green: A good question, Harry. They belong to *animal*. In this game, *animal* has a much wider meaning. It includes things that come from animals. Feathers, for instance,

	are *animal* because they are taken out of birds, and leather, because it is made from the skins of animals.
Rosa:	Ms. Green, we're quite clear about what *animal* means in this game. Can you explain what *vegetable* includes?
Ms.Green:	Certainly. *Vegetable* includes the kinds of vegetables we eat, such as beans, potatoes, cabbages, tomatoes and so on. In addition to the vegetables we eat, it also includes all kinds of living things such as grass and trees except *animal* we have just mentioned. Of course, it includes anything from these. Wood, for example, may be called *vegetable* in this game because it originates from trees.
Hans:	Obviously, mineral must have a very wide meaning in this game, too.
Ms.Green:	Yes. Generally speaking, when we use the word *mineral*, we mean things from mines: such as oil and coal, or any kind of inorganic things, such as metals like gold, silver, copper, iron and tin, that is to say, *mineral* in this game is a kind of non-living things. It is anything that is neither *animal* nor *vegetable*. Glass is mineral, so a window can be all mineral if the frame is made of steel, and it can be both *mineral* and *vegetable*, if the frame is made of wood. Must I explain the rules again?
Students:	No, you needn't. Your explanation is quite obvious to us.

Text B

PRE-READING TASK

1. Are you clear about the rules for "Twenty Questions"? If not, please read Text A once again.
2. In this game, oil belongs to _____.
   A. *animal*   B. *vegetable*   C. *mineral*   D. *unknown*
3. In this game, iron belongs to _____.
   A. *animal*   B. *vegetable*   C. *mineral*   D. *unknown*

Twenty Questions (I)

Ms. Green: Now, let's begin the game, shall we? The first object that I've thought of is mineral. Now, please ask questions, will you?
Harry: Can it be a famous building of any kind?
Ms. Green: No, it's not a building or something like that.
Hans: Is it made of some kind of metal?
Ms. Green: No.
Pedro: Some kind of rock or stone?
Ms. Green: No, it is neither rock nor stone.
Rosa: Is it very useful?
Ms. Green: Oh, yes.
Rosa: Is it a very large thing?
Ms. Green: No, quite small. You could put one of those in your handbag.
Harry: Can it be a pair of scissors?
Ms. Green: No. You should not have asked such a question. I told you it was not made of metal.
Anne: Could it be something made of plastics?
Ms. Green: I don't think plastics are the right word for the material.
Anne: Are you thinking of the material itself or of something made from this material?
Ms. Green: There are two words in the answer. One is the name of the material, and the other is the name of the thing.
Hans: Are there any these things in the room?
Ms. Green: Yes, quite a large number.
Pedro: Are they things we wear?
Ms. Green: Yes.
Harry: Which part of the body?
Ms. Green: Such questions should not be allowed to ask in the game. Harry, you ought to use your brains.
Harry: I'm sorry, Ms. Green. Well, are they worn above or below the waist?
Ms. Green: Below the waist.
Pedro: Can it be a pair of socks?
Ms. Green: It's something like that, but much longer.

Rosa: Then it must be stockings, I dare say.
Ms.Green: Yes, but you'll still have to give the name of the material.
Pedro: You said mineral, so it can't be cotton, and can't be wool, either. Is it rayon?
Ms.Green: Rayon is made partly from wood. That's vegetable.
Rosa: I know! It must be nylon stockings.
Ms. Green: Yes, you are right, Rosa. The object I thought of just now is nylon stockings. It is said that nylon is made from coal, air and water.
Students: Science and technology is really wonderful.
Ms.Green: We shall be dressed in artificial materials soon, perhaps. I'd rather have natural silk than artificial silk, but my elder sister says nylon blouses are much easier to wash.

Word List

1. European /juərəˈpiːən/ n. 欧洲人 a. 欧洲的
2. advance /ədˈvɑːns; (US) ədˈvæns/ n & v. 提高，提升；前进
3. adult /ˈædʌlt/ n. 成年人 a. 成年的，成熟的
4. experimental /ɪkˌsperɪˈmentl/ a. 实验的
5. game /ɡeɪm/ n. 游戏，比赛；（复）运动会
6. programme /ˈprəʊɡræm/ n. 节目；程序；规划 v. 安排节目；编程序；规划
7. web /web/ n. 网；环球网
8. site /saɪt/ n. 站点；地点，场所
9. website /ˈwebsaɪt/ n. 网址
10. robot /ˈrəʊbɒt/ n. 机器人；遥控设备；自动机械
11. artificial /ˌɑːtɪˈfɪʃəl/ a. 人工的，人造的；假的
12. intelligence /ɪnˈtelɪdʒəns/ n. 智能，智力，聪明
13. object /ˈɒbdʒɪkt/ n. 物体，目标；宾语 /əbˈdʒekt/ v. 反对，抗议
14. vegetable /ˈvedʒɪtəbl/ n. & a. 蔬菜(的)；植物(的)
15. mineral /ˈmɪnərəl/ n. 矿物，矿石
16. indicate /ˈɪndɪkeɪt/ v. 指出，显示；预示
17. include /ɪnˈkluːd/ v. 包括，包含
18. insect /ˈɪnsekt/ n. 昆虫 a. 虫子一样的

19. leather /ˈleðə(r)/ n. 皮革，皮革制品
20. feather /ˈfeðə(r)/ n. 羽毛，翎毛
21. potato /pəˈteitou/ n. 马铃薯
22. bean /biːn/ n. 豆，豆类
23. cabbage /ˈkæbidʒ/ n. 卷心菜，甘蓝
24. addition /əˈdiʃən/ n. 加，增加（物）
25. originate /əˈridʒineit/ v. 起源，发生
26. obviously /ˈɔbviəsli/ ad. 明显地
27. mine /main/ n. 矿，矿井 v. 挖掘，开采
28. inorganic /inɔːˈgænik/ a. 无机物的
29. metal /ˈmetl/ n. 金属
30. copper /ˈkɔpə(r)/ n. 铜；警察
31. silver /ˈsilvə(r)/ n. 银 v. 镀银
32. non-living /nɔnˈliviŋ/ a. 无生物的
33. frame /freim/ n. 结构，框架
34. plastic /ˈplæstik/ n. & a. 塑料(的)
35. obvious /ˈɔbviəs/ a. 明显的，显而易见的
36. handbag /ˈhændbæg/ n. 手提包
37. scissor /ˈsizə(r)/ n. 剪刀 v. 剪，剪去
38. material /məˈtiəriəl/ n. 材料，物资 a. 物质的，实质的
39. waist /weist/ n. 腰部；衣服的上身
40. sock /sɔk/ n. 短袜；鞋内衬底
41. stocking /ˈstɔkiŋ/ n. 长袜
42. wool /wul/ n. 羊毛，毛织品
43. rayon /ˈreiɔn/ n. 人造丝，人造纤维
44. partly /ˈpɑːtli/ ad. 部分地，几分
45. nylon /ˈnailɔn/ n. 尼龙
46. natural /ˈnætʃərəl/ a. 自然的；天赋的；正常的

Idioms and Expressions

1. as well as   以及，除……以外，也，又
2. in addition to   除……以外，又
3. web site   网站
4. on line   在线
5. artificial intelligence   人工智能
6. take it easy   别着急，沉住气
7. work out   想出，做出，计算出

8. be not sure about 对……没有把握
9. living thing 生物
10. non-living thing 非生物
11. be made of 由……(材料)制成
12. be made from 由……(原料)制成
13. be obvious to sb. 对某人是清楚(明显)的
14. be dressed in 穿着

Word Derivation

1. invite—invitation
2. explain—explanation
3. mine—mineral
4. obvious—obviously
5. use—useful—usefulness—usefully
6. wonder—wonderful—wonderfully
7. artifice—artificial—artificially
8. nature—natural—naturally
9. origin—originate—original—originally
10. organ—organic—inorganic

Notes to the Text

❶ Summer School 暑期学校，暑假(补习)学校
❷ the BBC English by radio programs BBC英语广播节目
BBC = British Broadcasting Corporation 英国广播公司
http = Hypertext Transfer Protocol 万维网服务程序中所用的超文本传递协议
www = World Wide Web 万维网
❸ Ms. Green is explaining the rules on how to play the language game.
格林女士正在解释怎样玩这个语言游戏的规则。
句中，介词 on 后接带有连接副词 how 的不定式作宾语。某些介词如 of，about，on 后面可以接带有连接代词(what，who，which)或连接副词(when，where，how)的不定式作宾语。
Would you please give us some advice on how to improve our English?
请就怎样提高英语水平给我们提些建议。
He is thinking about what to do next. 他正在考虑下一步做什么。
❹ Animal includes insects, birds, fishes, snakes as well as cats, dogs and so on.
动物不仅包括猫、狗等等，而且包括虫、鸟、鱼、蛇。

as well as 与 not only...but also... 比较：

The children are lovely as well as healthy.

The children are not only healthy but also lovely.

孩子们不仅健康，而且活泼。

❺ Can it be a pair of scissors?

有可能是一把剪刀吗？

a pair of scissors 一把剪刀   a pair of trousers 一条长裤

a pair of socks 一双短袜   a pair of stockings 一双长袜

❻ You needn't ask such a question. 你不必提这样的问题。

Such 是形容词，与不定冠词 a 或 an 连用时要放在冠词之前，但若与 all，any，few，no，one，several 等词连用时，则应放在后面。如：

Such a dictionary is quite enough. 比较：One such dictionary is quite enough.

这样的字典一本就足够了。

❼ Could it be something made of plastics?

它可能是塑料制成的物品吗？

句中，过去分词短语 made of plastics 作定语修饰复合不定代词 something。如：

Are you thinking this material itself or something made from this material?

你想的是材料本身呢，还是该材料制成的物品呢？

Exercises for Reading Comprehension

I. Answer the following questions.

1. What have the students in the Summer School been invited to do?
2. "Twenty Questions" is a language game in the BBC English by radio programmes, isn't it?
3. Can you play the game on line? How can you manage it?
4. In what condition will you lose the game?
5. Is the question "Where can we find it?" allowed to ask according to the rules?
6. Man in this game is a kind of animal, isn't he?
7. Does *animal* include leather and feathers in this game? Why/Why not?
8. *Vegetable* doesn't include wood in this game, does it?
9. What does the word *mineral* in the game mean?
10. Why needn't Mr. Green explain the rules again?
11. How small is the object that Ms. Green has thought of?
12. Why isn't it necessary for Harry to ask such a question, "Can it be a pair of scissors?"
13. Is it the object that people wear on hands?
14. The object Ms. Green has thought of is a pair of socks, isn't it?

15. Is there any *vegetable* in rayon according to the game?
16. Why is the material not rayon?
17. The object Ms. Green has thought of is nylon, isn't it?
18. What is nylon made from?
19. Ms. Green likes artificial silk better than natural silk, doesn't she?
20. Does her sister like the things made of nylon? Why/Why not?

II. Find the meaning of the words or expressions in Column (A) from those in Column (B).

(A)	(B)
1. except	A. have sth. or sb. as a cause or beginning
2. besides	B. silk-like material that is made partly from wood
3. include	C. a strong thread made from coal, air and water
4. originate	D. very clear, easy to see or understand
5. wear	E. apart from
6. artificial	F. in addition to, as well as
7. natural	G. made by people or false
8. obvious	H. not made or changed by people
9. nylon	I. be dressed in
10. rayon	J. have sth. or sb. as part of the total

III. Fill in the blanks with the words from the blocks, and be sure to use appropriate verb forms and appropriate singular or plural forms for nouns.

> explain, explanation;   invite, invitation;   organic, inorganic
> origin,   originate, original;   wonder, wonderful, wonderfully

1. Generally speaking, birds, beasts, trees and vegetables are _____ things, while iron, copper, tin, gold and silver are _____ things.
2. Do you know the _____ of the word "okay"? Some people say it _____ from an Indian tribe, and its _____ meaning is "it is so."
3. The teacher _____ the question we raised in class, and his _____ was quite obvious to us.
4. I _____ whether you went to the zoo yesterday. The panda and the tamer performed _____, and we really had a _____ time there.
5. They will _____ me to dinner tomorrow, and I have accepted their _____.

IV. Complete the sentences with the given expressions, and change the forms where necessary.

artificial intelligence	as well as	be dressed in	be made from
be made of	be not sure about	be obvious to sb.	in addition to
on line	living thing	non-living thing	take it easy	work out

1. With the development of information technology, it is possible to learn _____ through internet.
2. Nylon _____ coal, air and water, but the blouses _____ nylon.
3. I am sure of some of the English grammar rules, but I _____ their idiomatic usage.
4. Plants and animals are _____ whereas metals are usually _____.
5. _____. There is still some time for you to prepare for the exam.
6. He thought and thought, and at last he _____ the mathematical problem.
7. On Christmas, children _____ beautiful clothes.
8. The president _____ some officials is going to inspect the soldiers.
9. Although he was good at playing chess, he was defeated by a robot with high _____.
10. _____ the names on the list, there are other six doctors and nurses who are willing to fight against SARS.

V. Perform the language game "Twenty Questions" in groups according to the rules given by using the following sentence patterns.

1. The object that I've thought of is...
2. Is it...?
3. Can/Could it be...?
4. It must be..., I dare say.
5. Then it may / might / should / ought to be...
6. It can't be...
7. You should..., shouldn't you?
8. You needn't / shouldn't have asked such a question.
9. Such a question is not allowed to ask in this game.
10. Yes, the object I thought of is ...

Language Structure

The Modal Verbs（情态动词）

　　情态动词表示可能、必要、允许、愿望、猜测等意义。它们本身虽有一定词义，但不能独立用作谓语，后面要跟原形动词。情态动词本身一般没有人称和数的变化。

　　情态动词主要有七个，其时态变化只有现在式和过去式。但它们的现在式可以表示现在时和将来时，过去式除了表示过去时外，也可用于现在时，不过语气比较委婉，此外还有几个与情态动词同义的短语。列表如下：

词义	现在式	过去式	否定式	同义短语	
能够、会	can	could	cannot	be able to	be unable to
可以、许可、也许、可能	may	might	must not、may not	be allowed to	be not allowed to
必须、一定	must	had to	need not、must not	have to	don't have to
应当、要	shall	should	shall not	ought to	ought not to
愿意、会	will	would	will not	be going to	be not going to
需要	need	need	need not		
敢于	dare	dare	dare not		

情态动词的用法：

I. can / could

❶ 表示能力和客观的可能性。如：
You **can** ask questions with an "or" in the middle.
Ms. Green said that the students **could** ask questions with an "or" in the middle.

❷ 在否定句和疑问句中表示猜测、怀疑或惊异。如：
Can it be a pair of scissors?
What he said **could** not be true.

❸ "can / could + have + 过去分词"的结构表示对过去发生的行为的怀疑或不肯定。如：
Can he have seen me yesterday?
You can not have met him in the street just now, for he has gone to the United States.

II. may / might

❶ 表示请求、可以、允许，might 比 may 语气更委婉。如：
Wood **may** be called "vegetable" in this game.
Might I trouble you with a few questions?

❷ may 的否定式有两个：当回答由 may 引起的问题时，否定回答 must not 表示"不许"、"不应该"的意思。如果表示"可能不"的意思就用 may not，含有猜测语气。如：

—*May* I go now?

—Yes, you *may*. (No, you *mustn't*. 或 No, you *may not.*)

❸ "may （或 might)+have+过去分词"的结构，表示对过去发生行为的猜测，含有"可能会"、"也许是"的意思。如：

You *may* (*might*) have heard the language game in the BBC English by radio programs.

III. must / have to

❶ 表示必须、必要，must 表示的是说话人的主观看法，而 have to 则表示客观需要，have to 比 must 有更多的形式。如：

I said I *must* leave but I stayed.（主观看法）

At sometime or another, everyone of us *has had to* face the music.（客观需要）

❷ 当回答由 must 引起的问题时，其否定式有两个，否定答复用 needn't，表示"不必"、"用不着"的意思；否定式用 mustn't，则表示"不许"、"禁止"的意思，其语气比较强烈。如：

—*Must* I explain the rules again?

—No, you *needn't*.

You *mustn't* break the rules in this game.

❸ "must be+主语补足语"的结构通常表示猜测，一般用于肯定句，含有"一定"、"准是"的意思。若在否定句中，则用"cannot be+主语补足语"的结构，含有"不可能"、"准不是"的意思。如：

It *must be* a pair of stockings.

It *can't be* an apple.

❹ "must + have+过去分词"的结构，表示对过去发生行为的猜测，一般用于肯定句，含有"一定"、"准是"的意思；若在否定句中，则用"cannot + have+ 过去分词"，含有"不可能"、"准不是"的意思。如：

You *must have guessed* the object.

He *can't have done* it yesterday.

IV. shall / should / ought to

作为情态动词，should 的使用比 shall 广泛得多，should 并不一定表示过去时态，ought to 和 should 同义，只是语气更强而已。

❶ 表示"应该"、"必须"。如：

You *should* use your brains.

You *ought to* master computer science as the students who major in information technology.

❷ "should(或 ought to)+ be +主语补足语"的结构，表示推测或惊奇。如：

Then it should be something that comes from an animal.

It ought to be a kind of fish, shouldn't it (或oughtn't it)？

❸ "should + have +过去分词"的结构，表示过去应该做而实际上未做的动作或行为，其否定式则表示发生了不该发生的行为。如：

You should have finished the task. （实际上未完成）

You shouldn't have made such a mistake in your exam. （实际上已做了）

❹ shall用作情态动词时，表示决心、警告、命令、允诺等，用于陈述句的第二、第三人称中，在疑问句中则用于第一、第三人称，表示征求对方的意见。如：

You shall get the ticket this afternoon.

Shall he come in or wait outside?

V. will / would

❶ 表示意志、决心或愿望。如：

I *will* help him if he asks me to. （= I'm willing to help him...）

He wondered whether I *would* cooperate with him. （= I was willing to cooperate with him...）

❷ 表示习惯性行为，有"总是"、"惯于"的意思。如：

He *will* talk for hours without stop if you give him the chance.

He *would* go for a walk with his wife after supper.

❸ 用于第二人称作主语的疑问句，表示询问对方的意愿或提出请求，would较will语气委婉客气。如：

Would (Will) you please explain the rules to "Twenty Questions"?

VI. need 和 dare 这两个词只能算"半情态动词"，它们作情态动词时，一般用在否定句或疑问句中，如果用在肯定句中，它们一般只能做实意动词。试比较：

❶ You *needn't* explain the rules again because they are quite obvious to us.

(= You don't need to explain the rules again...)

—*Need* I come here this afternoon? (= Do I need to come here this afternoon?)

—Yes, you *must*. (No, you *needn't*.)

He needs to get a pair of leather shoes. （而不能说 He need get a pair of leather shoes.）

"needn't + have +过去分词"的结构表示"本来不必"做，但实际上已经发生的事情。如：

You *needn't* have asked such a question. （实际上已经问了）

❷ *Dare* he swim across the river? (= Does he dare to swim...?)

The old lady *daren't* walk alone at night. (= The old lady doesn't dare to walk alone...)

[注] "I dare say"常用作插入语，意为"恐怕"、"大概"。如：

It must be a pair of stockings, I dare say.

127

VII. 用作情态动词的短语

除上表所列的情态动词意义短语 be able to，have to，ought to 等之外，还有 had better，had best，would rather，cannot but 等。如：

You **had better** put on more clothes so that you may not catch a cold.

I **would rather** play "Twenty Questions" than watch TV programs.

Everyone **cannot but** be moved to tears.

Exercises for Language Structure

I. Complete the following sentences with the proper forms of modal verbs *must* and *have to*.

1. The last bus has left, and we _____ walk home.
2. You _____ try to be more careful with your work.
3. He said that he _____ study English hard, or he would fall behind.
4. I'm sorry to _____ tell you all about that, but you will see what I've done is for your good.
5. Wang Hong _____ have made her experiment now.

II. Complete the following sentences with the proper forms of modal verbs *had better* and *would rather*.

1. You _____ hurry up, otherwise you will be late for class.
2. The soldiers _____ die than surrender.
3. It's cold outside. You _____ put on more clothes when you go out.
4. You _____ not go about at lunch time.
5. I _____ watch TV than go to the movies this evening.

III. Choose the best answer.

1. She _____ the examination again since she had already passed it.
    A. needn't to take   B. needn't have taken
    C. mustn't take   D. didn't need to take
2. You _____ lead a horse to the water but you _____ not make it drink.
    A. will...can   B. may...can   C. will...may   D. can...may
3. No one _____ that to his face.
    A. dare to say   B. dare says   C. dare say   D. dare saying
4. Prof. Bradley, many students want to see you, _____ they wait here or outside?
    A. do   B. will   C. shall   D. are
5. It _____ be difficult to learn Japanese.
    A. shall   B. must   C. should   D. need

6. Would you like to watch a football match with me this afternoon? I _____ wait for you at the gate of the stadium.
   A. must   B. will   C. would   D. ought to
7. The old man _____ live in the village than in the city.
   A. prefers   B. likes to   C. would rather   D. had better
8. The English of the composition is too good. He _____ it by himself.
   A. must have to write   B. can't have written
   C. mustn't have written   D. can't be written
9. I _____ do it if I needn't face the music.
   A. would not rather   B. would rather not
   C. had not better   D. had better not
10. Must I come here again tonight? No, you _____.
    A. needn't   B. can't   C. mustn't   D. won't

IV. Find out which of the underlined parts in each sentence is not correct in written English.

1. What <u>do you like</u> <u>to do</u> this afternoon, <u>play basketball</u> or <u>go shopping</u> with me?
          A   B   C   D

2. You <u>didn't ought to</u> <u>have done</u> <u>such silly things</u>. You should <u>use your brains</u>.
              A   B   C   D

3. He was <u>a good swimmer</u> so he <u>can swim</u> to the river <u>bank</u> when the boat <u>sank</u>.
                  A   B   C   D

4. Sally <u>needsn't do</u> it <u>by herself</u> if she <u>doesn't</u> want <u>to</u>.
               A   B   C   D

5. I <u>don't believe</u> you <u>at all</u>, <u>for</u> what you said <u>mustn't</u> be true.
            A   B   C   D

6. Prof. Lee <u>isn't able to</u> be in New York <u>now</u>, <u>for</u> I saw him in the street <u>just now</u>.
                   A   B   C   D

7. Our class instructor <u>has made</u> a rule. He said that <u>all</u> the students <u>might</u> come <u>to class</u>
                               A   B   C   D
   on time.

8. Look! <u>What</u> you <u>have done</u>! You <u>would not</u> have been <u>so careless</u>.
              A   B   C   D

9. The boy <u>in the classroom</u> <u>had not better</u> <u>make</u> such a big <u>noise</u>.
                    A   B   C   D

10. I'm sorry I <u>couldn't get in touch with</u> him <u>before</u> he left. I <u>should tell</u> him about it
                          A   B   C   D
    earlier.

Practice and Improvement

Reading Skills

Go through the following passages quickly, and after that, take note of the time, do the exercises, check the answers to the exercises and calculate words per minute.

Speed Reading A

Notes: Before reading the passage, try to get familiar with the following words and expressions.

1. worm /wə:m/ *n.* 虫，蛆虫；蚯蚓
2. alive /ə'laiv/ *a.* 活着的；活泼的
3. raw /rɔ:/ *a.* 生的；未加工的
4. brain /brein/ *n.* 脑，头脑
5. use one's brains 动脑筋，想办法

Twenty Questions (II)

Ms.Green: Now, let's continue our games, shall we? The object I've thought of is an animal.
Rosa: Has it two legs?
Ms.Green: No.
Anne: Has it four legs?
Ms.Green: No.
Pedro: Is it an insect? Has it eight legs?
Ms.Green: No, it's not an insect, and an insect has six legs, not eight.
Hans: Has it any legs at all?
Ms.Green: It has no legs.
Harry: Then it might be a snake.
Ms.Green: No, not a snake.

Anne:	It may be a worm. A worm has no legs.
Ms.Green:	No, not a worm.
Hans:	Then it should be something from an animal. Is it leather or feathers?
Ms.Green:	No, neither leather nor feathers.
Pedro:	Can it be eaten?
Ms.Green:	Yes, it can be eaten.
Anne:	Then it ought to be a kind of fish, shouldn't it?
Ms.Green:	No, the object isn't a fish.
Rosa:	Is it alive?
Ms.Green:	That's a difficult question to answer. There's life inside it.
Hans:	It's something we can eat. Do we usually cook it or eat it raw?
Ms.Green:	It's generally cooked, but these things are sometimes eaten raw.
Rosa:	An apple? No, it can't be an apple. An apple is vegetable, not animal. Can you get these things everywhere or in only a few parts of the world?
Ms.Green:	Oh anywhere, I think.
Hans:	Is it wet or dry?
Ms.Green:	It's dry outside but wet inside.
Pedro:	Is it hard or soft?
Ms.Green:	Hard outside…
Harry:	Then it's soft inside. What color is it?
Ms.Green:	That's not a "Yes or No" question. You should use your brains, shouldn't you?
Hans:	Is it red?
Ms.Green:	No.
Hans:	Yellow?
Ms.Green:	Part of it is yellow.
Pedro:	Then I dare say it's an egg.
Ms.Green:	Yes, the object I thought of is a hen's egg. But you have asked me more than twenty questions, so you have lost the game.

(355 words)

Time:

Comprehension

I. Choose the best answer according to the passage.

1. An insect is an animal which has _____ legs.
   A. two   B. four   C. six   D. eight
2. Which of the things doesn't belong to *animal*?
   A. A snake.   B. A worm.   C. A fish.   D. An apple.
3. The object is _____.
   A. dry outside, wet inside; soft outside, hard inside
   B. wet outside, dry inside; hard outside, soft inside
   C. dry outside, wet inside; hard outside, soft inside
   D. wet outside, dry inside; soft outside, hard inside
4. Which of the statement is true?
   A. The object is red.   B. The object is yellow.
   C. Part of the object is red.   D. Part of the object is yellow.
5. The students lost the game because _____.
   A. they didn't find the answer
   B. they found the wrong answer
   C. they found the answer within twenty questions
   D. they found the answer with more than twenty questions

II. True or False:

(　) 6. Leather is something that comes from an animal.
(　) 7. It's difficult to say whether the object is alive or not.
(　) 8. People usually eat it raw.
(　) 9. We can get it everywhere.
(　) 10. Harry broke the rules in this game.

Correct rate: _____%
Reading speed: _____ wpm

Speed Reading B

Notes: Before reading the passage, try to get familiar with the following words and expressions.

1. **partner** /ˈpɑːtnə(r)/ *n.* 伙伴，伴侣； *v.* 与……合伙，与……组成一对
2. **magnificent** /mægˈnifisnt/ *a.* 宏伟的，华丽的
3. **grand** /grænd/ *a.* 豪华的，盛大的；主要的
4. **Roman** /ˈrəumən/ *n. & a.* 罗马的，罗马人（的）

5. Rome /rəum/ n. 罗马
6. Italy /ˈitəli/ n. 意大利
7. Venice /ˈvenis/ n. 威尼斯（地名），意大利城市
8. lean /liːn/ v. & n. 倾斜；依靠
9. tower /ˈtauə(r)/ n. 塔；城堡
10. Pisa /ˈpiːzə/ n. 比萨（地名），意大利城市
11. the Leaning Tower of Pisa 比萨斜塔
12. Galileo /ˌgæliˈleiːou/ 伽利略（意大利科学家，1564~1642）

Twenty Questions （Ⅲ）

Mr.Green: Would one of you like to take my place and answer the questions raised by your partners?
Rosa: May I take your place?
Ms.Green: Certainly, Rosa.
Rosa: I've thought of something. It's mineral.
Harry: It's something made of metal?
Rosa: No, it's not made of metal.
Pedro: Is the object natural or artificial?
Rosa: It is artificial.
Pedro: Was it made recently or a long time ago?
Rosa: A long time ago.
Hans: Is it a useful subject?
Rosa: I suppose it was useful when it was made, but I don't know if it's useful today.
Harry: Is it in England?
Rosa: No.
Pedro: In your country, Italy?
Rosa: Yes, it's in my country.
Pedro: It must be an old and famous building?
Rosa: Yes, that's a good guess.
Hans: Is it a magnificent palace?
Rosa: No, I'm afraid it is not.
Hans: Can it be a grand theatre?
Rosa: No.
Anne: You said it was made a long time ago. Are you thinking of some of the Roman ruins?

Rosa: No, it's not something that the Romans built.
Harry: What town in Italy do you come from?
Ms.Green: Harry, you are not allowed to ask that kind of question.
Harry: Sorry, Ms.Green. Rosa, are you from Rome or Venice?
Rosa: Neither.
Pedro: Did Galileo once teach in the university of your town?
Rosa: Yes! You must have guessed it.
Pedro: Did Galileo drop two heavy weights from the top of this building you're thinking of? You're from Pisa, aren't you?
Rosa: Yes. The object I thought of is the Leaning Tower of Pisa.

(272 words)

Time: _____

Comprehension

I. Choose the best answer according to the passage.

1. The thing that Rosa thought of is _____.
   A. a kind of metal   B. a natural object
   C. an artificial object   D. a useful subject
2. You can find the object in _____.
   A. Italy   B. Britain   C. France   D. England
3. The thing that Rosa thought of _____.
   A. is being made now   B. will be built soon
   C. was made just now   D. was made a long time ago
4. Rosa is _____ young woman.
   A. an English   B. an Italian   C. a German   D. a French
5. The old and famous building was _____.
   A. a magnificent palace   B. a grand theatre
   C. one of the Roman ruins   D. a leaning tower

II. True or False:

( ) 6. Ms. Green answered the entire questions raised by the students.
( ) 7. The object was useful when it was made, but it's really not useful now.
( ) 8. Many old famous buildings now become the Roman ruins in Italy.
( ) 9. Galileo once taught in the University of Pisa.
( ) 10. Galileo once dropped two heavy weights from the Leaning Tower of Pisa.

Cloze Procedure

Inviting sb. to the Theatre

Pedro: (1) you like to go to the theatre with me, Rosa?

Rosa: I'd like to go with you, but I (2) . I've promised to go to the theatre with Harry.

Pedro: Oh, well, you'll enjoy being with Harry, (3) ?

Rosa: I'm not sure. He's a very dull young man. What are you going to see at the theatre?

Pedro: "Hamlet," the play we all read last week. You (4) it very much.

Rosa: Yes, I enjoy reading the play by Shakespeare, but I'm sorry I can't go with you.

Pedro: It's a pity you can't go. Next week, perhaps.

Rosa: I wish I knew Harry's telephone number. I (5) phone and say I'm not well enough to go with him.

Pedro: Oh, that (6) be very kind, would it? You (7) break your promise.

Rosa: You're right. I (8) keep my promise to Harry. Let's go to "Hamlet" tomorrow, (9) .

Pedro: Need I call for you tomorrow evening?

Rosa: No, you (10) . Let's meet at the gate of the theatre at seven tomorrow evening.

Notes:

1. **dull** /dʌl/ *a.* 迟钝的，呆笨的；不活跃的
2. **Hamlet** /ˈhæmlit/ 哈姆雷特（莎士比亚悲剧剧名和该剧主人公）
3. **Shakespeare** /ˈʃeikspiə/ 莎士比亚（1564~1616）英国著名剧作家和诗人
4. **break one's promise** 违约
5. **keep one's promise** 守约
6. **call for** 邀约（某人）；拿取（某物）

Fill in the blanks with the best answers.

1. A. Would   B. Could   C. Had   D. Should
2. A. mustn't   B. may not   C. can't   D. wouldn't

3. A. will you   B. won't you   C. shall we   D. shan't we
4. A. may enjoy   B. might enjoy
   C. must enjoy   D. must have enjoyed
5. A. could   B. can   C. had   D. should
6. A. shouldn't   B. wouldn't   C. hadn't   D. couldn't
7. A. had better not   B. had not better
   C. would rather not   D. would not rather
8. A. may   B. might   C. must   D. had to
9. A. will you   B. won't you   C. shall we   D. shall I
10. A. need   B. must   C. needn't   D. mustn't

Speaking Skills

I. Warm-up Exercises: *Read the poem aloud.*

To（致—）

By Percy Bysshe Shelley （1792~1822）

I can not give what men call love:
But wilt thou accept not
The worship the heart lifts above
And the heaven rejects not.
And the desire of the moth for the star,
Of the night for the morrow
The devotion to something afar
From the sphere of our sorrow.

我不能给您
    人们所津津乐道的爱情，
您能否接受
    上苍也不会拒绝的崇敬。
犹如飞蛾扑向星星，
    又如黑夜向往黎明。
这种仰慕之心
    早已超越了人间的苦境。

——波西·比希·雪莱（1792~1822）

II. Conversation

Practice the dialogues with your partner, and then write a dialogue about invitation and appointment.

Dialogue 1   Taking a Ride in the Countryside

A: Hi, Jenny.
B: Hi, Frank. How're you doing?
A: Oh, not too bad. Say, are you doing anything on Saturday evening?
B: No, nothing special. Why?
A: Well, do you feel like going to the new restaurant for dinner?

B: That sounds like a good idea.

A: Terrific, what about taking a ride in the country first?

B: Sure, why not? Where shall we meet?

A: Why don't I pick you up at your house?

B: Okay. What time?

A: Does five o'clock suit you?

B: Fine. Well, see you at five, Saturday evening.

A: Right. See you then.

B: Bye.

Dialogue 2   Going to the Concert

A: Hello. Could I speak to Lisa Black, please?

B: This is Lisa speaking.

A: Hi, Lisa. This is Derek Jones. Do you remember—I'm from the International Trade Department.

B: Oh, of course, Derek. How are you?

A: Just fine, thanks. Oh, Lisa, I wonder if you'd like to go to a concert this Saturday evening.

B: I'd love to, Derek, really, but I'm sorry I can't. I have a previous appointment. Mary invited me to her birthday party.

A: Oh, I see. Well, could we make it some other time then?

B: Yes, I'd like that.

A: Well, are you free next Saturday evening, by any chance?

B: Next Saturday would be fine. What time does the concert start?

A: At half past seven, but we could have dinner together first.

B: That sounds very nice.

A: I'll pick you up at half past five at the school gate, okay?

B: Fine. I'll see you next Saturday then.

A: Right. I'm looking forward to it.

B: Me, too. Thank you so much for your invitation. Goodbye.

A: Ok, so long for now.

Notes:

1. **previous**   /ˈpriːvjəs/ a. 在前的，早先的
2. **appointment**   /əˈpɔintmənt/ n. 约会；指定
3. **pick up**   用车接人；掘地；捡起；获得；看到；加速
4. **by any chance**   万一；或许

Listening Skills

I. Directions: Listen to the following sentences. Tick the right words the speaker says.

1. A. piece   B. peace
2. A. guest   B. guessed
3. A. heard   B. heart
4. A. wear   B. where
5. A. learning   B. leaning
6. A. glass   B. grass
7. A. coal   B. goal
8. A. medal   B. metal
9. A. thin   B. thing
10. A. wash   B. watch

II. Directions: In this section, you will hear 10 short conversations. At the end of each conversation, a question will be asked about what was said. The conversation and question will be spoken only one time. After each question, there will be a pause. During the pause, you must read the four choices marked A, B, C and D, and decide which the best answer is, and then choose the corresponding letter.

1. A. At a hotel.   B. At the airport.
   C. At the doctor's office.   D. In a post office.
2. A. It was wonderful.   B. She enjoyed it very much.
   C. She would watch it again.   D. It was not good at all.
3. A. In England.   B. In China.   C. In India.   D. In the United States.
4. A. By train.   B. By bus.   C. By car.   D. By air.
5. A. The woman was trying to sleep.   B. The man was very quiet.
   C. The woman was making a loud noise.   D. The man was trying to sleep.
6. A. Two.   B. Three.   C. Four.   D. Six.
7. A. Saturday.   B. Sunday.   C. Wednesday.   D. Monday.
8. A. 2 pounds.   B. 3 pounds.   C. 4 pounds.   D. 5 pounds.
9. A. 9:30.   B. 12:00.   C. 11:50.   D. 2:20.
10. A. In a post office.   B. In a hotel.
    C. At a station.   D. At the airport.

III. Directions: In this section, you will hear a passage of about 90 words three times. There are about 20 words missing. First, you will hear the whole passage from the beginning to the end just to get a general idea about it. Then, in the second reading, write down the missing words during the pauses. You can check what you have written when the passage is read to you once again without the pauses.

At a Summer School __(1)__ for Europeans who __(2)__ their English, a group of __(3)__ have been invited to take part in "Twenty Questions," a global __(4)__ language game. Ms. Green is explaining the rules on how __(5)__ the language game.

You all know something about __(6)__, I'm sure. Some of you may have heard it in the BBC English __(7)__, or some of you may have contacted the website __(8)__ to play the game with the __(9)__ robot. The address of the __(10)__ is http://www.20q.net/.

Translation Skills

I. Translate the following into English.

1. 这些报纸和杂志不允许带出办公室。(be allowed to do)
2. 这些事实大家都很清楚。(be obvious to)
3. 动植物是生物，而矿物是非生物。(living things, non-living things)
4. 在这个游戏中，动物除包括鸟、兽、虫、鱼以外，还包括皮革和羽毛，因为它们出自生物。(as well as)
5. 尼龙是煤、水和空气制成的，而剪刀是用铁制成的。(be made of, be made from)

II. Translate the following into Chinese.

1. Ms. Green's sister would rather have nylon blouses because they are easier to wash.
2. You had better go there by bus, otherwise you would be late.
3. You must have played the global experimental language game.
4. He cannot have done such a thing, but his brother may have done it.
5. You needn't have taken the exam last week, for you passed it last term.

Writing Skills

I. Rewrite each of the sentences after the model.

Model A: *Animal* includes not only cats and dogs but also insects, birds, fishes, snakes and so on.

Animal includes insects, birds, fishes, snakes as well as cats, dogs and so on.

1. As a writer of science fictions, he must have not only strong imagination but also scientific knowledge.
2. Air can hold up not only tiny raindrops but also birds and planes.
3. We must grasp not only grammar rules but also idiomatic usage.
4. In this game, *mineral* includes not only things from mines like coal and oil but also

metals like gold and silver.

5. The goods win popular sales not only for their reasonable prices but also for their excellent quality.

Modal B：*Such questions are not allowed to ask in this game.*
Such questions mustn't be asked in this game.

1. You are not allowed to break the rules in this game.
2. Newspapers and magazines are not allowed to take out of the reading room.
3. The chart is not allowed to fill in ink.
4. You are not allowed to speak freely in class.
5. The passengers are not allowed to smoke in the non-smoking area.

II. Practical Writing
1. 请柬

请柬也称请帖（Invitation or Invitation Card），广泛用于宴会、晚会、舞会、婚礼以及各种开幕式、闭幕式等社交场合。全文要用第三人称语气。邀请者夫妇双全且同居一处，则应把夫妇的姓名都写上；被邀请者如夫妇双全且同居一处，也要用全称写上两者的姓名。

Invitation Card

Invitation Card

Mr. and Mrs. Robert Johnson
request the pleasure of the company of
Mr. and Mrs. George Bradley
at a welcome reception
in honor of the Chinese trade delegation
on Saturday, Dec.11, 2004
at 7 o'clock p.m.
at Hilton Hotel in West Street

RSVP

Telephone：
55168168

2. 回帖

回帖（Reply to Invitation），被邀请人收到正式请柬后，应及时答复，以表示接受或拒绝。如果接受，应先表示谢意，然后再写明应邀出席的时间和地点；如果谢绝，应先致以歉意，然后再说明不能出席的原因。回帖的格式与请柬的格式相同。

Reply to Invitation

Reply to Invitation

Mr. and Mrs. George Bradley
accept with pleasure
the kind invitation of Mr. and Mrs. Robert Johnson
to the welcome reception
in honor of the Chinese trade delegation
on Saturday, Dec.11, 2004
at 7 o'clock p.m.
at Hilton Hotel in West Street

Notes：
1. invitation /inviˈteiʃən/ n. 请帖，请柬；邀请
2. pleasure /ˈpleʒə(r)/ n. 愉快，高兴
3. reception /riˈsepʃən/ n. 招待会；接待，接受
4. delegation /deliˈgeiʃən/ n. 代表团；授权，委托
5. in honor of 向……表示敬意，为……欢迎
6. RSVP 法语缩写词，请帖用语（= please reply）

Exercise

Write an Invitation and a Reply to Invitation according to the Chinese given. You can model your writing on the above samples.

按照上面的格式分别写一张请柬和回帖：

1. 请柬

请　柬

兹定于2004年12月31日（星期五）晚上8时在教学楼320室举行除夕晚会。
恭请
戴维·布朗宁先生光临

财经系学生分会谨订

10点至12点举行舞会
请赐回音

2. 回帖

回　帖

因另有前约，抱歉不能参加财经系学生分会2003年12月31日（星期五）晚上8时在教学楼320室举行的除夕晚会。

戴维·布朗宁

A　Proverb

He that nothing questioneth, nothing learneth.
—Gosson

提不出问题，学不到东西。
——葛桑

Unit Six

FABLES ABOUT MICE

Reading Selection

Text A

PRE-READING TASK

1. Have you read any fables or fable books in English before?
2. Do you like reading fables? Why or Why not?
3. Can you tell a fable in English?

The Mouse King Marries His Daughter

Long, long ago, there was a mouse kingdom. The mouse king had a daughter, who was the most beautiful mouse in this castle. When she was old enough to be married, the mouse king called together all of his advisers and ministers to consult them.

"My daughter," he said, "is lovely and noble enough to marry just anyone, and I have decided to marry her to the greatest thing in the world. Now, will you please tell me whom she is to be married to?"

Mouse King 老鼠国王   Mouse Princess 老鼠公主   Mouse Bridegroom 老鼠新郎   The Wedding Ceremony 结婚典礼

(The Mouse King Marries His Daughter 鼠王嫁女)

At first, the mice didn't know what to say. After a while, a senior minister advised the mouse king that the sun was the greatest thing in the world.

"Then, I shall marry her to the sun." said the mouse king.

"But," objected the second, stroking his whiskers, "a cloud can cover the sun."

"You are right. Then, she ought to be married to the cloud."

"But," squeaked the third, "the rain is strong enough to burst through the clouds and destroy them."

"That's true. I have to wed her to the rain."

"But," cried the fourth, waving his tail, "no matter how hard the rain falls, it can not wash away the trees."

"Then the solution is simple. She must marry a tree."

"But," pointed out the fifth, "a strong wind can blow down the trees."

"Very true. The wind must be her husband then."

"But," remembered the sixth, scratching his ear, "no matter how hard the wind blows, it cannot blow away the earth."

"Then I have to marry her to the earth."

"But the earth is buried under the wooden floor of men's houses," said the seventh.

"Then she shall wed the wooden floor at once."

"But," said the prime minister at last, his eyes glittering, "strong as the wooden floor is, a mouse can bite his way through it."

"There is no doubt that a mouse is the greatest thing in the world!" the mouse king burst out cheering.

All the mice hailed excitedly, and that is how the mouse princess happened to marry a mouse.

Text B

PRE-READING TASK

1. *Do you think a mouse is really the greatest thing in the world?*
2. *What is the natural enemy of mice?*

3. Can you guess how the mice in the kingdom coped with the situation when their natural enemy came on the scene?

A Mice's Meeting

Once upon a time, there lived many mice in a castle. But one day, two cats, Felicia and Madeline, came on the scene and they killed many of the mice.

Then the mouse king called all his advisers to his palace so as to have a meeting. He said, "It's necessary for us to decide what to do about the two cats. They seem to be the most dangerous enemy of us."

The mice thought and thought, but no one gave any advice on how to deal with the cats. They found it very difficult to cope with the situation.

"Who will give me some advice on how to solve the problem?" the mouse king squeaked impatiently.

The mice looked at each other in blank dismay and kept silent.

Then the mouse king turned to his son-in-law, Wellington, to whom he just married his daughter, "What about your opinion?"

"I've got a good idea," the junior mouse said. "In order not to be caught by the cats, we must put two bells around their necks. When they come near, we'll hear the bell ring and run away to hide. So the cats will kill no more of us."

"What a splendid idea!" All the mice burst into cheers. They were excited for the young mouse to have put forward such a wonderful proposal. This would make it possible for them to deal with the cats.

Then the mouse king said, "It's very clever of you to think out such a good plan, Wellington, but who will bell the cats?"

No mouse replied. They pretended not to have heard what he said.

The mouse king raised his voice, "Who will put the bell around the cats' necks?" He waited, but still no one volunteered to do it.

Then he turned to Wellington once again, but this time the young mouse lowered his head and murmured, "I'm afraid—that I am—too young to do it."

At last, the mouse king said, "It's easier to say things than to do them."

Word List

1. fable /ˈfeibl/ n. 寓言；虚构的故事
2. mice /mais/ n. mouse 的复数形式
3. mouse /maus/ n. 老鼠；鼠标
4. kingdom /ˈkiŋdəm/ n. 王国
5. king /kiŋ/ n. 国王
6. castle /ˈkɑːsl；(US)ˈkæsl/ n. 城堡
7. adviser /ədˈvaizə(r)/ n. 顾问；指导老师
8. minister /ˈministə(r)/ n. 大臣，部长
9. consult /kənˈsʌlt/ v. 商议，请教；向……咨询
10. lovely /ˈlʌvli/ a. 可爱的，有趣的
11. noble /ˈnoubl/ a. 高贵的；崇高的 n. 贵族
12. advise /ədˈvaiz/ v. 劝告；建议
13. senior /ˈsiːnjə(r)/ a. 年长的；地位高的 n. 长辈；大学四年级学生
14. stroke /strouk/ v. 抚摸 n. 击，敲
15. whisker /ˈwiskə(r)/ n. 胡须，腮须
16. squeak /skwiːk/ v. & n. (发出)尖叫，吱吱叫
17. tail /teil/ n. & a. 尾巴(的)，尾部(的)
18. destroy /diˈstrɔi/ v. 破坏，毁坏，消灭
19. burst (burst, burst) /bəːst/ v. 爆发，爆裂
20. wed /wed/ v. 嫁，娶，结婚
21. solution /səˈluːʃən/ n. 解决方法；溶解，溶液
22. simple /ˈsimpl/ a. 简单的，朴素的；率直的；易受骗的
23. point /pɔint/ v. 指出，指向；瞄准 n. 要点；分数
24. scratch /skrætʃ/ v. 搔，抓；刮擦；涂抹
25. bury /ˈberi/ v. 隐藏；埋葬
26. wooden /ˈwudn/ a. 木制的
27. glitter /ˈglitə(r)/ v. & n. 闪光，闪烁
28. bite /bait/ v. & n. 咬；刺痛
29. cheer /tʃiə(r)/ v. & n. (使)欢快，发出(欢呼)
30. happen /ˈhæpən/ v. 碰巧，偶然
31. princess /ˈprinses/ n. 公主，王妃
32. scene /siːn/ n. 现场，场面；景色
33. advice /ədˈvais/ n. 忠告，建议；(商务) 通知
34. deal (dealt, dealt) /diːl/ v. 处理，应付 n. 交易
35. cope /koup/ v. 应付，处理
36. situation /sitjuˈeiʃən/ n. 情景；境遇；位置

37. impatiently /ɪmˈpeɪʃəntli/ ad. 不耐烦地，无耐性地
38. blank /blæŋk/ a. 空白的；无表情的 n. 空白，空格
39. dismay /dɪsˈmeɪ/ n. & v. 沮丧，惊慌
40. son-in-law n. 女婿
41. junior /ˈdʒuːnjə(r)/ a. 年少的；地位低的 n. 晚辈；大学三年级学生
42. bell /bel/ n. 钟，铃 v. 系铃于，装钟于
43. splendid /ˈsplendɪd/ a. 壮丽的，辉煌的；极好的
44. reply /rɪˈplaɪ/ n. & v. 答复，回答；报复；答辩
45. pretend /prɪˈtend/ v. 假装，装扮
46. volunteer /ˌvɒlənˈtɪə(r)/ v. 自愿 n. & a. 志愿(的)，志愿者
47. murmur /ˈmɜːmə(r)/ v. & n. (发出)咕哝；怨言；低沉连续的声音

Proper Names

Felicia /fəˈlɪsiə/ 菲丽西娅(女子名)
Madeline /meɪdlɪn/ 玛德琳(女子名)
Wellington /welɪŋtən/ 威林顿(男子名)

Idioms and Expressions

1. burst through 冲破
2. blow away 刮走，吹走
3. wash away 冲走，冲跑
4. point out 指出
5. bite one's way through 咬穿……而过
6. burst out 爆发
7. happen to (do) 碰巧做，偶然发生
8. once upon a time 从前
9. come on the scene 出现，登场
10. deal with 处理，对付，安排
11. cope with 处理，应付
12. in dismay 处于沮丧状况
13. turn to 转向，求助于；开始行动
14. burst into 爆发；闯入；突然出现
15. think out 想出，解决

Word Derivation

1. king—kingdom
2. prince—princess
3. solve—solution
4. situate—situation
5. love—lovely
6. wood—wooden
7. advise—advice—adviser
8. consult—consultant—consultation
9. patience—patient—impatient—impatiently
10. cheer—cheerful—cheerfully

Notes to the Text

❶ When she was old enough to be married, the mouse king called together all of his advisers and ministers to consult them. 当她到了足以出嫁的年龄，鼠王把所有的顾问和大臣召集在一起，和他们商量此事。

句中，she = the mouse king's daughter，在寓言故事中，往往把动植物比拟做人，用人称代词 he 或者 she；be married 表示状态。

enough 在这里是副词，修饰形容词或副词时，一般应放在形容词或副词之后。如：
This book is easy enough for me to read. 这本书很容易，我足可读懂。
You know well enough what I mean. 你足以了解我的意思。

❷ Now, please tell me whom she is to be married to. 现在，请告诉我她该嫁给谁。

句中，助动词 be 和不定式连用，作句子的谓语，表示计划、约定、职责和义务等。如：
The factory is to turn out 50,000 cars next year. 这家工厂计划明年生产五万辆轿车。
The president of Russia is to visit China next month. 俄罗斯总统定于下月访问中国。

❸ "But," objected the second, stroking his whiskers, "a cloud can cover the sun."
"但是，"第二只老鼠抚着胡须反对到，"云彩能遮住太阳。"

stroking his whiskers 是现在分词短语，作状语修饰谓语动词 objected，表示伴随情况和方式。又如：
"But," cried the fourth, waving his tail, "no matter how hard the rain falls, it can not wash away the trees." "但是，"第四只老鼠摇着尾巴喊道，"不管雨下得有多大，总不能把树冲跑。"

❹ "But," said the prime minister at last, his eyes glittering, "strong as the wooden floor is, a mouse can bite his way through it." "但是，"宰相眨巴着眼睛最后说道，"虽

然木质地板非常坚硬，但是老鼠能够咬穿地板而过。"

① his eyes glittering 是由名词+现在分词构成的复合结构，在句子中作状语，修饰谓语动词 said，表示伴随情况。如：

He fell to the ground, blood streaming from his nose. 他鼻子流着血，倒在地上。

② strong as the wooden floor is = though the wooden floor is strong，连词 as 引导让步状语从句时，往往将充当主语补语的形容词或作状语的副词置于句首。如：

Hard as the rain falls, it can not wash away the trees.

虽然雨下得很大，但不能冲跑树木。

❺ "There is no doubt that a mouse is the greatest thing in the world!" the mouse king burst out cheering. 鼠王顿时发出欢呼，"毫无疑问，老鼠是世界上最伟大的东西！"

burst out cheering =burst into cheers 突然发出欢呼 又如：

burst out crying =burst into tears 突然哭起来

burst out laughing=burst into laughter 突然笑起来

❻ All the mice hailed excitedly, and that is how the mouse princess happened to marry a mouse.

所有的老鼠都激动得欢呼起来，这就是老鼠公主为什么恰好嫁给一个老鼠的经过。

happen +不定式是"碰巧"、"恰好"的意思。又如：

I happened to be out when you made a telephone call to me. 你给我电话时，我碰巧外出了。

❼ Once upon a time, there lived many mice in a castle. 从前，有许多老鼠住在一个城堡里。

① once upon a time 意为从前，很久以前。往往用于故事或寓言的开头，交待故事发生的时间，类似的短语还有 long, long ago 等等。

② 表示"存在"的句型，有时谓语不用 be，而用 live, appear, come, lie, seem, stand 等动词，从而使句子更加生动。如：

There lies a purse on the ground. 地上有一个钱包。

There stand two big trees in front of the house. 房前有两棵大树。

❽ It's very clever of you to think out such a good plan. 你想出这样一个好计划，真聪明。

句中 it 是形式主语，介词 of+名词或代词（宾格）+to do 构成的不定式复合结构是实际主语，常用在以 bad, careless, clever, thoughtful, foolish, good, kind, nice, right, smart, wise, wrong 等表示心理特征的形容词作补语的句子中。这时 of 后面的名词或代词是不定式的逻辑主语，同时又与前面的形容词有主语和补语的关系。因此此句可改写为：

You are very clever to think out such a good plan. 又如：

It's thoughtful of you to meet me at the airport. 你到机场来接我真是考虑周到。

You are thoughtful to meet me at the airport.

❾ I'm afraid—that I am—too young to do it. 恐怕……我……太小，做不了此事。

句中，too...to do 是以不定式来修饰前面的副词 too，因而不定式含有否定的意思，可译为"太……而不能"。又如：

The news is too good to be true. 消息太好，恐不可靠。

He was too excited to speak. 他激动得说不出话来。

 Exercises for Reading Comprehension

I. Answer the following questions.

1. When and where did the story happen?
2. Who had a beautiful daughter in the mouse kingdom?
3. Why did the mouse king call together all of his advisers and ministers?
4. What did the mouse king say about his daughter?
5. What did his advisers and ministers do at first?
6. Who said that the sun was the greatest thing in the world?
7. A cloud can cover the sun, can't it?
8. Why did the prime minister's eyes glitter when he gave his advice to the mouse king?
9. Whom did the mouse king happen to marry his daughter to?
10. What can you learn from this fable?
11. What happened one day to the mice in a castle?
12. Why did the mouse king call his advisers to his palace?
13. The mice found it very easy to cope with the cats, didn't they?
14. Who gave a good idea finally?
15. Does the idea make it possible for the mice to deal with the cats?
16. What did the mouse king say to Wellington, his son-in-law?
17. Many mice volunteered to bell the cats, didn't they?
18. Why did the mice pretend not to have heard what the mouse king said?
19. What did Wellington say when the mouse king turned to him?
20. Do you agree to the saying, "It is easier to say things than to do them? Why / Why not?

II. Find words in the texts which mean approximately or the same as the following, using the given letters as a clue.

1. person who gives advice — a_____
2. cut into with the teeth — b_____
3. ask someone to learn what you want to know — c_____
4. short story that teaches something — f_____
5. shine brightly with small flashes of light — g_____
6. younger or of lower rank or position — j_____
7. country ruled by a king or queen — k_____
8. be against or feel dislike — o_____
9. older or of higher rank or position — s_____

10. marry   w_____

III. Complete the sentences with the given expressions, and change the forms where necessary.

> king, kingdom;   love, lovely;   solve, solution
> advice, advise, adviser;   patience, patient, impatiently

1. Once upon a time there was a small _____, which had a wise _____.
2. Ms. Green is a very kind and _____ teacher. She always enlightens her students with _____, and never treats her students _____.
3. A doctor is usually a good _____ to the patients. When a patient consulted Dr. Stuart last week, he _____ the patient to give up smoking, and the patient took his _____.
4. When I asked George how to _____ the difficult problem, he told me that there were three _____ to the problem.
5. Our motherland is so _____ that every one of us _____ her very much.

IV. Complete the following passage by using appropriate words listed below. Be sure to use singular or plural forms for nouns.

> blow away   blow down   burst into   burst out   burst through
> come on the scene   cope with   deal with   happen(to do)   in dismay
> once upon a time   point out   think out   turn to   wash away

1. Since you can't _____ the situation, I have worked out a plan _____ it.
2. _____, there was an old fisherman who lived in a small village.
3. When she heard the bad news, the girl _____ tears, that is to say, she _____ crying.
4. The storm yesterday _____ several large trees and _____ the clothes that were hanging on the line, and the small bridge nearby _____ by the flood.
5. After a heavy rain, the sun _____ the clouds and shone over the earth.
6. If you _____ to meet some problems in your studies, you can _____ your adviser for help.
7. When the famous singer _____, the audience burst into cheers and hailed her.
8. I must _____ a good idea to object to their carrying out this plan.
9. The wise leader _____ a way for the people to develop their country in the changing

world situations.

10. The ministers were all _____ when the prime minister asked them how to deal with the difficult political and economic situation.

Language Structure

The Infinitive （不定式）

不定式是动词的一种非限定形式，通常前面带有不定式符号to。不定式可以起名词、形容词和副词的作用，在句子中可以充当主语、宾语、补语、定语、状语等；同时不定式保留了动词的某些特征，如可以有宾语或状语（不定式和宾语或状语一起构成不定式短语），还可以有否定式、时态和语态等。

I. 不定式的用法

❶ 不定式不能单独作谓语，但可以与情态动词或助动词一起构成谓语。如：

I have *to wed her to the rain*. 我得把她嫁给雨。

Now, please tell me whom she is *to be married to*. 现在请告诉我她该嫁给谁。

❷ 作主语　不定式作主语时，常用先行词it代替，而将不定式移到句子后面去。如：

To see one time is better than to hear a hundred times. 百闻不如一见。

It is easier to say things than to do them. 说事容易做事难。

❸ 作宾语　不定式作宾语时，常用先行词 it 代替，而将不定式移到句子后面去。如：

I have decided *to marry her to the greatest thing in the word*. 我已决定把她嫁给世界上最伟大的东西。

The mice found it very difficult *to cope with the situation*. 老鼠们觉得很难应付这种情况。

[注] 有些动词后面只能接不定式作宾语，如 decide, determine, expect, fail, hope, pretend, promise, refuse, volunteer 等等。

❹ 作补语

① 作主语补语，放在联系动词后面。如：

The greatest happiness is *to work for the happiness of all*. 为全人类谋幸福是最大的幸福。

They seem *to be the most dangerous enemy of us*. 它们好像是我们最危险的敌人。

② 作宾语补语，放在宾语之后。如：

A senior minister advised the mouse king *to wed his daughter to the sun*. 一位老臣劝告鼠王把女儿嫁给太阳。

[注] 在 make, let, have, see, hear, watch, notice, feel 等动词后使用不定式作宾语补语时，要省略 to，但这种句子变为被动结构时，to 就不能省略。

The boss made the clerks *work overtime*. 老板迫使职员们加班工作。

The clerks were made to *work overtime*. 职员们被迫加班工作。

❺ 作定语 不定式作定语时，一般放在所修饰的名词或代词之后。如：

Is this the best way *to deal with the problem*? 这是处理该问题的最佳办法吗？

There is nothing *to worry about*. 没有什么可发愁的。

❻ 作状语 不定式作状语，表示行为的目的、结果和原因等。如：

① 作目的状语 如：

One day, a mother mouse and her babies went out *to play in the open field*.

一天，母老鼠和小老鼠到户外去玩。

Then the mouse king called all the advisers and ministers to his palace *so as to have a meeting*. 然后，鼠王召集所有的顾问和大臣到他的宫殿去开个会。

In order to catch up with others, she decided to study even harder.

为了赶上别人，她决定更努力地学习。

② 作结果状语 如：

My daughter is lovely and noble enough *to marry just anyone*. 我的女儿又美丽又高贵，足以和任何人匹配。

I'm afraid—that I am—too young *to do it*.

恐怕……我……太年轻了，还做不了这件事。

The cat was so frightened *as to run away*. 猫吓得逃跑了。

③ 作原因状语或是在哪方面存在谓语所表示的情况。如：

I'm very glad to see you.

She is always ready to help others.

II. 不定式的复合结构 由"介词 for + 名词（或代词宾格）+ to do"构成，在句中可以充当以下成分：

❶ 作主语 不定式复合结构作主语时常用先行词 it 代替，而将实际主语放在句子后面。如：

It was dangerous *for him to come out for a meal*. 他出外用餐是很危险的.

He knew that it was safe *for him to go out*. 他知道到外面去是安全的.

❷ 作宾语 不定式复合结构作作宾语常用先行词 it 代替，而将实际主语放在句子后面。如：

This would make it possible *for them to deal with cats*.

这就使他们有可能对付猫了。

I think it not necessary *for you to fight over such a bell*.

我认为你们为这样一只铃铛大打出手是没有必要的。

❸ 作补语 如：

It is *for you to decide*. 此事由你决定。

❹ 作定语 如：

The first thing *for you to do* is to make out a study plan.

你们要做的第一件事是制定一个学习计划。

It's time *for us to go over our lessons*. 是我们复习功课的时候了。

❺ 作状语 如：

The problem is too difficult *for them to solve*.

这个问题太难了，他们解决不了。

They handed in their exercises just in time for *the teacher to correct*.

他们正好及时交上了作业，让老师批改。

III. 连词 whether，连接代词 what，which，who，连接副词 when，where，how + 不定式结构，这种结构可以在句子中充当以下成分：

❶ 作主语 如：

Where to hold the conference hasn't been decided.

❷ 作宾语 在 advise，decide，discuss，find out，forget，know，learn，show，teach，tell 等动词后，常用这种结构作为宾语。如：

At first the mice didn't know *what to say*.

[注] 不定式一般不能用作介词的宾语，但这种结构可用在某些介词如 of，on，about 后作介词宾语。如：

But no one gave any advice on *how to deal with the cats*.

但是没有人对怎样对付猫提出任何建议。

Everyone has his own idea of *how to do it*. 每个人对如何做这件事都有自己的想法。

❸ 作补语 如：

The problem now is *how to have a good command of English* as soon as possible.

问题是如何尽快地掌握英语。

❹ 作状语 如：

I'm not sure *what to do next*. 我对下一步做什么没有把握。

IV. 不定式的时态和语态　　不定式有时态和语态的变化，现以 **learn** 为例，列表如下：

时态＼语态	主动式	被动式
一般式	to learn	to be learned
进行式	to be learning	—
完成式	to have learned	to have been learned
完成进行式	to have been learning	—

❶ 不定式的时态

① 不定式一般式所表示的动作一般在谓语动词所表示动作之后发生。如：

The doctor advised the patient *to give up smoking*. 医生建议这位病人戒烟。（to give up smoking 的动作发生在谓语动词 advised 之后）

② 不定式进行式表示动作正在进行，与谓语所表示的动作同时发生。如：

He pretended *to be listening carefully*. 他装着一副认真听讲的样子。(to be listening carefully 与谓语动词 pretended 同时发生）

③ 不定式完成式所表示的动作发生在谓语动词所表示的动作之前。如：

They were excited for the young mouse *to have put forward such a wonderful proposal*. 小老鼠提出这样一个奇妙的建议，他们都激动不已。(to have put forward such a wonderful proposal 发生在谓语 were excited 状态之前）

④ 不定式完成进行式在谓语动词之前发生，并一直延续到谓语动词发生时。如：

The scientists are reported *to have been making researches on space travel*. 据报道这些科学家一直在从事宇航研究。

❷ 不定式的语态 不定式的逻辑主语是不定式所表示的动作的承受者时，一般要用被动形式。不定式的被动式有两种形式：

① 不定式一般式的被动式 如：

He preferred *to be given heavier work to do*. 他宁愿承担更繁重的工作。

The books and magazines are not allowed *to be taken out of the reading room*. 这些书籍和杂志不许携带出阅览室。

② 不定式完成式的被动式 如：

Ham was said *to have been trained in a space school*. 据说哈姆曾在宇航学校受过培训。

Prof. Bradley was delighted *to have been invited to the evening party*. 被邀参加晚会，布莱德利教授非常高兴。

V. 不定式的否定形式一般是在不定式符号 **to** 前加否定副词 **not** 或 **never**。如：

In order not to be caught by the two cats, we must put two bells around their necks. 为了不让这两只猫抓住我们，我们必须在她们颈上系两个铃铛。

They pretended not to have heard what the mouse king said. 他们假装没听见鼠王说了些什么。

Exercises for Language Structure

I. Point out each infinitive in the following sentences and then tell its function.

1. The rain is strong enough to burst through the clouds and destroy them.
2. When she was old enough to be married, the mouse king called together all his advisers and ministers to consult them.
3. We found it difficult to finish the work on time.
4. The doctors are trying their best to save the patients who suffered from SARS.
5. Jane, I have something important to tell you.
6. Our main task is to build our motherland into a prosperous country.

7. When to visit the Great Wall has not been decided yet.

8. It is necessary for us to grasp science and culture.

9. The mice were having a meeting to discuss how to deal with the cats.

10. When they come near, we'll hear the bell ring and run away to hide.

II. Complete the sentences with the infinitive.

1. Enough has been said on _____ （怎样学习词语掌故）.

2. _____ （如何处理这个问题） is for you to decide.

3. The cat happened _____ （看见老鼠在田里玩耍）.

4. The teacher often tells us _____ （上学不要迟到）.

5. He gave me some advice on _____ （怎样提高英语水平）.

6. He got up early _____ （以便准时赶上火车）.

7. When she heard the news, she didn't know _____ （是哭还是笑）.

8. It's not easy _____ （防止污染）.

9. This novel is said _____ （已被译成了英语）.

10. There are a lot of oral exercises _____ （供我们在课上练习）.

III. Choose the best answer.

1. Did you notice him _____ the road?
   A. across   B. cross   C. to cross   D. crossed

2. _____ defend his motherland, he joined the army.
   A. In order that   B. In order to   C. So that   D. So as to

3. He was _____ to help me at the moment.
   A. too busy   B. so busy   C. very busy   D. enough busy

4. Ms. Green, would you be _____ to explain the rules again?
   A. too kind   B. so kind   C. so kind as   D. as kind as

5. Mr. Green advised me to practice more _____.
   A. so as to make not mistakes   B. so as to not make mistakes
   C. not so as to make mistakes   D. so as not to make mistakes

6. He didn't know _____ to stay or to leave here.
   A. whether   B. if   C. either   D. weather

7. The little boy found _____.
   A. with no one to play   B. no one with to play
   C. no one to play with   D. no one to play

8. There isn't any difference between the two. I really don't know _____.
   A. where to choose   B. which to choose
   C. to choose what   D. to choose which

9. You don't need _____ about her. She is safe at home now.
   A. to be worrying   B. to be worried

C. to worrying D. to have worrying
10. I think it careless _____ so many mistakes.
   A. for he to make B. for him to make
   C. of he to make D. of him to make

IV. Find out which of the underlined parts in each sentence is not correct in written English.

1. <u>Almost</u> <u>everyone</u> fails <u>passing</u> <u>his driver's test</u> at first.
     A   B   C   D

2. The article was <u>so difficult</u> <u>to understand</u> that I <u>had to</u> have my teacher <u>to explain it</u>.
                  A   B   C   D

3. <u>As soon as</u> he saw the young child <u>fell into</u> the river, he <u>jumped into</u> it <u>to save him</u>.
     A   B   C   D

4. The building <u>is said</u> <u>to have destroyed</u> <u>in a fire</u> two months <u>ago</u>.
             A   B   C   D

5. The teacher <u>asked</u> Harry <u>didn't</u> to make <u>such</u> a noise <u>in class</u>.
          A   B   C   D

6. Mr. Harris dislikes <u>playing</u> football, but he <u>likes</u> <u>to watch</u> others <u>to play it</u>.
              A   B   C   D

7. There are <u>still</u> <u>a lot of</u> difficulties <u>for they</u> <u>to overcome</u>.
       A B   C   D

8. She <u>was heard</u> <u>sing</u> <u>a sweet song at the party</u> <u>last night</u>.
       A   B   C   D

9. He said, "It's quite <u>late</u> now. You <u>had better</u> <u>to leave</u> <u>at once</u>."
                  A   B   C   D

10. When he graduated <u>from</u> a college, he asked <u>to send</u> <u>to work</u> <u>in the western areas</u>.
                   A   B   C   D

Practice and Improvement

Reading Skills

Go through the following passages quickly, and after that, take note of the time, do the exercises, check the answers to the exercises and calculate words per minute.

Speed Reading A

Notes: Before reading the passage, try to get familiar with the following words and expressions.

1. peace /piːs/ n. 和平，安宁
2. softly /ˈsɔftli/ ad. 柔软地，温柔地
3. starve /staːv/ v. (使)……饿死
4. jingle /ˈdʒiŋgl/ v. & n. (发出)铃铛声
5. unfair /ʌnˈfɛə(r)/ a. 不公平的
6. dash /dæʃ/ v. 猛冲，猛撞 n. 破折号；冲撞
7. equally /ˈiːkwəli/ ad. 同等地；公平地
8. cheat /tʃiːt/ n. & v. 欺骗
9. appear on the scene 出现，登场
10. run after 追赶，追逐
11. cheat sb. into doing sth. 欺骗某人做某事

A Mouse and Two Cats

Once upon a time, in a mouse kingdom there was a smart mouse, Wellington, who lived in a beautiful castle and married the mouse king's lovely daughter. Every day, he ate good food and lived a comfortable life. But one day, two cats, Felicia and Madeline, appeared on the scene, and they killed many mice. From that day on, he had no peace. Every time the cats saw him step out of the hole in the wall, they would run after him, so he was only safe when they were not around. But they walked so softly that he didn't know when they were around. It was dangerous for him to come out for a meal. He had to do something to deal with the cats, or he would be starved to death. They had a meeting to discuss how to cope with the situation. Though he put forward a good proposal, no one volunteered to bell the cats.

One evening, Wellington came out of his hole with a bright silver bell. The junior mouse walked up to Felicia and said, "Is this a lovely bell, Felicia? Ah, yes my dear, I thought you would like it. I found it in the wall and right away I thought of you. Well, if you put this bell around your neck, you'll be the most beautiful cat in the castle!"

Felicia was delighted when she looked at the bell. "Well, you'll make your sister Madeline look like an old hen." That was about all Wellington needed to say. Not a moment later, Felicia was running proudly around the castle with the bell jingling at her neck.

Next, Wellington walked up to Madeline. "Hello, Madeline," he squeaked, "did you see the silver bell around your sister's neck? Oh, you did? And you just let her walk around the castle and do nothing about it? Why, it's unfair for your sister to wear the bell, not fair, I say. Your sister is becoming the pet of the castle. Listen, you are twice as lovely as she is. With the bell, no cat in the castle will be more beautiful than you. Oh, here comes your sister, and I had better go to hide now."

The mouse dashed back to his hole and waited to see whether his plan was working. A minute later, he found that the two cats were fighting over the bell. Once again Wellington went out of his hole. He carried another bell and dashed into the middle of the fight.

"Look," he shouted, "I've found another bell just like the first one. I think it not necessary for you to fight over such a bell." He handed the bell to Madeline. "Now you both look equally beautiful." Madeline put the bell around her neck and the two cats were satisfied and walked away. Wellington was quite satisfied, too, because the two cats were cheated into wearing the bells.

From that day on, when he heard the bells, he knew that the cats were coming. And when he didn't hear the bells, he knew that it was safe for him to go out. He did not have to worry about Felicia and Madeline any more.

(540 words)

Time: _____

Comprehension

I. Choose the best answer according to the passage.

1. Wellington didn't know when the two cats were around because _____.
   A. his eyes were blind
   B. his ears were deaf
   C. they walked very softly
   D. they walked very slowly

2. Wellington _____ the silver bell around her neck.
   A. told Felicia to put
   B. asked Felicia to put

C. made Felicia put　　　　　　　　D. cheated Felicia into putting

3. Felicia was _____ when she looked at the silver bell.

   A. angry　　　B. excited　　　C. satisfied　　　D. disappointed

4. When he found that the two cats were fighting over the bell, Wellington dashed into the middle of them so as to _____ .

   A. stop them from fighting　　　　B. watch them fighting
   C. see whether his plan was working　　D. give another bell to Madeline

5. The mouse said to Felicia, "Well, you'll make your sister look like an old hen." In this sentence, "look like an old hen" means look _____ .

   A. beautiful　　　B. lovely　　　C. noble　　　D. ugly

II. True or False:

(　) 6. The mouse lived a happy life before the two cats came on the scene.

(　) 7. Wellington told Madeline that she was much more beautiful than Felicia.

(　) 8. Wellington was disappointed when he saw the two cats fight over the bell.

(　) 9. Wellington made the two cats wear the silver bells by force.

(　) 10. Wellington was a clever mouse who was good at observation and thinking.

Correct rate: _____ %

Reading speed: _____ wpm

Speed Reading II

Notes: Before reading the passage, try to get familiar with the following words and expressions.

1. bilingual　/baiˈliŋgwəl/　a. 能说两种语言的
2. crawl　/krɔːl/　n. & v. 爬行，缓慢行进
3. bowwow　/ˈbauwau/　n. 狗吠声
4. in no time　立即，很快

The Bilingual Mouse

One day a mother mouse and her babies went out to play in an open field. They were having a good time when suddenly a hungry cat came on the scene! The cat hid behind a big tree and then crawled forward through the tall grass until she could almost hear the mice talking. Before the mother mouse and her babies knew what had happened, the cat jumped from the hiding-place and started to run after them.

The mother mouse and her babies ran away at once. They hurried towards their home, which was under a few large stones, but the baby mice were too frightened to run very quickly. Closer and closer the cat came. In no time, the cat would be upon them. What was to be done?

The mother mouse stopped running, turned round and shouted to the cat, "Bowwow! Bowwow!" just like an angry dog. The cat was so frightened as to run away.

The mother mouse turned to her babies and said, "Now you see how important it is to learn a second language."

(182 words)
Time: _____

Comprehension

I. Choose the best answer according to the passage.

1. A bilingual mouse can speak _____.
   A. only one language　　　B. two languages
   C. its mother tongue　　　D. its native language

2. The cat hid behind a big tree so as to _____.
   A. crawled forward through the tall grass
   B. hear the mice talking
   C. climb the big tree
   D. catch the mice suddenly

3. When the mother mouse shouted to the cat, "Bowwow! Bowwow!" the cat ran away because it _____.
   A. was afraid of the mother mouse
   B. was afraid of the baby mice
   C. was afraid of an angry dog
   D. didn't want to run after the mice

4. The mother mouse told her babies that it was very important _____ to learn a second language.
   A. for they　　B. for them　　C. of they　　D. of them

5. The sentence "The cat was so frightened as to run away" means _____.

A. the cat was so frightened that she ran away
B. the cat was so frightened that she didn't run away
C. the cat was so frightened that she might run away
D. the cat was so frightened that she couldn't run away

II. True or False:

( ) 6. One day, a mother mouse and her babies went out to play in the open air.
( ) 7. They enjoyed themselves very much, and at that time a hungry cat suddenly appeared.
( ) 8. The mice's hole was made of a few large stones.
( ) 9. The baby mice were so frightened that they could not run very quickly when they saw the cat.
( ) 10. The mother mouse fought bravely against the cat like an angry dog and saved her babies.

Correct rate: _____ %
Reading speed: _____ wpm

Cloze Procedure

The Town Mouse and the Country Mouse

One day a country mouse invited a town mouse, one of his close friends, __(1)__ him a visit. The country mouse had nothing __(2)__ his guest but some roots of wheat because it was winter and the field was bare. The town mouse said to his friend, "It is foolish __(3)__ the life of ants here. In my house, there is plenty of good food. You had better __(4)__ with me, and you'll have a share of my food."

So the country mouse went to town with his friend. As soon as they arrived, the town mouse took out plenty of bread and cheese __(5)__. The country mouse was very delighted __(6)__ such good food, and he expressed his thanks in warm words. Just as they were beginning to eat, someone burst into the room, and they both __(7)__ and ran off as fast as they could to a hole. They had badly begun their dinner again when someone entered the room __(8)__ something out of the room. The two mice were more frightened than before, and ran away to hide themselves. At last the country mouse, __(9)__ to death, said to his good friend: "Though you prepared such good food for me, I have __(10)__ it by yourself. I prefer my bare field and roots of wheat so that I could live in safety, and without fear."

Notes:

1. **entertain** /ˌentəˈteɪn/ v. & n. 招待，款待
2. **root** /ruːt/ n. 根，根部　v. （使）生根，扎根
3. **bare** /beə(r)/ a. 赤裸的，无遮蔽的

Fill in the blanks with the best answer.

( ) 1. A. to pay   B. pay   C. paying   D. paid
( ) 2. A. to entertain B. entertain   C. entertaining   D. entertained
( ) 3. A. for you live B. for you to live C. because you live D. of you to live
( ) 4. A. to go   B. go   C. going   D. gone
( ) 5. A. for his friend ate   B. of his friend ate
       C. for his friend to eat   D. of his friend to eat
( ) 6. A. see   B. to see   C. have seen   D. to have seen
( ) 7. A. to squeak   B. squeak   C. squeaking   D. squeaked
( ) 8. A. so to take   B. to take   C. not to take   D. taking
( ) 9. A. to have almost starved   B. to starve almost
       C. to have starved   D. to have been starved
( ) 10. A. leave you enjoy   B. to leave you enjoy
       C. leave you to enjoy   D. to leave you to enjoy

Speaking Skills

I. Warm-up Exercise: *Read the poem aloud.*

A Birthday

By Christina Rossetti （1830~1894）

My heart is like a singing bird	我的心像欢唱的小鸟
Whose nest is in a watered shoot;	鸟巢筑在水汪汪的嫩尖；
My heart is like an apple-tree	我的心像芳香的果树
Whose boughs are bent with thickest fruit;	硕果累累把枝干压弯；
My heart is like a rainbow shell	我的心像雨后的彩虹
That paddles in a halcyon sea;	如桨划过平静的大海；
My heart is gladder than all these	我的心欢悦远胜于此哟
Because my love is come to me.	人间真爱正向我撒来。

——克里斯蒂娜·罗塞蒂（1830~1894）

II. Conversation

Practice the dialogues and then write a dialogue about "Directions and Instructions" and practice it with your partner.

Dialogue 1   Where Is the Bookshop?

A: Excuse me. I'm looking for the shopping center.

B: Well, there isn't a shopping center here. I mean, what sort of shop do you want?

A: I want to buy a couple of fairy tales books for my daughter.

B: What you really want is a bookshop, isn't it?

A: Yes, a bookshop.

B: Let me see. Oh, there's one on Castle Street. Do you know Castle Street?

A: No, I'm a stranger here.

B: Are you walking or driving?

A: Walking.

B: Well, go down this street, and take the first turn on the right.

A: First on the right.

B: Yes. Then second left.

A: First right, then second left.

B: That's right. On the corner there's an electrical goods shop. They sell radios, TV sets and fridges. That's on the corner, where you turn. You can't miss it.

A: OK.

B: Turn left at this electrical goods shop, and walk down till you come to a clothes shop. A big men's clothes shop. And just after that there's your bookshop.

A: I see.

B: Opposite it there's a bank. So if you look out for the clothes shop and the bank, you know you're in the right place.

A: And it's on the same side as the bank?

B: No. Opposite it. It's just after the clothes shop, on the same side. It may be next door to it, or one door away, but it's just after it.

A: Let's see. Down here, first right, then second left at an electrical goods shop.

B: That's right.

A: Then it's just after a men's clothes shop, near a bank?

B: That's it.

A: Thank you very much.

B: You're welcome.

Dialogue 2   Where Is the Central South University?

A: Excuse me, I want to get to Central South University. Can you tell me if Bus No. 12 is the right bus to take?

B: Yes. Take Bus No. 12, but you'll have to change to another bus to get to the university.

A: Oh dear, where do I change buses?

B: Well, when you get to the Maple Hotel, you should get off Bus No. 12. Go directly across the main road and you'll see a bus stop. Wait there for Bus No. 5. It will take you directly to the Central South University. It will be on your right. You can't miss it.

A: I see—take Bus No. 12, get off at the Maple Hotel, cross the main road, and then change to Bus No. 5.

B: That's right. You can't go wrong.

Notes:

1. stranger /ˈstreɪndʒə(r)/ n. 外地人，陌生人；门外汉
2. electrical /iˈlektrɪkl/ a. 电的
3. fridge /frɪdʒ/ n. 电冰箱
4. opposite /ˈɔpəzɪt/ a. 对面的，对立的，相反的 prep. 在……的对面
5. maple /ˈmeɪpl/ n. 枫树，枫木

Listening Skills

I. Directions: *Listen to the following sentences. Tick the right words the speaker says.*

1. A. scene   B. seen
2. A. piece   B. peace
3. A. hole   B. whole
4. A. advise   B. advice
5. A. wear   B. where
6. A. new   B. knew
7. A. wash   B. watch
8. A. bag   B. back
9. A. cheers   B. tears
10. A. quiet   B. quite

II. Directions: *In this section, you will hear 10 short conversations. At the end of each conversation, a question will be asked about what was said. The conversation and question will be spoken only one time. After each question, there will be a pause. During the pause, you must read the four choices marked A, B, C and D, and decide which the best answer is, and then choose the corresponding letter.*

1. A. Couple.   B. Strangers.   C. Boss and employees.   D. Friends.
2. A. Three.   B. Twelve.   C. Nine.   D. Fifteen.
3. A. She didn't sleep well.   B. She went to bed late.
   C. She couldn't fall asleep.   D. She didn't sleep last night.
4. A. He posted the letter.   B. He lost the letter.
   C. He didn't know about the letter. D. He forgot to post the letter.
5. A. She doesn't mind.   B. The man should not smoke.
   C. She doesn't smoke.   D. She allows the man to smoke.
6. A. She has won a prize, too.   B. She doesn't show much interest.
   C. She is glad to hear that.   D. She has already known it.
7. A. On foot.   B. By taxi.   C. By their own car.   D. By bus.
8. A. She will say goodbye.   B. She will stay for a cup of tea.
   C. She will be late for work   D. She will go to the railroad station.
9. A. She attended a party,   B. She lost her way.
   C. She met with an accident.   D. She failed to attend the party.
10. A. He heard of that, too.   B. He will not believe it unless he sees it.
    C. He saw it with his own eyes.   D. He believed it was true.

III. Directions: *In this section, you will hear a passage of about 90 words three times. There are about 20 words missing. First, you will hear the whole passage from the beginning to the end just to get a general idea about it. Then, in the second reading, write down the missing words during the pauses. You can check what you have written when the passage is read to you once again without the pauses.*

The mother mouse and her babies __(1)__ at once. They hurried __(2)__ their home, which was __(3)__ a few large stones, but the baby mice were __(4)__ to run very quickly. Closer and closer the cat came. __(5)__, the cat would be upon them. What was to be done? The mother mouse __(6)__, turned round and shouted to the cat, "Bowwow! Bowwow!" just like __(7)__. The cat was so frightened as to run away. The mother mouse __(8)__ her babies and said, "Now you see __(9)__ it is to learn __(10)__."

Translation Skills

I. Translate the following into English.
1. 他太年轻了，现在还不能应付这一工作。
2. 他们终于想出了对付困难的好办法。
3. 当这位影星登场时，观众爆发出阵阵欢呼。
4. 听到这个消息时，玛丽突然放声大哭起来。

5. 昨天我在街上碰巧遇到了约翰。

II. Translate the following into Chinese.

1. The teacher advised the students not to read on bed.
2. He seemed to have known the news.
3. This new method makes it possible for us to finish the task within a couple of days.
4. Prof. Bradley gave us some advice on how to improve our English.
5. She is a nice person to work with.

Writing Skills

I. Rewrite each of the sentences after the model.

Model A：*You are clever to think out such a good plan.*

It's clever of you to think out such a good plan.

1. You are nice to invite me to the party.
2. You are foolish to turn down the proposal.
3. Pedro is so kind to think so much of us.
4. Harry is silly to ask such a question in the game.
5. Wendy is so smart to consider the problem so carefully.

Model B：*The mice didn't know what they could say at first.*

The mice didn't know what to say at first.

1. I don't know which shirt I shall choose.
2. Please show me how I can do that.
3. I wonder whether I'll watch TV or go to the movies this evening.
4. Please tell us when we'll leave for New York.
5. We want to know where we are going to have a conference.

II. Practical Writing

明信片（Postcard）是向亲友传递简要信息或表达问候或祝贺的简短信函，通常写法比较简单。在明信片的右面通常写上收信人的姓名和地址，地址的排列顺序应由小到大，左面写上寄信人简明扼要的话语。一般来说，明信片没有必要写上寄信人的地址，但要签署写信人的姓名。

明信片　　　　　　　POSTCARD

POSTCARD

Nov.28, 2004

Many Happy Returns of the day to you!
And I wish you always happy and gay.
　　　　　　　　Yours
　　　　　　　　Li Ming

Mr. George Hill
266 Seaside Road
Boston, MS28345
United States

Stamp

Exercise

Write a postcard according to the Chinese given. You can model your writing on the above postcard.

根据所给的材料，按照上面的格式给詹尼·罗丝女士写一封明信片。地址：英国利物浦市场街168号；邮编：LV 28SR；内容：祝圣诞快乐，新年愉快！

POSTCARD

Stamp

A Proverb

To strive, to seek, to find, and not to yield.

　　　　　　　　　　　　—Tennyson

奋斗，探索，发现，而不要放弃。

　　　　　　　　　　　　——丁尼生

Unit Seven

STORIES ABOUT THOMAS EDISON

Reading Selection

Text A

PRE-READING TASK

1. Have you heard of Thomas Edison?
2. How many inventions did he make? Can you name one or two of his inventions?
   A. A few.   B. Dozens of.   C. Hundreds of.   D. Thousands of.
3. In your opinion, what qualities should an inventor possess?

The World's Greatest Inventor

Thomas Edison was a great American inventor who made great contributions to the mankind. In his life, he made hundreds of inventions, including the electric bulb, and the world's first talking machine, the phonograph.

Even when he was a little boy, he was always trying to find out how things worked. Being proud of Thomas Edison, Sam Edison liked to talk

After long and hard work, Edison felt tired and fell asleep at his working table.

Edison was demonstrating his tinfoil phonograph in his laboratory in 1878.

(Genius is one percent inspiration and ninety-nine percent perspiration.)

about his son to his friends or neighbors.

"He is always asking about things," with a pipe in his mouth, Sam Edison was talking to a friend, Captain Bradley. "I expect he's gone to the farm to bother the people there with his questions."

"The other week he went to a grain store, and climbed to the top to watch the grain pouring into the barn. He leant over too far and fell in. If one of the men hadn't seen him and pulled him out, he would have been killed."

The captain laughed now and then, while listening to his words.

"Then there was time he wanted to know how a bees' nest in the hedge worked. He looked in and nothing happened, so he began to prod it with a stick. Just then a goat came and pushed him into the bees' nest, but the bees did not like it a bit. When he came running home, his face and hands all swelled up."

"That boy will go a long way," Captain Bradley said. "It's good for him to find out things, as long as he does no harm."

"He never does any harm to others—except to himself and his clothes." Having finished his chat with his neighbor, Sam Edison wrinkled up his nose and sniffed. "Can you smell something burning?" he asked, getting to his feet.

"There's smoke over there," the captain said, his finger pointing to a farm in the distance. Accompanied by his friend, Sam Edison hurried towards the farm.

"Why, there's my son, running as if a wild animal chased after him."

The "wild animal" was a very angry farmer.

"Set my farm on fire!" he was roaring, his face covered with sweat.

Sam Edison went into a house and then came out with a long stick in his hand.

"Why did you do it?" he asked in a terrible voice, with his eyes wide open.

"I wanted to see what would happen," he answered and felt uneasy with his father staring at him. Sam Edison took him by the hand and led him down the street.

That's how the world's greatest inventor was publicly beaten in the market place, at the age of six in the year 1853.

Text B

PRE-READING TASK

1. Do you know who created the world's first industrial-research laboratory?
2. When was the world's first industrial-research laboratory set up?
   A. In 1850s.   B. In 1860s.   C. In 1870s.   D. In 1880s.
3. What was the first invention in the laboratory?

Talking Tinfoil

In 1876, Thomas Edison created the world's first industrial-research laboratory in Menlo Park, New Jersey. Then he began to work on an invention. It was a machine that he hoped would talk.

"Talk!" cried one of his assistants, "how could a machine talk?"

"Just wait," the inventor said with a smile on his face. "One of these days, I'll show you that it can be done."

The decision having been made, Edison started working at once. With his assistants helping him, he made one experiment after another. Soon Edison was ready to try out his new machine. "Bring me some tinfoil," Edison said to one of his assistants, "and today you'll see the talking machine."

Having been given such a good chance, his assistants all stopped their work and came in front of Edison's working table. A strange-looking little machine was on the table. They observed the experiment being carried on. Edison wrapped a sheet of tinfoil around a part of the machine. It was shaped like a tube. Then Edison started turning a crank, and the tube wrapped in tinfoil turned round and round. Bending over the little machine, Edison shouted as loud as he could:

"Mary had a little lamb,
Its fleece was as white as snow.
And everywhere that Mary went,
The lamb was sure to go."

Edison stopped cranking, and turned the machine back to its starting point. His assistants burst into laughter now, for they felt amused to hear Edison reciting the old rhyme. With the tube turning round and round, a voice was heard clearly.

"Mary had a little lamb,
Its fleece was as white as snow..."

These were the first words ever recorded. Edison was right. He finally made a talking machine, the first phonograph, or gramophone. It was one of his most important inventions.

Word List

1. contribution /ˌkɔntriˈbjuːʃən/ n. 贡献，捐献
2. electric /iˈlektrik/ a. 电的，用电的，电动的
3. bulb /bʌlb/ n. 灯泡
4. phonograph /ˈfounəɡrɑːf/ n. 留声机，唱机
5. demonstrate /ˈdemənstreit/ v. 展示，示范；证明，论证
6. tinfoil /ˈtinfɔil/ n. 锡箔，锡纸
7. neighbor /ˈneibə(r)/ n. 邻居，邻国
8. pipe /paip/ n. 烟斗；管道，输送管 v. 以管道输送
9. expect /iksˈpekt/ v. 期待，期望；料想
10. bother /ˈbɔðə/ v. 打扰，烦扰
11. barn /bɑːn/ n. 粮仓
12. nest /nest/ n. 巢，窝 v. 筑巢，巢居
13. hedge /hedʒ/ n. 树篱；矮树
14. prod /prɔd/ v. 戳；刺激
15. swell /swel/ v. 肿胀；增大
16. wrinkle /ˈriŋkl/ v. 起皱 n. 皱纹
17. sniff /snif/ v. 嗅出，闻；用力吸气
18. distance /ˈdistəns/ n. 远处；距离，间隔
19. accompany /əˈkʌmpəni/ v. 伴随，陪同
20. chase /tʃeis/ v. & n. 追逐，追赶；跟踪
21. roar /rɔː(r)/ n. & v. 吼叫，咆哮
22. sweat /swet/ n. 汗；水珠，湿气
23. uneasy /ʌnˈiːzi/ a. 拘束的，不自在的；忧虑的，担心的
24. stare /steə(r)/ v. 盯，凝视
25. publicly /ˈpʌblikli/ ad. 公开地，公然地，当众地
26. decision /diˈsiʒən/ n. 决定，决策
27. observe /əbˈzɜːv/ v. 观察，观测；遵守；评述，说

28. crank /kræŋk/ n. 曲柄 v. 转动(曲柄)
29. bend (bent,bent) /bend/ v. (使)……弯曲；专心于 n. 弯曲
30. lamb /læm/ n. 羔羊
31. fleece /fli:s/ n. 羊毛
32. laughter /ˈlɑːftə(r); (US) ˈlæftər/ n. 笑，笑声
33. amuse /əˈmjuːz/ v. 逗……乐(笑)，给……娱乐
34. recite /riˈsait/ v. 背诵，朗诵
35. rhyme /raim/ n. 韵律，押韵；押韵的诗词
36. gramophone /ˈgræməfoun/ n. 留声机

Proper Names

1. Thomas Edison　托马斯·爱迪生
2. Sam Edison　萨姆·爱迪生
3. Bradley　布莱德利
4. Menlo Park　门罗公园
5. New Jersey　新泽西(美国州名)

Idioms and Expressions

1. make a contribution to 对……做出贡献
2. be proud of 为……而骄傲(自豪)
3. fall in 掉下，坍塌
4. now and then 时而，不时
5. not a bit 一点也不，毫不
6. swell up 肿胀起来
7. go a long way 大有作为
8. do harm to 对……有害
9. point to 指着，指向
10. in the distance 在远处
11. chase after 追逐，追赶
12. stare at 凝视，盯着看
13. work on 从事于；继续工作
14. one...after another 相继，一个又一个
15. try out 试验，试行
16. carry on 进行；处理；坚持下去

Word Derivation

1. contribute—contributor—contribution—contributive
2. demonstrate—demonstrator—demonstration—demonstrative
3. decide—decision—decisive
4. electric—electricity—electrify—electrician
5. public—publicity—publicize—publicly
6. distance—distant—distantly
7. ease—easy—uneasy—uneasily
8. amuse—amusement—amused—amusing
9. assist—assistance—assistant
10. laugh—laughter

Notes to the Text

❶ He is always asking about things. 他总爱寻根究底。

现在进行时和 always, constantly, all the time 等副词或短语连用时,常可表示一种感情色彩,如厌烦、赞叹等。如:

The children are always making troubles.(表示厌烦)

这些孩子总是捣蛋。

She is always thinking of others. (表示赞叹)

她总是想着别人。

❷ With a pipe in his mouth, Sam Edison was talking to a friend, Captain Bradley.

萨姆·爱迪生含着烟斗,正在和一位朋友布莱德利船长交谈。

介词 with 后面可跟复合结构构成短语,常见的复合结构可由名词(或代词宾格)+ 介词短语、形容词或分词等构成,通常用来作状语,表示伴随情况、行为方式、原因和条件等等。如:

Sam Edison went into a house and then came out with a long stick in his hand. 萨姆·爱迪生走进了一座房子,然后拿着一根长棍走了出来。

He was roaring, with his eyes wide open. 他咆哮着,眼睛瞪得溜圆。

❸ If one of the men hadn't seen him and pulled him out, he would have been killed.

要不是有人看见,把他拉了出来,他就没命了。

句中 hadn't seen...would have been killed 是虚拟语气,表示与过去事实相反的假设。又如:

If Edison had not been curious about things, he would not have become an inventor.

要是爱迪生不对事物充满好奇,他就不可能成为发明家。

❹ That boy will go a long way. 那孩子会很有出息的。

go a long way 大有作为，很有帮助

❺ Then there was the time he wanted to know how a bees' nest in the hedge worked. 还有一次，他想知道树篱中的蜂窝是怎么回事。

句中，he wanted to know how a bees' nest in the hedge worked 是省去关系副词 when 的定语从句；当先行词为 time 时，关系副词 when 可以省略。如：

Come any time you like. 你随便什么时候来都行。

❻ Why, there's my son, running as if a wild animal chased after him. 哎呀，那是我的儿子，他飞跑着，好像后面有只野兽在追逐似的。

句中，as if 所引导从句的谓语动词用的是虚拟语气。又如：

The weather is so cold now. It seems as if it was (were) winter already. 天气很冷，仿佛已经是冬天了。

They talked as if they had been friends for years. 他们谈话很投缘，就好像是多年的老朋友似的。

❼ Sam Edison took him by the hand and led him down the street.

萨姆·爱迪生抓住他的手，领着他向大街走去。

注意英语中这一说法和汉语不同，英语中把接收动作的人作为直接宾语，而用介词短语来说明接触到人体的某一部位。又如：

to pull him by the arm　拉住他的胳膊（不是 pull his arm）

to hit him on the head　击中他的头部

to strike him in the face 打在他的脸上

❽ It was a machine that he hoped would talk.

他希望这是一台会说话的机器。

句中，he hoped 是插入语。

❾ A strange-looking little machine was on the table. 一台模样古怪的小机器放在工作台上。

strange-looking 是一个合成词，由形容词 + 现在分词构成。又如：

good-looking 好看的，fine-sounding 动听的

Exercises for Reading Comprehension

I. Answer the following questions.

1. How many inventions did Edison make in his life?
2. What was Thomas Edison always trying to do when he was a little boy?
3. Why did Sam Edison like to talk about his son to his friends or neighbors?
4. Was Thomas Edison fond of asking about things when he was a little boy?
5. Why did Thomas Edison fall into the barn?
6. How did Captain Bradley act while listening to Sam Edison?
7. What happened when Edison began to prod the bees' nest with a stick?
8. Who was chasing after Thomas Edison? And why?

9. Why did Edison set the farm on fire?
10. His father didn't beat him, did he?
11. When and where did Edison set up a big, new laboratory?
12. What did Edison begin to work on in his new lab?
13. Was one of his assistants very surprised to hear about the talking machine?
14. What did Edison ask one of his assistants to bring him?
15. How did the little machine on the table look like?
16. Why did Edison shout as loud as he could to the little machine?
17. Can you recite the old rhyme Edison shouted to the machine?
18. Why did his assistants burst into laughter?
19. Was the experiment successful?
20. What was the name of the talking machine?

II. Find the meaning of the words or expressions in Column (A) from those in Column (B).

(A)	(B)
1. accompany	A. shout with anger
2. bother	B. far away
3. market	C. cause trouble to
4. recite	D. run after
5. roar	E. fix one's eyes on
6. chase after	F. say aloud from memory
7. in the distance	G. public place where people meet to buy and sell goods
8. now and then	H. go with
9. stare at	I. experiment with something in order to test it
10. try out	J. from time to time

III. Complete the sentences with the given expressions, and change the form where necessary.

be proud of   carry on   chase after   go a long way
in the distance   make a contribution to   now and then
one...after another   stare at   try out

1. Things nearby seem big; things _____ seem small.
2. The scientist is awarded Nobel Prize this year, for he _____ the researches of new energy.

3. That boy is very clever, and the neighbors expect that he _____.
4. Having made _____ experiment _____, the doctors succeeded in inventing a new medicine to cure SARS.
5. The weather is changeable, and it rains _____, so you had better take an umbrella with you.
6. We _____ being college students in the new century.
7. The naughty boy felt uneasy with the whole class _____ him.
8. Every time when the mouse stepped out of its hole, the cats would _____ it.
9. No matter how hard it may be, he is determined _____ with this work.
10. You can't join the basketball team if you don't _____.

IV. Fill in the blanks with the words listed below, and be sure to use appropriate verb forms and appropriate singular and plural forms for nouns.

> assist, assistance, assistant; amuse, amusement, amusing, amused
> decide, decision, decisive; laugh, laughter; public, publicly, publicity

1. As soon as Mr. Johnson finished his joke, the audience burst into _____, that is to say, they burst out _____.
2. They _____ to develop a new product, and it is _____ for them to take actions at once after the _____ has been made.
3. The scientist needed some _____ in his experiment, so he asked one of his _____ to help him, but all of them stopped their work _____ him in the experiment.
4. The _____ for the new film was very successful; some famous actors appeared on the scene _____ when it was first shown to the _____.
5. To succeed in producing a film, you must try _____ the audience. If your film is _____, that is to say, if the audience feels _____ at your film, they will pay for the _____.

V. Complete the following passage by using appropriate words listed below, and be sure to use singular or plural forms for nouns.

> bother   electric   laboratory   phonograph   record
> ask about   be proud of   carry on   go a long way   hundreds of

Thomas Edison was born in 1847 in the United States. As a little boy, he was fond of __(1)__ things. He liked __(2)__ people with his questions, but

177

his father __(3)__ him and expected that he would __(4)__. When he grew up, he became interested in inventions. In 1876, he built __(5)__ at Menlo Park, New Jersey in order __(6)__ with his experiments. Soon he invented __(7)__ or gramophone. The word "phonograph" means something that can __(8)__ sound. Some scientists before Edison had thought of machines which would do this, but Edison was the first to make a machine which actually worked. He also invented the __(9)__ lamp, with which people could use electricity to light up their homes. By the time Edison died in 1931, he had made __(10)__ inventions.

Language Structure

The Participle（分词）

分词是动词的一种非限定形式。分词有现在分词（The Present Participle）和过去分词（The Past Participle）两种。现在分词由动词+ -ing 构成；规则动词的过去分词由动词+ -ed 构成，不规则动词的过去分词没有统一的构成规则。

分词可以起副词和形容词的作用，在句子中可以作补语、定语或状语等成分。同时分词仍然保留着动词的某些特征，如可以有宾语或状语，带有宾语或状语的分词叫做分词短语。分词还有否定式、时态和语态等。

I. 分词的用法

❶ 作补语 现在分词作补语时，多表示主语或宾语所具有的特征和属性，而过去分词作补语时，则多表示主语或宾语所存在的状态。如：

It was *amusing* to hear Edison reciting the old rhyme.（主补）听爱迪生朗诵古诗真令人发笑。

Don't get *excited*, boys.（主补）孩子们，别激动。

The other week he went to a grain store, and climbed to the top to watch grain *pouring into the barn*.（宾补）不久前的那个星期，他到一家粮店去了，并爬上屋顶观看粮食倒进粮仓。

Edison had fourteen miles of wire *laid into these trenches*.（宾补）爱迪生叫人在这些深沟里埋设了14英里长的的电线。

［注］在复合宾语中，用不定式和用现在分词意义有所不同。不定式表示事情发生了，指事情发生的全过程；而现在分词则表示动作和谓语动词所表示的动作同时发生，指事情正在发生的过程中。如：

I saw him *make the experiment*. 我看见他做了这个试验。（说明做试验这回事）

I saw him *making the experiment*. 我看见他正在做这个试验。（说明做试验的情景）

❷ **作定语**　单个分词作定语时，一般放在所修饰词的前面，但有时也可放在所修饰词的后面。如：

Today you'll see the *talking* machine. 今天你们将看到会说话的机器。

The *tired* inventor leant back in his chair and closed his eyes for a moment. 这位疲惫的发明家靠着椅子闭了一会儿眼睛。

Can you smell something *burning*? 你闻到了东西烧焦的气味吗？

The experience *gained* would be useful to the future experiments. 已获取的经验对进一步的试验很有用处。

分词短语作定语时，一般应放在所修饰词的后面。如：

Edison lived in a room *facing the street*. 爱迪生住在临街的房间。

Then Edison started turning a crank, and the tube *wrapped in tinfoil* turned round and round. 然后爱迪生开始转动曲柄，接着，包着锡箔的管状物便不停地旋转起来。

❸ **作状语**　分词作状语时，可以表示方式、伴随情况、原因、时间、让步或条件等。如：

Bending over the little machine, Edison shouted as loud as he could.（表示行为方式）
俯身对着小机器，爱迪生尽力高喊起来。

Accompanied by his friend, Sam Edison hurried towards the farm.（表示伴随情况）
在朋友的陪同下，山姆·爱迪生匆匆向农场走去。

Being proud of Thomas Edison, Sam Edison liked to talk about his son to his friends or neighbors.（表示原因）
由于对托马斯·爱迪生感到自豪，山姆·爱迪生喜欢和朋友或邻居谈及自己的儿子。

[注] 分词作状语时，有时为了强调分词的状语意义，可以在分词前面加上 as, as if, as though, if, though, when, while, unless 等连接词。如：

The captain laughed now and then, *while listening to his words*.（表示时间）
这位船长一边听他讲，一边不时发出笑声。

Though tired, he kept working on the invention.（表示让步）
他虽然疲劳了，仍继续致力于发明。

If looking around us, we can see many Edison's inventions.（表示条件）
如果我们观察周围，爱迪生的发明便处处可见。

II. 分词的复合结构

分词的复合结构由"名词（或代词）+分词"构成，在句子中作状语，表示行为方式、伴随情况、时间、原因或条件等。如：

"There's smoke over there," the captain said, *his finger pointing to a farm in the distance*.（表示行为方式）"那里有一股烟，"船长指着远处的一个农场说道。

"Set my farm on fire!" he was roaring, *his face covered with sweat*.（表示伴随情况）
"竟敢点火烧我的农场！"他咆哮着，满脸是汗。

[注] 有时也可用介词"with +名词（或代词宾格）+分词"构成短语，它在句子中所起的作用和分词的复合结构基本相同。如：

He felt uneasy *with his father staring at him*.(表示原因)
由于父亲盯着他，他感到很不自在。
With the switch turned on, the bulb glowed brightly.(表示时间)
开关打开后，灯泡放出明亮的光芒。

III. 分词的时态和语态

现在分词有一般式和完成式。及物动词的现在分词有主动式和被动式。过去分词一般表示完成的或被动的动作，只有一种形式。现将现在分词的形式列表如下：

现在分词	及物动词 learn		不及物动词 rise
	主动形式	被动形式	主动形式
一般式	learning	being learned	rising
完成式	having learned	having been learned	having risen

❶ 现在分词的时态
① 现在分词一般式所表示的动作与谓语动词所表示的动作一般同时进行。如：
When he came *running* home, his face and hands all swelled up.
当他跑回家时，脸和手都肿了。
With the machine turning round and round, a voice was heard clearly.
随着机器的不停旋转，大家清晰地听到了一个声音。
② 现在分词完成式所表示的动作往往在谓语动词所表示的动作之前完成。如：
Having finished his chat with his neighbor, Sam Edison wrinkled up his nose and sniffed.
和邻居闲聊完毕之后，萨姆·爱迪生皱起鼻子闻了闻。
The clouds having disappeared, the sun shone again. 乌云消散之后，太阳重放光芒。

❷ 现在分词的语态
① 现在分词一般式的被动式表示一个被动动作与谓语动词所表示的动作同时进行。如：
They observed the experiment *being carried on*. 他们观察这个试验进行下去。
This was another experiment *being made* in the laboratory. 这是在这个实验室进行的又一次试验。
② 现在分词完成式的被动式表示一个被动动作发生在谓语动词所表示的动作之前。如：
Having been given such a good chance, his assistants all stopped working and came in front of his working table. 由于给了这样一个良机，他的助手都停下工作，来到爱迪生的工作台前。
The decision having been made, Edison started working at once.
做出决定之后，爱迪生立即开始了工作。

IV. 分词的否定形式 分词的否定形式由"否定副词+分词"构成。如：

Not having received her answer, I made a telephone call to her.
由于没有收到她的答复，我给她挂了一个电话。

Never tired of her job, the secretary dealt with everything carefully.
这位秘书对工作从不厌烦，总是细心地处理每件事情。

V. 现在分词和过去分词的区别

❶ 语态上不同，现在分词表示主动，而及物动词的过去分词则表示被动。试比较：

I found the servant *cleaning the room*. 我发现服务员正打扫房间。
I found the room *thoroughly cleaned*. 我发现房间被彻底打扫过了。
Who is the man *speaking to our monitor*? 与我们班长讲话的人是谁？
What is the language *spoken in Canada*? 加拿大讲什么语言？

❷ 时态上不同，现在分词表示正在进行的动作，而过去分词表示已经完成的动作。试比较：

the *developing* country 发展中国家　the house *being built* 正在修建的房子
the *developed* country 发达国家　　 the house *built*　已经建好的房子

Exercises for Language Structure

I. Fill in the blanks with the correct participial forms of the given verbs.

1. Swimming is _____ (interest). I'm really _____ (interest) in swimming.
2. The bike _____ (lose) hasn't been found yet.
3. He often receives letters _____ (write) in English.
4. _____ (finish) his work, he went home on foot.
5. _____ (make) of plastics, the machine is light.
6. Any matter, when _____ (heat) to a high temperature, becomes a source of light.
7. _____ (not do) it well enough, they tried it again.
8. The officer, _____ (follow) by a group of guards, inspected the defense works.
9. I saw a _____ (wound) soldier _____ (lie) in the battle field.
10. When he returned home, he found the window open and something _____ (steal).

II. Point out each participle or participial phrase in the following sentences and tell the function.

1. This is the building set up hundreds of years ago.
2. Looking into the window, he found a strange-looking machine lying on the table.
3. The problem being discussed is very important.
4. "Can you smell something burning?" he asked, getting to his feet.

5. These were the first words ever recorded.
6. Though interested in everything, Edison took interest in electricity most of all.
7. Tonight, lit by many electric bulbs, the hall was as bright as day.
8. He looked disappointed when the experiment failed of success.
9. All things considered, his proposal sounds more reasonable.
10. Not a moment later, Felicia was running proudly around the castle with the bell jingling at her neck.

III. Choose the best answer.

1. _____ a very bad cold, he stayed in bed.
   A. To suffer   B. To suffer from   C. Suffering   D. Suffering from
2. Power stations make use of _____ water to produce electricity.
   A. falling   B. fallen   C. filling   D. filled
3. Tired of the big noise, _____.
   A. the door shut   B. the door was shut
   C. he shut the door   D. he had shut the door
4. I heard them _____ in the next room.
   A. talked loudly   B. to talk loudly   C. talking loudly   D. talking aloud
5. The "picture writing" _____ long, long ago is hard for us to understand today.
   A. draw   B. to draw   C. drawing   D. drawn
6. _____, we went swimming in the river.
   A. Being a hot day   B. The day to be hot
   C. It a hot day   D. The day being hot
7. Alice, _____ where to find the book, asked her mother where the book was.
   A. not to know   B. knowing not   C. unknown   D. not knowing
8. He waited and waited, but the door remained _____.
   A. locking   B. locked   C. lock   D. to lock
9. On National Day, everywhere you see people in their holiday dresses, their faces _____ with smiles.
   A. shine   B. shone   C. shining   D. to shine
10. _____ her things into the bag, Nancy hurried to the railroad station.
    A. Put   B. Putting   C. Had put   D. Having put

IV. Find out which of the underlined parts in each sentence is not correct in written English.

1. The news was so surprised to us all that some of us didn't believe it at first.
                        A   B   C   D
2. Because of my poor English, I'm afraid that I can't make myself understanding.
   A   B   C   D

3. Having caught in the heavy rain, he was wet to the skin.
      A   B   C   D

4. With the old man led the way, we set off on foot into the dark night.
                 A   B   C   D

5. There is something wrong with your car, so you had better have it repairing.
                     A   B   C   D

6. The woman talked with the foreign visitors is our class advisor.
              A B   C   D

7. Mother was pleased to look at the face of her asleep baby.
          A   B   C   D

8. Because the ground was covered with falling snow, there were few people walking outside.
                   A   B   C   D

9. The children taken their seats, the old man began to tell them stories.
          A   B C   D

10. With the problem solving, he went on to work at another.
                A   B   C   D

Practice and Improvement

Reading Skills

Go through the following passages quickly, and after that, take note of the time, do the exercises, check the answers to the exercises and calculate words per minute.

Speed Reading A

Notes: Before reading the passage, try to get familiar with the following words and expressions.

1. flicker /ˈflɪkə(r)/ v. & n. 闪烁不定，忽隐忽现
2. candle /ˈkændl/ n. 蜡烛
3. steady /ˈstedi/ a. 稳固的，稳定的 v. 使……稳定，使……稳固
4. glow /gloʊ/ v. 发光，发热
5. seal /siːl/ v. 封，密封 n. 封条，密封
6. gain /geɪn/ v. 获得，赢得 n. 利益，收获
7. further /ˈfɜːðə(r)/ a. 更远的，进一步的 ad. 更远地，进一步地

8. tightly /ˈtaitli/ ad. 紧密地；牢固地；严格地
9. thread /θred/ n. 线；思绪
10. rub /rʌb/ v. 擦，摩擦
11. lampblack /ˈlæmpblæk/ n. 灯烟，灯黑
12. blacken /ˈblækən/ v. 变黑，使……变黑；诽谤
13. hairpin /ˈhɛəpin/ n. 发夹
14. clay /klei/ n. 粘土，泥土
15. bake /beik/ v. 烤，烘
16. furnace /ˈfəːnis/ n. 炉子，熔炉
17. switch /switʃ/ n. 开关，电键 v. 转换
18. produce /prəˈdjuːs/ v. 生产，产生，制作 n. 产物，农产品
19. break apart 断开
20. go out 出外；熄灭；过时

A Safe and Bright Light

Thomas Edison sat in his laboratory, thinking about a new kind of light. This was another experiment being made in his laboratory. Though tired, he kept working on it. He hoped this kind of light would burn brighter and safer than the gas light used at that time.

Gas lights flicker like candle lights, and there was always a danger of fire. Edison wanted a light that would be steady and safe.

"Electricity is the answer," he said to himself. "But how?" The problem had bothered him for a long time.

He thought, "There is nothing hard about the problem." But it must be something that will glow for a long time. It's no use if it burns right up, so the bulb must be sealed tightly, for even a tiny bit of air will make the light go out.

Edison smiled. The experience gained would be helpful to the further experiments. Then he remembered hundreds of things he had tested inside the glass bulbs, but when he turned on the electricity, everything he tested had either broken apart or burned right up.

The tired inventor leant back in his chair and closed his eyes for a moment. His fingers touched some cotton thread that lay on his working-table. Suddenly he thought out an idea.

He did not go home at all that night. Instead, he slept right at his desk.

"Mr. Edison, you're here early again," one of his assistants said.

"No," said the inventor, rubbing his eyes. "Let's say that I stayed late. There's something I want to try."

Edison found some small pieces of cotton thread, and put them in lampblack and carefully bent the blackened thread into the shape of hairpins. Then he set each of them into a small clay dish.

"Here," he called to one of his assistants, "bake these in the furnace so they'll get hard. Some of the thread may break, but I hope one will come out strong enough for us to use."

Several hours later, the hairpins were taken out of the furnace. Edison chose one that looked very strong. He put it inside a glass bulb.

"Now, let's begin to test the bulb," he ordered. With the switch turned on, the bulb glowed brightly. It did not flicker. The men in the laboratory crowded around Edison's working table.

"Don't get excited, boys." Edison said. "Perhaps this bulb will burn up just as the others did."

Edison and his assistants watched the lamp burning. Minute after minute, it glowed brightly. Then hour after hour, and then, late the next day, it went out. It had burned for forty hours.

With the problem solved, Edison produced a great number of lamps. Soon people's houses were lit by electricity.

(475 words)

Time: _____

Comprehension

I. Choose the best answer according to the passage.

1. At that time _____ were used widely.
   A. the gas lights
   B. the candle lights
   C. the electric lights
   D. the new kind of lights

2. Hundreds of things that Edison tested in the bulbs had _____ broken apart _____ burned right up.
   A. both...and
   B. either...or
   C. neither...nor
   D. not only....but also

3. "Electricity is the answer." This sentence means _____.
   A. electricity can put out fire
   B. electric light will be steady and safe
   C. electricity will make gas lights safer
   D. electricity is a danger of fire

4. One of his assistants was asked to bake some pieces of cotton thread in the furnace in order to _____ them.

  A. blacken   B. break   C. burn   D. shape

5. The story tells us that _____.

  A. it is easy to make an invention

  B. it was clever of Edison to find out the right material for the light bulb

  C. Edison failed to invent the electric light because it burned only forty hours

  D. though he failed in his invention at first, Edison kept working on it until he succeeded

II. True or False：

( ) 6. Before the electric light bulb was invented by Edison, people used the candle lights.

( ) 7. The bulb must be sealed tightly so as to keep the air out of it.

( ) 8. The assistant thought that Edison had slept at home the night before.

( ) 9. His assistants had little interest in the experiment of electric light.

( ) 10. The light didn't go out until late the next day.

Correct rate: ____ %

Reading speed: ____ wpm

Speed Reading B

Notes: Before reading the passage, try to get familiar with the following words and expressions.

1. power　/ˈpauə/　n. 动力，电力，功率
2. provide　/prəˈvaid/　v. 提供
3. generator　/ˈdʒenəreitə(r)/　n. 发电机，发生器
4. steadily　/ˈstedili/　ad. 稳固地，稳定地
5. trench　/trentʃ/　n. 深沟，渠
6. connect　/kəˈnekt/　v. 连接，连结，联系
7. praise　/preiz/　v. 赞扬，表扬　n. 赞美，称赞
8. connect ...to/with　与……连结，和……联系

Light for the City

  Edison and his assistants came to New York to set up an electric power system. They hoped it would provide enough electricity to light up a part of the great city.

  They brought several machines with them. These were called

generators, which produced electricity power for lamps in Edison's building.

Soon there were lights for the building. Edison lived in a room facing the street. The light burned brightly and steadily and he was used to working over night. People often came and stopped their horse-drawn carriage to look. Everyone knew that Thomas Edison was in town.

First, the inventor and his assistants produced several large generators. A great deal of power would be needed to light up even a small part of the city.

Then the workers were busy digging deep trenches in the hard earth below the city streets. Edison had fourteen miles of wire laid into the trenches. The wire connected each building to a generator.

Setting up an electric power system was not an easy job. It took a year and a half. In September, 1882, the job was finished.

A small group of men stood around Edison inside the power house. The big moment came at last. The inventor, taking a deep breath, pulled a switch. The electric lights flashed up.

"Very good! Very good!" a man nearby shouted to praise Edison for what he had done.

"Sir," said Edison, "this is only the beginning!" And Edison was right. Soon Edison's lamp were lighting up cities all over the world.

(661 words)

Time：_____

Comprehension

I. Choose the best answer according to the passage.

1. The generators they brought with them could produce as much electricity as _____ needed.
   A. Edison's building B. a small part of the city
   C. the whole city D. the world

2. At that time carriages _____ by horse could be seen in the street.
   A. draw B. drew C. drawn D. drawing

3. Trenches were dug to _____.
   A. set up generators B. lay wires
   C. build city streets D. build a power house

4. It took a year and a half to _____.

    A. set up the electric system   B. produce several large generators

    C. dig the deep trenches   D. lay fourteen miles of wire into the trench

5. Edison took a deep breath before pulling a switch, which showed that he was _____.

    A. excited   B. frightened   C. uneasy   D. light-hearted

II. True or False:

( ) 1. Edison and his assistants came to New York to set up a laboratory.

( ) 2. Thomas Edison was well-known in New York when he set up the electric power system.

( ) 3. Digging the trenches and laying the wires are only part of the work of setting up the electric power system.

( ) 4. The switch was fixed in the deep trenches.

( ) 5. New York was the first city in the world lit by electricity.

                                              Correct rate: _____ %

                                              Reading speed: _____ wpm

Cloze Procedure

Edison's Inventions

    __(1)__ around us, we can see many of Edison's inventions. The electricity __(2)__ in our rooms is one of his greatest inventions. He developed the telephone which rings in our rooms. Records playing songs and music were also invented by him. He made the first __(3)__ pictures.

    It wasn't always easy for Edison __(4)__ new things. It was very difficult for him to make the first electric lights. He needed to make hundreds of tests. At first, it wasn't easy for him to find the right materials, but at last he did, and the world became brighter.

    Though __(5)__ in everything, Edison took interest in electricity most of all. He wanted to know __(6)__ it. He worked very hard to find possible ways to use it.

    Edison's experiments with electricity __(7)__ the world greatly. Today, with great trains __(8)__ on electricity, we can travel much faster. With our homes and the streets of town and village __(9)__ by electric lamps, we live a comfortable life. Radio and television run on it. Science uses it every day.

Though ___(10)___ how to explain electricity now, we have learned to use it in many ways. Records, shining lights and ringing telephones are very common now. Edison's inventions have kept the world warm.

Fill in the blanks with the best answers.

( ) 1. A. If looking   B. If looked   C. Whether looking   D. Whether looked
( ) 2. A. to shine   B. shine   C. shining   D. shone
( ) 3. A. to move   B. move   C. moving   D. moved
( ) 4. A. to find   B. find   C. finding   D. found
( ) 5. A. interested   B. interesting   C. interest   D. interests
( ) 6. A. how to use   B. how using   C. what to use   D. what using
( ) 7. A. has changed   B. have changed
      C. having changed   D. have been changed
( ) 8. A. to run   B. ran   C. run   D. running
( ) 9. A. to light   B. light   C. lit   D. lighting
( ) 10. A. not known   B. not knowing   C. known as   D. knowing not

Speaking Skills

I. Warm-up Exercise: *Read the poem aloud.*

A Psalm of Life (人生颂)(Excerpts)

By Henry Wadsworth Longfellow (1807~1882)

VI	第六节
Trust no Future, howe'er pleasant!	莫信未来好,
Let the dead Past bury its dead!	过去任埋葬。
Act-act in the glorious present!	努力有生时,
Heart within and God o'er head!	心诚祈上苍。
IX	第九节
Let us then be up and doing,	众生齐奋发,
With a heart for any fate;	顺逆不介意。
Still achieving, still pursuing,	勤勉而戒躁,
Learn to labor and to wait.	探索又进取。

——亨利·瓦兹沃斯·朗费罗（1807~1882）

II. Conversation

Practice the dialogues with your partner and then write a dialogue about visit and introduction.

Dialogue 1 Meeting a Visitor at the College Gate

A: Welcome to our school, Mr. Ford. I'm very glad to meet you again.

B: I'm very glad to meet you too, Mr. Li.

A: I'm very happy to have you visit us today.

B: Thank you for your invitation. I have heard about your polytechnic many times and I always wondered what kind of college it was. And now I am here to have a look at it with my own eyes.

A: I would like to show you around the campus. Which place are you most interested in?

B: Well, I would like to see your network center.

A: Okay. Let's go.

Dialogue 2 Showing a Visitor around the Campus

A: Now, Mr. Ford, how do you like this college?

B: Well, I think it is small in size and it has all these beautiful buildings.

A: Which building do you like best?

B: The laboratory building. It's got the best facilities that I have ever seen.

A: Yes, many students like it. They often go to it to make experiments in class or after class so as to improve their practical ability. Some students even have made a few inventions before their graduation.

B: Mm... Wonderful! What do they do in their spare time?

A: All kinds of things. There are a lot of different kinds of clubs and societies to join. And some students meet their friends at the Union, some go to the library to study.

B: Where is the library?

A: It's just next to the Students' Center where the Union holds many activities. Shall we walk there, Mr. Ford?

B: Yes, I'd like to. How many students do you have, Mr. Li?

A: I think we have about five thousand.

B: What kinds of students come here?

A: Well, there are all kinds. I'll explain it to you when we come back to the office later.

Notes:

1. **campus** /ˈkæmpəs/ *n.* 校园
2. **polytechnic** /ˌpɔliˈteknik/ *n.* 职业学院，工艺学校 *a.* 工艺的
3. **network** /ˈnetwəːk/ *n.* 网络，网状物

4. **facility** /fəˈsiliti/ n. 设备，设施；便利，简易
5. **practical** /ˈpræktikl/ a. 实际的，实践的，实用的，应用的
6. **graduation** /grædʒuˈeiʃən/ n. 毕业，毕业典礼；刻度，等级
7. **activity** /ækˈtiviti/ n. 活动，活跃，行动，行为
8. **show around** 带领……参观
9. **be interested in** 对……感兴趣

Listening Skills

I. Directions: Listen to the following sentences. Tick the right words the speaker says.

1. A. weak   B. week
2. A. sweat   B. sweet
3. A. let   B. lit
4. A. hours   B. ours
5. A. loud   B. laughed
6. A. labors   B. neighbors
7. A. heard   B. hurt
8. A. light   B. right
9. A. seem   B. seen
10. A. fourteen   B. forty

II. Directions: In this section, you will hear 10 short conversations. At the end of each conversation, a question will be asked about what was said. The conversation and question will be spoken only one time. After each question, there will be a pause. During the pause, you must read the four choices marked A, B, C and D, and decide which the best answer is, and then choose the corresponding letter.

1. A. 2 pills.   B. 3 pills.   C. 5 pills.   D. 6 pills.
2. A. The man worked hard.   B. The man has passed the test.
   C. The man ought to have worked hard.   D. The man will never succeed.
3. A. 9:30.   B. 10:10.   C. 9:00.   D. 8:50.
4. A. In a hospital.   B. In a post office.
   C. At the railway station.   D. At the airport.
5. A. Make it an inn.   B. Sell it.
   C. Rent it out.   D. Paint it.
6. A. It was good.   B. It was worth seeing.
   C. He wanted to see it again.   D. It was bad.
7. A. He doesn't understand what she said.

191

C. He is going there, too.

D. He is also a newcomer in the city.

8. A. On a bus.   B. At a bank.   C. In a restaurant.   D. At a party.

9. A. The man wanted to buy a car for a long time.

   B. The man doesn't like a car, but his wife does.

   C. The man's wife doesn't like a car.

   D. The man can afford to buy a car at last.

10. A. The man and his wife enjoyed their holiday very much.

    B. The man's wife was quite disappointed with him.

    C. The man's wife didn't enjoy the holiday.

    D. The man was quite disappointed with his wife.

III. Directions: *In this section, you will hear a passage of about 90 words three times. There are about 20 words missing. First, you will hear the whole passage from the beginning to the end just to get a general idea about it. Then, in the second reading, write down the missing words during the pauses. You can check what you have written when the passage is read to you once again without the pauses.*

"In order to make a light, something has to __(1)__ in the gas bulb," he thought. "There is __(2)__ about the problem." But it must be something that will glow for a long time. It's no use if it __(3)__, so the bulb must be sealed __(4)__, for even a tiny bit of air will make the light __(5)__.

Edison smiled. The experience __(6)__ would be helpful to the __(7)__. Then he remembered hundreds of things he had tested __(8)__ the glass bulbs, but when he __(9)__ the electricity, everything he tested had either __(10)__ or burned right up.

Translation Skills

I. Translate the following into English.

1. 我们都应该为祖国的四化建设做出贡献。
2. 进行试验时，助手们不时向爱迪生请教。
3. 战斗中，他腿部受了伤，不久就肿了起来。
4. 由于全班同学盯着他，他感到很不自在。
5. 他指着远处的山说："我的家就在那儿。"

II. Translate the following into Chinese.

1. Early in the next morning, the assistant found him still standing in front of the working table.

2. Accompanied by the assistants, the scientist is going to inspect our factory.
3. Having missed the bus, we had to go home by taxi.
4. The river being too wide, we can't swim across it.
5. The astronaut having returned to the earth, the doctor gave him a checkup.

Writing Skills

I. Rewrite each of the sentences after the model.

Model A: *As he was proud of Thomas Edison, Sam Edison liked to talk about his son to his friends or neighbors.*

Being proud of Thomas Edison, Sam Edison liked to talk about his son to his friends or neighbors.

1. If you turn to the left, you will find the post office.
2. After I had done my homework, I went to bed.
3. While she was waiting for the bus, Alice read a science fiction.
4. As Mother was ill, Mary had to stay at home to look after her.
5. The assistants who were working in the laboratory were very promising young men.

Model B: *He hoped this kind of light would burn brighter and safer than the gas light which was used at that time.*

He hoped this kind of light would burn brighter and safer than the gas light used at that time.

1. Suddenly there appeared a young woman who was dressed in green.
2. When it was seen from the hill, the city looked more magnificent.
3. Though he was tired, he kept working on his invention.
4. After his work had been finished, he wrote a report.
5. As the problem has been settled, we could make use of the energy of the sun.

II. Practical Writing

名片(Calling Card 或 Visiting Card)通常用于社交场合，用来向他人介绍自己的姓名和身份。名片上一般应有姓名、工作单位、职务、职称、地址、电话、传真以及电子邮件地址等等。

名片 　　　　　Calling Card

Galaxy Trade Corporation

Kate McKenna
Sales Manager
Senior Economist

Postcode CA32565
P. O. Box 176
Los Angeles, United States

Cable 5785 Galtra
Tel：36785860-018
Fax：36785865
Email：kmk@yahoo.net
Mobile：15623452233

Notes：

1. **manager** /ˈmænidʒə(r)/ n. 经理，管理人员
2. **economist** /iːˈkɔnəmist/ n. 经济师，经济学家
3. **postcode** /ˈpoustkoud/ n. 邮编
4. **cable** /ˈkeibl/ n. 电报，电缆
5. **fax** /fæks/ n. 传真
6. **net** /net/ n. 网，网络；净利，实价
7. **mobile** /ˈmoubail/ n. 移动电话 a. 可移动的

Exercise

Write a Calling Card according to the materials given. You can model your writing on the above writing.

按照上面的格式给湖南三一集团出口(export)部经理王海鸿高级经济师写一张名片。

地址：长沙市五一路185号
邮编：410007
电话：(0731)5567686   移动电话：13909778168
传真：(0731)5567685
电挂：3985 长沙
电子邮件：whh@263.net

A Proverb

Genius is one percent inspiration and ninety-nine percent perspiration.

—T. A. Edison

天才是百分之一的灵感和百分之九十九的汗水。

——爱迪生

Unit Eight

LIFE IN THE COUNTRYSIDE

Reading Selection

Text A

PRE-READING TASK

1. Do you like the life in the countryside? Why/Why not?
2. Can an illiterate person run a farm today?
3. What knowledge is required as a successful farmer today?

The Modern Farmer

Robert Kent succeeds in running a large farm outside a big city. In America today, it's dangerous running a farm without science and technology. As a modern farmer, Mr. Kent has to be an agriculturist, a technician and an accountant. After graduating from a high school, Mr. Kent studied agriculture at a university, where he learned not only soil, weather

Mr. Kent is driving a tractor in the fields, monitoring the crops with GPS (全球定位系统).

A lot of cows are raised in the barn of Mr. Kent's farm.

(Mr. Kent succeeds in running a large modern farm outside a big city.)

and climate, plant and animal cultivation but also economic management, computer science, international trade and even environmental protection.

As Mr. Kent's farm is such a large one, he must employ some workers. These employees, about 80 in all, are assigned to a number of posts in various parts of the farm.

Some of the employees work in the fields, where hay and corn grow. Their jobs are plowing fields, adding fertilizer to the soil, preventing crops from harmful insects and diseases, and getting in crops. Of course, most of the jobs are done by computers and machines.

As agriculture in America today is hi-tech, Mr. Kent often drives a large tractor in the fields, monitoring the crops with Global Positioning System (GPS)(全球定位系统). GPS is connected with satellites and his computer and can help him examine fields for crop damage, map soil conditions, and look for changes in the environment that could affect farming.

Some of the employees work in the barns. They are responsible for breeding, feeding and milking cows. All the milking on Mr. Kent's farm is also done by computerized machines. Twice a day, morning and evening, the cows are led to the barn where the milking machines are fixed. The milk that comes from the cows goes through tubes to a large vat where it is cooled, and then it will automatically be carried to the processing plant.

Some of the employees work in the processing plant, where raw milk is changed into pasteurized milk. The processing plant is also fixed with computerized machines, some of which are quite complicated and expensive. After the milk has gone through the various machines, it is cooled, bottled and stored in a refrigerator, ready for delivery.

Early every morning, the trucks pull up to the loading dock and pick up the milk that is to be delivered to homes and stores in the big city. The milk must be sent to the city very early so that it can be placed on the doorsteps in time for breakfast and in the stores before they open for business. Mr. Kent hires fifty men, more than half of his employees, as truck deliverers, and each of them is assigned to a different part of the big city.

Mr. Kent enjoys working with his employees. Sometimes he examines the soil conditions in the fields, sometimes he milks cows in the barn, and sometimes he delivers milk to homes and stores in the big city. Mr. Kent believes that, as an employer, he must be familiar with any job he assigns to his employees so that he can run his farm more efficiently. However, he spends most of his time in operating his computer, which is connected to the weather data from the weather station, the moisture detectors in the soil, the grain prices on the world market, and the cash flow into and out of his account.

Mr. Kent is fond of talking about those days when the farm was very small, and his father was able to run it by himself. But he knows that he must expand his farm. The days of the small farms are gone, especially near big cities.

Text B

PRE-READING TASK

1. In your opinion, what are the features of farming today?
2. Which accounts for most of the work in U.S. farming today, computer work or physical labor?
3. How many people can an American farmer feed today?
      A. About 80.   B. About 100.   C. About 120.   D. About 150.

Computerized Machinery in Modern Farming

There is no denying the fact that computerized machinery plays an important part in modern farming today. Since new factories and towns have been built on good farm land, there are now fewer farms to serve the increasingly larger population, so the farms must be more efficient in order to produce as much food as possible for the increasing population.

Two hundred years ago, ninety-five percent of American workers were farmers, and agriculture was America's biggest industry. Today less than two percent of American workers are farmers, and yet agriculture is still one of the biggest industries in America. American farmers used to grow only enough food to feed their families and animals; now each farmer grows enough to feed 120 other people. All of these should be attributed to computerized machinery. It is said that farming in America today is three-fourths computer operation and one-fourth physical labor.

Many of the beautiful sights of farming are disappearing now. Though some people prefer horses' plowing to tractors' running in the fields, yet they have to agree that tractors are more efficient than horses.

Computerized machinery in modern farming means the use of modern machinery with high intelligence on farms. By using the machines, the farmers can save both time and labor but bring in big profit. For example, in modern orchards, even the picking of fruit is done by computerized machines. Under the control of the computer, a special tractor with a long arm shakes fruit off from the trees. As the ripe fruit drop, they are caught by a special device. And even the sorting of the fruit is done by the tractor, too. Then the fruit is packed into wooden boxes before being carried to the cities. Only three men are needed to operate this tractor, but they can pick about thirty tons of fruit in just one day.

Computerized machinery is praised for having made great contributions to modern farming, but what's troubling some farmers is their not having proper farming machines for some special farming jobs. Though great efforts have been made, the problem is far from being settled.

Word List

1. **countryside** /ˈkʌntriˈsaid/ n. 农村，乡下
2. **succeed** /səkˈsiːd/ v. 成功；继承，接替
3. **agriculturist** /ægriˈkʌltʃərist/ n. 农学家，农场经营者
4. **technician** /tekˈniʃən/ n. 技师，技术员

5. accountant /əˈkauntənt/ n. 会计师，会计员
6. graduate /ˈgrædjueit/ v. 毕业　n. 毕业生
7. cultivation /kʌltiˈveiʃən/ n. 培育，耕作；培养，教养
8. environmental /invairənˈmentl/ a. 环境的，周围的
9. protection /prəˈtekʃən/ n. 保护
10. employ /imˈplɔi/ v. 雇佣；使用
11. employee /emplɔiˈiː/ n. 职工，员工，雇员
12. assign /əˈsain/ v. 指派，布置，指定
13. various /ˈvɛəriəs/ a. 不同的，各种各样的
14. hay /hei/ n. 干草
15. fertilizer /ˈfəːtilaizə(r)/ n. 肥料
16. disease /diˈziːz/ n. 疾病，弊病
17. harmful /ˈhɑːmful/ a. 有害的，伤害的
18. monitor /ˈmɔnitə(r)/ v. 监控，监视　n. 班长；监控器
19. hi-tech /ˈhaitek/ a. 高科技的
20. tractor /ˈtræktə(r)/ n. 拖拉机
21. position /pəˈziʃən/ v. 定位，安置　n. 位置，职位；立场；阵地
22. system /ˈsistəm/ n. 系统，体系；制度；秩序
23. connect /kəˈnekt/ v. 连接，联合
24. satellite /ˈsætəlait/ n. 卫星，人造天体
25. damage /ˈdæmidʒ/ n. & v. 损害，伤害
26. environment /inˈvairənmənt/ n. 环境，外界
27. affect /əˈfekt/ v. 影响；感动；侵袭
28. responsible /risˈpɔnsibl/ a. 有责任的，可依赖的，负责的
29. breed /briːd/ v. 繁殖；教养　n. 品种，种类
30. vat /væt/ n. & v. （装进）大桶，大缸
31. automatically /ɔːtəˈmætikli/ ad. 自动地
32. process /ˈprɔses/ v. 加工，处理　n. 过程，程序，步骤
33. pasteurize /ˈpæstəraiz/ v. 消毒，灭菌
34. complicated /ˈkɔmplikeitid/ a. 复杂的，难解的
35. refrigerator /riˈfridʒəreitə(r)/ n. 电冰箱；冷藏库
36. delivery /diˈlivəri/ n. 交付，递送
37. load /loud/ v. 装载，装货　n. 装载量，工作量，负荷，负载
38. dock /dɔk/ n. 码头，装货坞
39. deliver /diˈlivə(r)/ v. 交送，投递；发表
40. deliverer /diˈlivərə(r)/ n. 递送人
41. employer /imˈplɔiə(r)/ n. 雇主，老板
42. efficiently /iˈfiʃəntli/ ad. 效率高地，有能力地
43. operate /ˈɔpəreit/ v. 操作，控制；作业，运行；经营，管理；对……动手术

44. moisture /ˈmɔistʃə(r)/ n. 潮湿，湿气
45. detector /diˈtektə(r)/ n. 探测器，发现者
46. computerize /kəmˈpjuːtəraiz/ v. 使计算机化，用计算机处理
47. machinery /məˈʃiːnəri/ n. （总称）机器，机械
48. deny /diˈnai/ v. 否认，拒绝
49. population /pɔpjuˈleiʃən/ n. 人口
50. efficient /iˈfiʃənt/ a. 效率高的，有能力的
51. attribute /əˈtribjuːt/ v. 加于，归结于 n. 品质，属性
52. operation /ɔpəˈreiʃən/ n. 操作，运转；经营，业务；运算；手术
53. efficiency /iˈfiʃənsi/ n. 效率，功效
54. profit /ˈprɔfit/ n. 利润，益处 v. 有益于，有利于；得到，获益
55. orchard /ˈɔːtʃəd/ n. 果园
56. device /diˈvais/ n. 装置，设备；设计，图案
57. pack /pæk/ v. 捆扎，把……打包 n. 包，小盒
58. effort /ˈefət/ n. 努力；成就

Idioms and Expressions

1. succeed in （干……）成功
2. graduate from 毕业于
3. in all 总计，一共
4. be assigned to 分配于，指定为
5. get in 收获
6. be connected with(to) 与……连接，和……有联系
7. be responsible for 对某事负责
8. be responsible to 对某人负责
9. pull up 停下，阻止；拔起
10. play a part in 在……方面起作用
11. be attributed to 把……归结于，归功于
12. physical labor 体力劳动
13. in search of 寻求，查究
14. bring in 获得；引进，产生
15. far from 远没有，远未

Word Derivation

1. employ—employer—employee—employment

2. deliver—delivery—deliverer
3. efficiency—efficient—efficiently
4. economy—economics—economical—economically
5. agriculture—agricultural—agriculturist
6. industry—industrial—industrialist
7. finance—financial—financially
8. environment—environmental
9. graduate—graduation
10. protect—protection—protective

Notes to the Text

❶ As a modern farmer, Mr. Kent has to be an agriculturist, a technician and an accountant.

作为一个现代农民，肯特先生必须既是一个农学家，一个技术员，又是一个会计师。

❷ These employees, about 80 in all, are assigned to a number of posts in various parts of the farm. 这些员工，总计约有80人，被分配到农场的各个部门担任不同的工作。

句中，about 80 in all 作同位语，对前面的名词 These employees 作进一步的解释。

❸ GPS is connected with satellites and his computer and can help him examine fields for crop damage, map soil conditions, and look for changes in the environment that could affect farming. 全球定位系统与卫星和计算机连接，可以帮助他检查田野里庄稼的受损情况，画出土壤状况图，寻找可能影响农作物的环境变化。

❹ The milk must be picked up very early so that it can be on the door steps in time for breakfast and in the stores before they open in business. 清早，必须装运牛奶，以便及时送到订户门前，不误早餐，并在商店开门营业前送进商店。

❺ However, he spends most of his time in operating his computer, which is connected to the weather data from the weather station, the moisture detectors in the soil, the grain prices on the world market, and the cash flow into and out of his account. 然而，他大部分时间都用于操作计算机，计算机连接着气象台的天气资料、土壤中的湿度监测器、世界市场的谷物报价和进出他账户的现金流量。

❻ There is no denying the fact that computerized machinery plays an important part in modern farming. 无可否认，计算机化的机械在现代农业中起着非常重要的作用。

这是使用动名词的一个常见句型，句中动名词短语 denying the fact 为主语，后接 that 引到的同位语从句，对 fact 进行进一步的说明和解释，相当于 It is impossible to deny the fact that... 又如：

There is no knowing how long the fight against terrorism will last. 反对恐怖主义的斗争要持续多久，目前尚不清楚。

❼ It is said that farming in America today is three-fourths computer operation and one-fourth physical labor. 据说，当今美国的农业，四分之三是计算机操作，四分之一是体力劳动。

句中 It 是形式主语，实际主语为 that 引导的主语从句。计算机操作 (computer operation) 包括了解天气情况、土壤状况、作物生长情况、农场的经营管理、世界市场的谷价变化等等。

Exercises for Reading Comprehension

I. Answer the following questions.

1. Is Robert Kent an agriculturist, a technician, an accountant or a modern farmer?
2. What subjects did he learn about at a university?
3. How many employees does he have?
4. What are the employees' jobs in the field and how are the jobs done?
5. What does Mr. Kent often do in the field?
6. Can you describe the function of GPS on Mr. Kent's farm?
7. How is the milk processed in the barns?
8. Why must the milk be picked up very early in the morning?
9. Does Mr. Kent spend most of his time in working with his employees?
10. What topic is Mr. Kent fond of talking about?
11. What plays an important part in modern farming?
12. Why must the farms be more efficient?
13. What was the biggest industry in America two hundred years ago? And what about today?
14. The American farmers used to grow only enough food to feed their families and animals, didn't they?
15. How many people can each American farmer feed now?
16. Why is it that many of the beautiful sights of farming are disappearing now?
17. Some people prefer horses' plowing to tractors' running in the fields, don't they?
18. What is meant by computerized machinery in modern farming?
19. How much fruit can three farmers pick with a computerized tractor in one day?
20. What is computerized machinery praised for?

II. Find words in the texts which mean approximately the same as the following, using the give letters as a clue.

1. science or practice of farming   a_____
2. illness or disorder   d_____
3. use or hire a person as a paid worker   e_____
4. causing harm or damage   h_____
5. put things onto a truck or a ship   l_____

6. water in the form of steam or mist

7. piece of ground with fruit trees

8. fill a bag, box etc. with things

9. ready to be gathered and used

10. different

m_____
o_____
p_____
r_____
v_____

III. Fill in the blanks with the words from the block, and be sure to use appropriate verb forms and appropriate singular or plural forms for nouns.

> agriculture, agricultural;   deliver, deliverer, delivery
> economical, economics, economically, economy
> efficiency, efficient, efficiently;   employ, employee, employer

1. A person who hires others is _____, and a person hired is _____.
   Mr. Kent _____ about 80 men as workers on his farm.

2. In search of _____, most of the jobs are done by _____ machinery, which makes Mr. Kent run his farm more _____.

3. When the bottled milk is ready for _____, each truck _____ is responsible for _____ the milk to a different part of the city.

4. Mr. Kent studied _____ at a university, so he can deal with financial problems and run his farm very _____. He always practices _____ so as to expand his farm because a large farm can make _____ use of various farm machines.

5. _____ is still one of the biggest industries in America today, and _____ products, such as corn and cotton, are very important to industries in the cities.

IV. Complete the sentences with the given expressions, and change the forms where necessary.

> be assigned to   be attributed to   be connected with
> be responsible for far from   get in   graduate from
> in search of   physical labor   succeed in

1. It is fall now, and the farmers are busy _____ crops.

2. After _____ a senior middle school, he studied at a vocational college.

3. Now many factories make use of robots and computers in their production _____ efficiency.

4. When he heard the news, he was delighted _____ being angry.

5. A lot of exercises will _____ the students so that they can have a good command of this subject.
6. Mr. Green _____ running the branch company to the board of directors (董事会).
7. If they _____ developing the new product, it will bring in huge profits.
8. On this farm, heavy _____ has been replaced by computerized machinery.
9. Susan thought that her success _____ hard work.
10. He told me that his computer _____ a university web site through internet so that he could learn the course on line.

Language Structure

The Gerund（动名词）

动名词也是动词的一种非限定形式，由动词+ -ing 构成。动名词可以起名词的作用，在句中可以充当主语、补语、宾语和定语；同时，它还保留着动词的特征，如可以有宾语或状语，动名词和宾语或状语一起构成动名词短语，还有否定式、时态和语态等。

I. 动名词的用法

❶ 做主语 动名词（短语）做主语时，可以用先行词 it 作形式主语，而将实际主语放在句子的后面。如：

There is no d*enying the fact* that computerized machinery plays an important part in modern farming. 无可否认计算机化的机械在现代农业中起着重要的作用。

Living in a modern Asian city is not very different from living in an American city. 生活在一个现代化的亚洲城市和生活在一个美国城市没有什么不同。

In America today, it's dangerous *running a farm without science and technology.* 在当今美国，不懂科学技术办农场是很危险的。

❷ 作补语 如：

Their jobs are *plowing the fields, adding fertilizer to soil, and getting in crops.* 他们的工作是耕地、施肥以及收获庄稼。

Seeing is *believing.* 百闻不如一见。

❸ 作宾语 在带有宾补的句子中，动名词（短语）做宾语时，可以用先行词 it 作形式宾语，而将实际宾语放在宾补的后面。如：

Mr. Kent enjoys *working with his employees.* 肯特先生喜欢和他的员工一起工作。

Then Edison started *turning a crank*, and the tube wrapped in tinfoil turned round and round.

接着爱迪生开始摇动曲柄，包着锡箔的管状物不停旋转起来。

He felt it no use *discussing the problem with them at the moment.*

他觉得此刻和他们讨论此问题毫无用处。

[注] 有些动词后面常常接动名词作宾语，如：admit，avoid，consider，deny，enjoy，excuse，finish，mind，practice，suggest，can't help 等。

❹ 作介词宾语　如：

Robert Kent succeeds in *running a large farm outside a big city*. 罗伯特·肯特在大城市郊外成功地经营着一家大型农场。

After *graduating from a high school*，he studied agriculture at a university. 高中毕业后，他在一所大学攻读农学。

❺ 作定语　如：

The cows are led to the barn where the *milking* machines are fixed. 这些奶牛被牵引到装有挤奶器的牛棚。

The *processing* plant had a number of machines，some of which are quite advanced and expensive. 加工厂有许多机器，其中有些机器相当先进和昂贵。

[注] 动名词和现在分词作定语时的区别：动名词和现在分词在形式上完全相同，都可以作定语。动名词作定语时，表示它所修饰的名词的功能和用途；现在分词作定语时，表示它所修饰名词的状态和特征。试比较：

a sleeping car = (a car for sleeping) 一辆卧车

这里 sleeping 是动名词，修饰 car，说明 car 的用途，是供睡觉用的。

a sleeping baby = (a baby who is sleeping) 一个正在睡觉的男孩

这里 sleeping 是现在分词，作定语修饰 baby，说明 baby 处于睡觉的状态中。

the working table = (the table for working) 工作台

the working people = (the people who work) 劳动人民

动名词修饰名词，只有动名词有句子重音；现在分词修饰名词，两者都有句子重音。

II. 动名词的复合结构

动名词的复合结构由物主代词或名词所有格加动名词构成，在句子中可做主语、补语和宾语等。如：

Tom's arriving late made them very angry.（作主语）

汤姆姗姗来迟使得他们非常生气。

What we worry about is *your relying too much on us*.（作补语）

我们所担心的是你太依赖我们了。

Though some people like *horses' plowing instead of tractors' running in the fields*，yet they have to agree that tractors are more efficient than horses.（作宾语）

虽然有些人用马耕地，而不喜欢拖拉机在田野奔跑，然而他们不得不承认拖拉机比马的效率高。

[注] 在口语和非正式书面语中，这种结构如不在句首，往往用人称代词代替物主代词，用名词普通格代替所有格。如：

I don't mind *him going with me*. 我不介意他和我一起去。

I remember *the old man once telling us a fable about mice*. 我记得这位老人曾给我们

讲过一个关于老鼠的寓言。

III. 动名词的时态和语态

动名词有时态和语态的变化。现以 learn 为例，列表如下：

时态 \ 语态	主动形式	被动形式
一般式	learning	being learned
完成式	having learned	having been learned

❶ 动名词的时态

① 动名词的一般式表示一般性的动作，或是与谓语动词所表示的动作同时发生的动作。如：

Mr. Kent is fond of talking about those days when the farm was small, and his father was able to run it by himself. 肯特先生喜欢谈论过去的那些日子，当时农场很小，他父亲能独自经营。

They are responsible for breeding, feeding and milking the cows. 他们负责繁殖、喂养奶牛并为这些奶牛挤奶。

② 动名词的完成式表示该动作发生在谓语动词所表示的动作之前。如：

Computerized machinery is praised for *having made* great contributions for modern farming.

人们赞扬计算机化的机械为现代化农业做出了贡献。

❷ 动名词的语态 当动名词的逻辑主语是动名词所表示动作的承受者时，一般要用被动式。

① 动名词一般式的被动式 如：

Though great efforts have been made, the problem is far from *being settled*.

虽然已做出了巨大努力，但是问题远没有解决。

② 动名词完成式的被动式 如：

I don't remember *having ever been given a chance* to try this method.

我不记得谁曾给我机会来尝试这个方法。

IV. 动名词的否定形式（**not** + 动名词）如：

What's troubling some farmers is their not having proper farming machines for some special farming jobs. 某些农民感到苦恼的是他们没有适合特殊农活的机器。

I regret not having given you timely assistance. 我后悔没有给你及时的帮助。

V. 名词化的动名词 动名词有时可以进一步名词化，从而具有更多的名词特点，它可以有自己的冠词，可以有定语修饰等。

In modern orchards, even *the picking of fruit* is done by machines.

在现代果园，甚至连水果的采摘也是机器干的。

We should give our campus *a thorough cleaning* to prevent SARS.

为了预防非典型肺炎，我们应该把校园好好打扫一下。

Exercises for Language Structure

I. Point out each gerund or gerundial phrase in the following sentences and then tell its function.

1. All the milking on Mr. Kent's farm is also done by computerized machines.
2. My favorite sport is skating on the ice.
3. He thought it no good drinking too much.
4. This cool milk is kept in the vat until it is taken to the processing plant.
5. Far from reading the letter, he did not open it.
6. The heavy rain prevented us from starting off on time.
7. He doesn't like people smoking in his office.
8. They denied giving any further information to the policemen.
9. My friend can't understand his being made fun of like that.
10. Air pollution is known for having done great harm to plants and animals.

II. Fill in the blanks with the correct gerundial forms of the given verbs.

1. Have they finished _____ (clean) the barns?
2. There is no _____ (joke) about such matters.
3. He didn't mind _____ (leave) at home.
4. Then the fruit is packed into wooden boxes before _____ (carry) to the big cities.
5. What I felt uneasy about was my _____ (not come) here on time.
6. The scientist was praised for _____ (make) such a great contribution to the research of this field.
7. The girl made a living by _____ (sell) flowers at the corner of the street.
8. I apologized for _____ (not keep) my promise.
9. Do you mind my _____ (read) your paper?
10. He had some difficulty in _____ (explain) the rules to WTO clearly.

III. Rewrite the sentences after the model, using a gerund after the given prepositions.

Model: *It takes Mr. Kent most of his time to deal with the financial problems on his farm.*
Mr. Kent spends most of his time in dealing with the financial problems on his farm.

1. John plays football very well. (at)

2. He went forward and didn't look behind even for once. (without)

3. I am sure that he will come on time. (of)

4. We are proud that we are the college students of the new century. (of)

5. He got in touch with me, and he sent me an email. (by)

6. Excuse me. I come late for the meeting. (for)

7. Before you repair the computer, you must turn it off first. (before)

8. He warned me not to swim there, for the water has been polluted. (against)

9. After he joined the army, he fought bravely in many battles. (after)

10. He felt a great delight while he was helping others. (in)

IV. Choose the best answer.

1. You must practice _____ the car if you want to find a job.
   A. drive   B. to drive   C. driving   D. driven

2. I wonder why Wendy avoids _____ us.
   A. see   B. to see   C. saw   D. seeing

3. I hope you succeed _____ Peter pass the exam this time.
   A. helping   B. to help   C. at helping   D. in helping

4. In this community (社区), people are used to going to bed early and _____ up early in the morning.
   A. rising   B. getting   C. to rise   D. to get

5. He didn't seem to mind _____ TV while he was writing an experiment report.
   A. their watching   B. they watching   C. that they watch   D. them to watch

6. Mr. Smith prefers watching football games _____ football by himself.
   A. than playing   B. to playing   C. than play   D. to play

7. Prof. Bradley has many hobbies, one of which is _____ stamps.
   A. to collect   B. collect   C. collecting   D. collected

8. Seeing the photos, she couldn't help _____ the days when she was in a senior middle school.
   A. thinking of   B. to think of   C. think of   D. thought of

9. Since I'm very busy, I'm sorry that I can't help _____ the problem at the moment.
   A. dealing with   B. to deal with   C. dealt with   D. being dealt with

10. _____ English well helped him find a good job.
    A. He knowing   B. Him knowing   C. His knowing   D. Himself knowing

V. Find out which of the underlined parts in each sentence is not correct in written English.

1. I couldn't help to laugh when I saw the naughty boy making faces.
      A   B   C   D

2. Since what you said is right, I am considering to take your advice.
　　　　A　　　　B　　　　　　　C　　　　　　　D

3. He suggested spending two hours in practice spoken English with Prof. Bradley a
　　　　　　　　A　　　　　　　　　　B　　　　C　　　　　　D
week.

4. Jack going there won't be of much help, so he had better stay at home.
　　A　　　　　　　　　　　B　　　　　　　　C　　　　D

5. It is necessary his returning the book to the library before it is due.
　A　　　　　　B　　　　　　　　C　　　　　　　D

6. I remember to see you reading the magazine yesterday. Have you finished reading it?
　　　　　　　A　　　　B　　　　　　　　　　　　C　　　　　　　　　D

7. I don't mind waiting for her but I don't feel like to stand outside in the cold.
　　　　　　　A　　　　　　　　　　B　　　C　　　　　　　D

8. I don't object to climb mountains, but I have little interest in climbing mountains.
　　　　　　A　　　　　　　　　　　　　B　　　C　　　　D

9. Don't stop to do the work because of my not being able to solve the problem.
　　　　　A　　　　　　B　　　　　　　C　　　　　　D

10. The teacher was busy at his desk to correct the test papers.
　　　　　　　A　　　B　　　　C　　　　　　　D

Practice and Improvement

Reading Skills

Go through the following passages quickly, and after that, take note of the time, do the exercises, check the answers to the exercises and calculate words per minute.

Speed Reading A

Notes: Before reading the passage, try to get familiar with the following words and expressions.

1. similar /ˈsɪmɪlə(r)/ a. 相似的，类似的
2. beyond /bɪˈjɒnd/ prep. 在……的外边，远于；超出　ad. 在更远处
3. church /tʃɜːtʃ/ n. 教堂，教会
4. method /ˈmeθəd/ n. 方法，办法
5. digital /ˈdɪdʒɪtl/ a. 数字的，数码的，用数字显示的

6. **lonely** /ˈlounli/ *a.* 孤独的，寂寞的；偏僻的

7. **be similar to** 与……相似

Farm Life in the United States

All big cities are quite similar to each other. Living in a modern Asian city is not very different from living in an American city. The same cannot be said about living on farms, however.

In many parts of the world, farmers and their families live in villages. In the United States, however, each farm family lives on its own fields, often beyond the sight of any neighbors. Instead of traveling from a village to the fields every morning, American farmers stay on their land throughout the week. They travel to the nearest town on Saturdays for shopping or on Sundays for church. Their children ride on buses to large schools which serve all the farm families living in the area. In some areas, there are small schools serving a few farm families and the children walk to school. Of course, life keeps changing for everyone, including farmers. Today there are cars, refrigerators, digital TV sets and computers. And of course there are modern computerized machines for farming. All of these have changed farm life.

For many years, farming in America was often a lonely way of living. Farmers had to deal with their own problems, instead of getting assistance from others. They learned to try new methods, and trust their own ideas instead of following older ways.

(224 words)

Time：_____

Comprehension

I. Choose the best answer according to the passage.

1. Living in a modern Asian city is _____ living in an American city.
   A. the same as   B. quite different from
   C. similar to   D. not alike to

2. In the United States each farm family lives on its own fields, often _____
   A. with their neighbors   B. near their neighbors
   C. apart from their neighbors D. close to their neighbors

3. American farmers usually _____ throughout the week.
   A. go from the village to the fields every morning
   B. remain on their own land

C. go to the nearest town for shopping

   D. go to the nearest town for church

4. There are small schools serving a few families, and the children go to school _____.

   A. by bus　　　B. by bike　　　C. on foot　　　D. on horseback

5. From the passage we know that American farmers _____.

   A. feel lonely　　　　　　　B. get help from others

   C. trust themselves　　　　　D. follow older ways

II. True or False:

( ) 6. Living on an Asian farm is similar to living on an American farm.

( ) 7. In the United States farm families live far away from each other.

( ) 8. Cars, refrigerators, digital TV sets and computers as well as modern machines have changed American farm life.

( ) 9. Farmers in the United States help each other to deal with problems.

( ) 10. They keep on learning new knowledge and trust themselves.

Correct rate: _____%

Reading speed: _____wpm

Speed Reading B

Notes: Before reading the passage, try to get familiar with the following words and expressions.

1. **nation** /ˈneiʃən/ *n.* 国家，民族
2. **suburb** /ˈsʌbəːb/ *n.* 市郊，郊区
3. **product** /ˈprɔdəkt/ *n.* 产品，产物；乘积
4. **particularly** /pəˈtikjuləli/ *ad.* 尤其；独特地；显著地
5. **Midwest** /ˈmidwest/ *n.* 中西部（地区）
6. **gradually** /ˈɡrædʒuəli/ *ad.* 逐渐地，逐步地
7. **transfer** /trænsˈfəː(r)/ *v. & n.* 转移，迁移；转让，过户；调动，转学
8. **value** /ˈvæljuː/ *n.* 价值，估价，评价　*v.* 估价，评价，重视
9. **harvest** /ˈhɑːvist/ *v. & n.* 收获，收割
10. **mechanical** /miˈkænikl/ *a.* 机械的，机械学的，力学的；机械似的，呆板的
11. **leisure** /ˈliːʒər/ *n.* 空闲，休闲，安闲
12. **chore** /tʃɔː(r)/ *n.* 杂事，杂活
13. **development** /diˈveləpmənt/ *n.* 发展，开发，研制；生长，进化；新成就
14. **convenience** /kənˈviːnjəns/ *n.* 方便，便利；方便的用具、器械等
15. **take in** 吸收；接受；收容；理解
16. **in addition** 此外，另外

17. in the dark 在黑暗中；秘密
18. in one's leisure time 在空闲时

Country Living

The picture of the United States as a nation of small farmers is no longer true. Two hundred years ago, most of the people in the nation did live on farms, but this has been changing in the past fifty years. Now most of the country's population lives in cities and their suburbs, which have taken in most of the population increase in the period since World War II.

However many people still live in the countryside. It still plays a very important part in American life. Farmers produce most of the food that we eat or sell to foreign countries, and in addition, other farm products like corn and cotton are very important to industry in the cities.

Another change which is taking place in American country living is a change in the size of farms. This is particularly true in the farm area of the Midwest, where the small, one-family farms are gradually disappearing, while large farms are taking their place. Large farms can make more efficient and economic use of various modern farm machines.

One thing that is not changing, however, is the manner of life lived by those who still make their living from the soil. The work is hard and the hours are long. For example, a farmer in the Midwest has to begin to work very early in the morning, long before the sun is up. He has to dress in the dark and go down to the barn and milk the cows. After transferring the milk into cans and loading the cans onto his truck, he is able to return to the house for his breakfast. This is usually a large meal, with meat and potatoes. Having finished his breakfast, he will have to deliver the milk to the processing plant in a nearby town, which buys his milk, either for bottling or for changing it into dried milk.

Having sold his milk, the farmer will return to the farm. He may have any one of the jobs to do in the winter. He may have to transfer his stored grain from one barn to another, hoping in this way to increase the value of the grain. The drier the grain is, the higher will be the price he will get. There may be some mechanical repair work on one of the farm machines. There may be even some field work to do, though this is more likely as spring comes. In summer, there will be corn to grow, hay to cut, or weeds to get rid of. Then in the fall the crops have to be harvested. So no matter what the season may be, there is always something for the farmer to do in the daytime.

Perhaps the evening meal is usually the largest meal in the day, and the one which can be taken in his leisure time. But in order to do so, it is necessary for the farmer to have finished doing the evening chores, which means another round of feeding and milking the cows, cleaning the barn and storing the milk in a refrigerator.

In the evening he probably has to spend some time in operating his computer. With the help of his computer, he can take care of his accounts, get to know weather conditions, recent development in agriculture, as well as the latest grain prices on the world market, for running a farm today is quite a complicated operation. After doing that, he can sit back and enjoy watching TV. It is modern conveniences like cars, refrigerators, computers and digital TV sets that have brought farm life much closer to other American living forms.

(661 words)
Time: _____

Comprehension

I. Choose the best answer according to the passage.

1. The picture of the United States as a nation of small farmers is _____.
   A. true   B. false   C. gone   D. kept

2. Another change which is taking place in American country living is that the farms _____.
   A. are becoming smaller   B. are getting larger
   C. are run by one family   C. are disappearing

3. The farmers who make their living from the soil have to work from morning to evening _____.
   A. in winter   B. in spring
   C. in summer and fall   D. all the year round

4. In the summer there will be _____.
   A. corn to grow   B. hay to cut   C. weeds to get rid of   D. A, B and C

5. Running a farm in America today is _____.
   A. an easy job   B. a great delight
   C. a complicated operation   D. a mechanical process

II. True or False:

( ) 6. Most of American people now live in the cities and their suburbs.
( ) 7. The manner of life lived by American farmers is changing quickly.
( ) 8. If it's a winter, a farmer will have little work to do.
( ) 9. Having watched TV in the evening, the farmer may spend some time in operating his computer.
( )10. Modern conveniences like cars, refrigerators, computers and digital TV sets have made farm life different from other American living forms.

Correct rate: _____ %
Reading speed: _____ wpm

Cloze Procedure

Fighting against Harmful Insects with Insects

In __(1)__ against harmful insects, one of the most efficient and economic methods is __(2)__ large numbers of their natural enemies. Among them are many of the parasites (寄生虫) __(3)__ in or on these harmful insects.

Recently, the __(4)__ of egg parasites to get rid of insects harmful to rice has been widely employed and much experience about it __(5)__.

These parasites are put in the fields __(6)__ their eggs when the insects are breeding. Ten days or so after hatching (孵化), the young parasites live on the harmful insects' eggs and __(7)__ them.

Much attention has been paid to this research by the agriculturists of the __(8)__ areas. They __(9)__ some experiment stations in charge of further __(10)__ the breeding of these parasites.

Fill in the blanks with the best answer.

( ) 1. A. fight   B. to fight   C. fighting   D. fought
( ) 2. A. breed   B. breeding   C. to breed   D. bred
( ) 3. A. live   B lived   C. to live   D. living
( ) 4. A. breed   B. breeding   C. to breed   D. bred
( ) 5. A. has already gained   B. having already gained
      C. has already been gained   D. having already been gained

(　) 6. A. to lie　　　B. to lay　　　C. lying　　　D. laying
(　) 7. A. destroy　　B. destroying　C. destroyed　D. to destroy
(　) 8. A. rice-grow　B. rice-grew　　C. rice-growing　D. rice-grown
(　) 9. A. have set up　　　　　　　　B. have been set up
　　　　C. having set up　　　　　　　D. having been set up
(　) 10. A. experiment　　　　　　　　B. experimenting
　　　　C. to experiment　　　　　　　D. experimented

Speaking Skills

I. Warm-up Exercise: *Read the poem aloud.*

Saying Goodbye to My Friend（送友人）

By Li Bai (701~762)

The green mount before the northern city stands,　　　青山横北郭，
　　The clear river goes round the eastern lands,　　　　白水绕东城。
We have to part now at this memorial place,　　　　　　此地一为别，
　　And you alone will have a remote domain to face.　　孤篷万里征。
Like a cloud, you wanderer may float here and there,　　浮云游子意，
　　My deep affection to you the sunset should always bear,　落日故人情。
We wave to each other and say goodbye,　　　　　　　挥手自兹去，
　　The horse sadly gives out neigh and sigh.　　　　　萧萧斑马鸣。

—李白（701~762）

II. Conversation

Practice the dialogues with your partner and then write a dialogue about departure and farewell.

Dialogue 1　Seeing Prof. Bradley off at the Airport

A: Here we are at the airport, Prof. Bradley.

B: It's very kind of you to come and see me off, Wang Hong.

A: It's my pleasure. It's a pity that you have to go now.

B: Well, I've certainly had a wonderful time here, and I'm deeply impressed by the students I have taught. They study hard, respect their teachers, help and learn from each other.

A: Thank you. We all appreciate your teaching here, Prof. Bradley. Under your guidance, we have improved a lot in our English study. We sincerely hope that you will come again and continue to teach us next term.

B: Oh, I'll be glad to if I get the chance.

A: Please give my best regards to your wife and your son, Bob. I do hope that they'll pay a visit to China someday soon.

B: Thank you. I'll do that.

A: At your request, we have booked the ticket of Flight CA 537 for you, business class, window seat. Here is your ticket.

B: Thank you. Is it non-stop flight to Vancouver?

A: No, it has a stopover at the Singapore Airport. Oh, it's time for you to go through the check-in formalities. Boarding is at Gate 9. May you have a pleasant journey!

B: Thank you. Good-bye.

A: Good-bye and take care.

Dialogue 2　Seeing a Friend off at the Railroad Station

A: Here we are at the railroad station.

B: It's very nice of you to come and see me off.

A: It's my pleasure. It's a pity that you are leaving so soon.

B: Well, I've certainly had an excellent time here, and I'm deeply impressed by what I have seen and heard during this visit. My trip to China has been both enjoyable and productive.

A: It's been a great pleasure to have you with us. We hope you'll come here more often in the future.

B: Oh, I'll be glad to if I have the chance.

A: Please give my best regards to your colleagues. I do hope that they'll pay a visit to China someday soon.

B: Thank you. I'll do that. It's time for us to say good-bye now. Thank you for your help.

A: I'm looking forward to seeing you again. May you have a pleasant journey!

B: Thank you. Good-bye.

A: Good-bye and all the best!

Notes:

1. appreciate　/əˈpriːʃieit/ v. 感激，欣赏；涨价，升值
2. sincerely　/sinˈsiəli/ ad. 真诚地
3. non-stop　/ˈnɔnˈstɔp/ a. 直飞的，中途不停的
4. stopover　/ˈstɔpouvə(r)/ n. 中途停留
5. board　/bɔːd/ v. 上(船、车、飞机)　n. 木板，纸板；董事会，委员会
6. impress　/imˈpres/ v. 留下印象；盖印
7. enjoyable　/inˈdʒɔiəb(ə)l/ a. 令人愉快的，可享受的

8. productive /prəˈdʌktiv/ a. 多产的,有成果的;生产的
9. give one's best regards to   向……问好/致意
10. take care   保重

Listening Skills

I. Directions: Listen to the following sentences. Tick the right words the speaker says.

1. A. roar   B. raw
2. A. pool   B. pull
3. A. horses   B. houses
4. A. hours   B. ours
5. A. quiet   B. quite
6. A. led   B. red
7. A. food   B. foot
8. A. safe   B. save
9. A. price   B. prize
10. A. chores   B. shores

II. Directions: In this section, you will hear 10 short conversations. At the end of each conversation, a question will be asked about what was said. The conversation and question will be spoken only one time. After each question, there will be a pause. During the pause, you must read the four choices marked A, B, C and D, and decide which the best answer is, and then choose the corresponding letter.

1. A. By plane.   B. By bus.   C. By car.   D. By train.
2. A. She doesn't know his music.   B. She likes Bach better than Beethoven.
   C. She doesn't like him.   D. She likes him better than Bach.
3. A. Why should he?   B. He doesn't like her.
   C. That's fine.   D. Why does she ask?
4. A. Changed her mind.   B. Changed her professor.
   C. Seen the professor.   D. Left school.
5. A. It doesn't matter which color the man chooses.
   B. It's a difficult decision.
   C. She doesn't like either color.
   D. The man should choose a different room.
6. A. Cream and sugar.   B. Nothing.   C. Cream.   D. Sugar.
7. A. He knows all his friends well.   B. He writes a lot.
   C. He has a lot of time.   D. He has a lot of friends.
8. A. A shop assistant.   B. The man's wife.

C. The man's secretary. D. A shopper.
9. A. The first speaker. B. Jane. C. The second speaker. D. Anne.
10. A. In a restaurant. B. On a farm. C. In a clinic. D. In an office.

III. **Directions**: *In this section, you will hear a passage of about 90 words three times. There are about 20 words missing. First, you will hear the whole passage from the beginning to the end just to get a general idea about it. Then, in the second reading, write down the missing words during the pauses. You can check what you have written when the passage is read to you once again without the pauses.*

In the evening he probably has to spend some time in ___(1)___. With the help of his computer, he can ___(2)___ his accounts, get to know ___(3)___, recent developments in agriculture, as well as the latest ___(4)___ on the world market, for ___(5)___ today is quite ___(6)___. After doing that, he can sit back and ___(7)___. It is modern ___(8)___ like cars, refrigerators, computers and ___(9)___ that have brought farm life much closer to other ___(10)___.

Translation Skills

I. **Translate the following into English.**
1. 大学毕业后，他经商成功了。
2. 史密斯先生对董事会负责管理这座加工厂。
3. 通过使用计算机，工厂能节省大量的时间和劳动，从而获取巨额利润。
4. 为了生产尽可能多的粮食，我们必须有效地管理农场。
5. 我们把所取得的成就归功于计算机化的管理。

II. **Translate the following into Chinese.**
1. Mr. Kent spends most of his time in dealing with the financial problems of his farm.
2. After being bottled, the pasteurized milk is delivered to various stores.
3. What bothers Mr. Brown is his not having enough raw materials.
4. There is no denying the fact that science and technology plays an important part in developing national economy.
5. Computerized machinery is praised for having made great contributions to modern farming.

Writing Skills

I. Rewrite each of the sentences after the model.

Model A: *In America today, running a farm without science and technology is dangerous.*

In America today, it is dangerous running a farm without science and technology.

1. Your trying to cheat me is no good.
2. Getting everything ready in time is very difficult.
3. Walking in the storm is unpleasant.
4. Crying over the spilt milk is no use.
5. Your saying anything now is a waste of time.

Model B: *It is impossible to deny the fact that computerized machinery plays an important part in modern farming.*

There is no denying the fact that computerized machinery plays an important part in modern farming.

1. It is impossible to go out in the storm.
2. It is impossible to say how long the war is going to last.
3. It is impossible to tell what will happen.
4. It is impossible to get on with him.
5. It is impossible to know when he will arrive.

II. Practical Writing

电子邮件(Electronic Mail 或缩写为 email)是书写、输送、读取全部电子化的信函。电子邮件通常由三个部分组成：邮件头（Head）、正文（Message）和签名（Signature）。邮件头通常由发件时间（计算机自动生成）、收件人的姓名（发件人输入）、寄件人的姓名(计算机自动生成)和主题行(发件人输入)四个部分组成；正文是邮件的具体内容，其书写方式和普通英文书信基本相同；签名写在邮件的最后一行，有时附有发件人的通信地址和电话号码。

电子邮件　　　　　**Electronic Mail**

Date: Thu. Dec 23　2004　19:25:38
From: Nancy White 〈nc@163.net〉
To: Edward Green 〈edgn@yahoo.com〉
Subject: Spending Christmas Together

Dear Edward,

　　I made a ring to you this afternoon, but you were not available. And tomorrow is Christmas, so we'd like to invite you to the English Evening held by the Branch Students' Union of English Department. Please phone us if you accept the invitation.

Yours,
Nancy
Telephone: 2821051

Exercise

Write an e-mail according to the materials given. You can model your writing on the above writing.

按照以上格式以爱德华·格林的名义向 Nancy White 发一个电子邮件。

内容:邀请 Nancy White 后天到岳麓山(Mount Yuelu)共度元旦。

A Proverb

Science and technology is the primary productive force.

—Deng Xiaoping

科学技术是第一生产力。

——邓小平

REVISION II

Test Paper 2

(For Unit5~Unit8)
(to be finished within 120 minutes)

Part I. Listening Comprehension (15%)

Section A. Directions: *Listen to the following sentences. Tick the right words the speaker says.* (5%)

1. A. right   B. write
2. A. palace   B. place
3. A. caught   B. court
4. A. one   B. won
5. A. sights   B. sites
6. A. sweat   B. sweet
7. A. glass   B. grass
8. A. cheers   B. tears
9. A. labor   B. neighbor
10. A. placed   B. praised

Section B. Directions: *In this section, you will hear 10 short conversations. At the end of each conversation, a question will be asked about what was said. The conversation and question will be spoken only one time. After each question, there will be a pause. During the pause, you must read the four choices marked A, B, C and D, and decide which the best answer is, and then choose the corresponding letter.* (5%)

11. A. At home. B. At the hospital. C. In prison. D. In a kindergarten.
12. A. She baked the cake herself.   B. She wants the man to bake the cake.
    C. The bakery made the cake for her.   D. The cake required no baking.
13. A. He doesn't know Sam.   B. Everyone knows about it.

C. Sam doesn't tell him.   D. Sam earned the money himself.
14. A. She called the man.   B. She took a plane.
    C. She saw her aunt off.   D. She went to meet her aunt.
15. A. The man's appetite.   B. The man's health.
    C. The problem of the man.   D. The man's family.
16. A. A bath.   B. A bathing room.
    C. A single room with bath.   D. A double room.
17. A. He used to work hard.   B. He seldom works hard.
    C. He always works hard.   D. He's hard working now.
18. A. He's never said that.   B. John will get a new bike from him.
    C. He's joking with John.   D. He has no money.
19. A. She likes him.   B. She thinks he's talkative.
    C. She doesn't think highly of him. D. She thinks he's a good man.
20. A. She feels sorry.
    B. She won't believe it.
    C. She is surprised.
    D. She wants to know how Lily broke her leg.

Section C. Directions: *In this section, you will hear a passage of about 90 words three times. There are about 20 words missing. First, you will hear the whole passage from the beginning to the end just to get a general idea about it. Then, in the second reading, write down the missing words during the pauses. You can check what you have written when the passage is read to you once again without the pauses. (5%)*

Mr. Kent enjoys __(21)__ his employees. Sometimes he examines the __(22)__ in the fields, sometimes he milks cows in the barn, and sometimes he __(23)__ to homes and stores in the big city. Mr. Kent believes that, __(24)__, he must be familiar with any job that __(25)__ his employees so that he can run his farm more __(26)__. However, he spends most of his time in __(27)__, which is connected to the __(28)__ from the weather station, the __(29)__ in the soil, the grain prices on the world market, and the __(30)__ into and out of his account.

Part II. Grammar and Vocabulary (30%)

Section A. *Fill in the blanks with proper prepositions.* (10%)

31. In this game, animal stands _____ any kind of living things except plants, such as grass and trees.
32. Her explanation on the rules is quite obvious _____ the adult students.
33. The rain is strong enough to burst _____ the clouds and destroy them.
34. It's necessary for us to decide what to do _____ the two cats.
35. The mice looked at each other _____ blank dismay and kept silent.
36. Just then a goat came and pushed him _____ the bees' nest, but the bees did not like it a bit.
37. He answered and felt uneasy with his father staring _____ him.
38. With his assistants helping him, Edison made one experiment _____ another.
39. In America today, it's dangerous running a farm _____ science and technology.
40. _____ using the machines, the farmers can save both time and labor but bring in big profit.

Section B. *Write the words in the right column according to the meaning in the left column, using the given letters as a clue.* (10%)

41. made by people or false	a	_____
42. cause trouble to	b	_____
43. ask someone to learn what you want to know	c	_____
44. use or hire a person as a paid worker	e	_____
45. causing damage or injury	h	_____
46. have sth. or sb. as part of the total	i	_____
47. put things onto a truck or a ship	l	_____
48. public place where people meet to buy and sell goods	m	_____
49. ready to be gathered and used	r	_____
50. older or of higher rank or position	s	_____

Section C. *Choose the best answer.* (10%)

51. How many times have I told you _____ football on the street?
    A. do not play   B. not to have played   C. not to play   D. not playing
52. He offered to _____ her a hand as the suitcase was too heavy for her to carry.

  A. help   B. show   C. borrow   D. lend
53. I remember _____ the book to you the other day when I met you on my way to the library.
  A. returned   B. returning   C. to return   D. being returned
54. Many chemical fertilizer plants have been set up. _____ agriculture output has rapidly increased.
  A. They lead to   B. As a result,   C. So it makes   D. So that
55. Don't _____ the speaker now; he will answer your question later.
  A. influence   B. affect   C. inspect   D. interrupt
56. She is not used to _____ in public.
  A. speak   B. be speaking   C. speaking   D. spoken
57. I'd like to go on holiday but I can't _____ the time.
  A. afford   B. spend   C. take   D. cost
58. She felt _____ at his joke.
  A. amuse   B. to amuse   C. amusing   D. amused
59. Hard work will definitely _____ to success.
  A. cause   B. result   C. lead   D. take
60. You should _____ the car before you buy it.
  A. keep   B. inspect   C. take   D. investigate
61. It _____ be difficult to learn Japanese.
  A. shall   B. must   C. should   D. need
62. The English of the composition is too good. He _____ it by himself.
  A. must have to write   B. can't have written
  C. mustn't have written   D. can't be written
63. There isn't any difference between the two. I really don't know _____.
  A. where to choose   B. which to choose
  C. to choose what   D. to choose which
64. The police promised to _____ the matter as soon as possible.
  A. look into   B. look up   C. look through   D. look for
65. Much _____ has been done to the natural environment.
  A. injury   B. hurt   C. harm   D. destroy
66. As an inventor, he is very curious _____ the things around him.
  A. about   B. of   C. at   D. for
67. They did very well in the English speech contest; _____ there is much room for improvement.
  A. therefore   B. moreover   C. however   D. otherwise
68. The "picture writing" _____ long, long ago is hard for us to understand today.
  A. draw   B. to draw   C. drawing   D. drawn
69. Tired of the big noise, _____

A. the door shut B. the door was shut
C. he shut the door D. he had shut the door

70. _____ English well helped him find a good job.
A. He knowing B. Him knowing
C. His knowing D. Himself knowing

Part III. Reading Comprehension (30%)

Directions: There are 3 passages in this part. Each passage is followed by some questions. For each of them there are four choices marked A, B, C and D. You should decide on the best choice.

(I)

The earthworm is a useful animal. Out of the ground, it is food for other animals. In this ground, it makes rich soil for fields and gardens.

Earthworms dig tunnels (隧道) that loosen the soil and make it easy for air and water to reach the roots of plants. These tunnels help keep the soil well drained (排水).

Earthworms drag dead leaves, grass and flowers into their burrows (洞穴). When this plant material decays, it makes the soil more fertile.

No other animal is so useful in building up good topsoil. It is estimated that in one year fifty thousand earthworms carry about eighteen tons of soil to the surface of an acre of land. One worm may add three quarters of a pound of earth to the topsoil.

71. The best title for this passage is _____.
A. Fertilizing the Soil B. How Earthworms Improve the Soil
C. Working Underground D. How Earthworms Carry Topsoil

72. Which of the following is NOT the use of earthworms' digging tunnels?
A. The soil gets loosened. B. Air and water can reach the roots of the plants.
C. The soil is kept drained. D. The weeds are destroyed.

73. The plant material carried underground by earthworms makes soil _____.
    A. well drained   B. more fertile   C. easier to plow   D. uneven
74. The amount of topsoil that one worm may bring to the surface is about _____.
    A. three pounds   B. three quarters of a pound
    C. a quarter of a pound   D. eighteen tons
75. The passage says that _____.
    A. good crops will grow where there are earthworms
    B. worms sometimes harm the soil
    C. worms do more to improve the soil than any other animals
    D. worms are most useful as food for other animals

(II)

Can you imagine how difficult life would become if all supplies of paper suddenly disappeared? Banks and post offices, schools and colleges would be forced to close. Food manufacturers would be unable to pack or label their products. There would be no magazines, newspapers or books. And we would no longer be able to write to our friends.

Those would be only a few of the troubles of a paperless world. Everywhere we turn we find paper. Without it our modern world would come to a standstill (停止). Paper is the life-blood of industry, the bringer of news, and the distributor of knowledge. It wouldn't be much fun chipping out our letters on a table of stone, or writing up schoolwork on slates (石板)!

76. If ever a day comes when paper is in short supply, _____.
    A. people would live normally as before
    B. the world would come to an end
    C. the paper industry would increase production
    D. people would have to make great adjustments
77. Banks, post offices, schools and colleges _____ if all supplies of paper suddenly disappeared.
    A. would be willing to close   B. would be unable to function
    C. would have to buy more computers D. would increase their business
78. According to this passage, paper is _____.
    A. the foundation of the industry   B. the sender of news
    C. the media of knowledge   D. all of the above
79. Which of the following statements is NOT the trouble of a paperless world described

in this article?

A. People would not be able to read newspapers or magazines.

B. People would be unable to communicate through letters.

C. The air pollution would become more serious.

D. Food producers would have to look for other materials to pack their products.

80. Which of the following statements cannot be inferred from this article?

A. Paper plays a very important function in people's life.

B. A serious paper shortage would affect a country's literacy.

C. Without paper the pollution of our environment would become less serious.

D. The development of our society would be hindered by a serious paper shortage.

(Ⅲ)

Television, the modern wonder of electronics, brings the world into your own home in sight and sound. And the word "television" means seeing far.

Television works in much the same way as radio. In radio, sound is changed into electromagnetic waves that are sent through the air. Experiments leading to modern television took place more than a hundred years ago. By the 1920s inventors and researchers had turned the early theories into working models. Yet it took another thirty years for TV to become an industry.

The influence of TV on the life of the people is incalculable: it can influence their thoughts and their way of life. It can also add to their store of knowledge. Educational TV stations offer teaching in various subjects. Some hospitals use TV for medical students to get close-up views of operations. At first television programs were broadcast in black-and-white. With the development of science and technology, the problem of how to telecast them in full color was solved and by the middle 1960s, the national networks were broadcasting most of their programs in color.

The programs that people watch are not only local and national ones. Since the launching of the first communications satellite, more and more programs are telecast "live" from all over the world. People in San Francisco were able to watch the 1964 Olympic Games in Tokyo. And live telecasts now come from outer space. In 1969, the first astronauts to land on the moon televised their historic "moon walk" to viewers on the earth. Since then, astronauts have regularly sent telecast to the earth.

81. The launching of communications satellites made it possible for people in San Francisco to _____.

   A. get close-up views of operations   B. store knowledge
   C. watch the 1964 Olympic Games in Tokyo   D. watch national programs

82. The development of science and technology made it possible for television programs to be telecast _____.

   A. in full color   B. in San Francisco   C. in Tokyo   D. in black-and-white

83. The word "incalculable" means _____.

   A. easy to tell   B. very great   C. difficult to tell   D. very small

84. Television is said to be the modern wonder of electronics, because _____.

   A. it influences people's way of life
   B. it makes people see far
   C. it brings the world into people's own home in sight and sound
   D. it works as radio

85. Television became an industry in _____.

   A. 1950   B. the 1960s   C. the 1920s   D. the 1950s

Part IV. Translation (10%)

Direction: In this part, there are five sentences, which you should translate into Chinese. These sentences are all taken from the reading passages you have just read in the Test Paper.

86. No other animal is so useful in building up good topsoil like earthworms.
87. Can you imagine how difficult life would become if all supplies of paper suddenly disappeared?
88. Paper is the life-blood of industry, the bringer of news, and the distributor of knowledge.
89. Television works in much the same way as radio.
90. Since the launching of the first communications satellite, more and more programs are telecast "live" from all over the world.

Part V. Practical Writing (15%)

给美国加利福尼亚大学商学院财经系的Robert Swift教授发一封电子邮件，了解他对美国的最新经济发展的分析（analysis）。对方的Email：rtst@yahoo.com。

Appendixes

APPENDIX I

Irregular Verbs

Infinitive	Past Form	Past Participle
be	was, were	been
bear	bore	born, borne
beat	beat	beaten
become	became	become
begin	began	begun
bend	bent	bent
blow	blew	blown
break	broke	broken
breed	bred	bred
bring	brought	brought
broadcast	broadcast, broadcasted	broadcast, broadcasted
build	built	built
burn	burnt, burned	burnt, burned
buy	bought	bought
catch	caught	caught
choose	chose	chosen
come	came	come
cost	cost	cost
cut	cut	cut
dig	dug	dug
do	did	done
draw	drew	drawn
dream	dreamt, dreamed	dreamt, dreamed
drink	drank	drunk

drive	drove	driven
eat	ate	eaten
fall	fell	fallen
feed	fed	fed
feel	felt	felt
fight	fought	fought
find	found	found
fly	flew	flown
forget	forgot	forgotten, forgot
freeze	froze	frozen
get	got	gotten, got
give	gave	given
go	went	gone
grow	grew	grown
hang	hung, hanged	hung, hanged
have	had	had
hear	heard	heard
hide	hid	hidden, hid
hit	hit	hit
hold	held	held
hurt	hurt	hurt
keep	kept	kept
kneel	knelt, kneeled	knelt, kneeled
know	knew	known
lay	laid	laid
lead	led	led
learn	learnt, learned	learnt, learned
leave	left	left
lend	lent	lent
let	let	let
lie	lay, lied	lain, lied
light	lit, lighted	lit, lighted
lose	lost	lost
make	made	made
mean	meant	meant
meet	met	met
melt	melted	molten, melted
mistake	mistaken	mistaken
misunderstand	misunderstood	misunderstood

pay	paid	paid
prove	proved	proved, proven
put	put	put
read	read [red]	read [red]
retell	retold	retold
ride	rode	ridden
ring	rang	rung
rise	rose	risen
run	ran	run
see	saw	seen
sell	sold	sold
send	sent	sent
shake	shook	shaken
shine	shone, shined	shone, shined
shoot	shot	shot
show	showed	shown, showed
sing	sang, sung	sung
sit	sat	sat
sleep	slept	slept
smell	smelt, smelled	smelt, smelled
spend	spent	spent
spread	spread	spread
stand	stood	stood
strike	struck	stricken, struck
sweep	swept	swept
swell	swelled	swollen, swelled
swim	swam	swum
take	took	taken
teach	taught	taught
tell	told	told
think	thought	thought
throw	threw	thrown
understand	understood	understood
wake	woke, waked	woken, waked
wear	wore	worn
wed	wed, wedded	wed, wedded
win	won	won
write	wrote	written

APPENDIX II

Presupposed Words and Phrases

根据教育部高等教育司《高职高专教育英语课程教学基本要求》的规定，学生在学习本书之前必须掌握下列1000个词汇及有关短语：

I. Words

A

a/an	able	about	above	accept
across	address	afraid	after	afternoon
age	ago	air	all	almost
alone	along	already	also	although
America	American	among	angry	animal
another	answer	any	anybody	anything
April	arm	army	around	arrive
as	ask	at	aunt	away

B

B. C.	baby	back	bad	bag
ball	banana	bank	basket	basketball
bath	bathroom	be	beat	beautiful
beautiful	because	become	bed	bedroom
before	behind	believe	bell	belong
beside	best	better	between	big
bird	birth	birthday	birthday	bit
black	blackboard	blue	boat	body
book	bookshop	boring	born	borrow
boss	both	bottle	bowling	box
boy	brave	bread	break	breakfast
bridge	bright	bring	brother	build
building	burn	bus	busy	but
buy	by	bye-bye		

C

call	can	card	care	careful
carry	cat	catch	centre/center	certain

certainly, chair, chance, change, cheap
chicken, child, china, Chinese, choice
choose, cinema, city, class, clean
clear, clever, climb, clock, close
clothes, cloud, coat, cock, coffee
come, computer, consider, cook, cool
corner, correct, cough, count, country
cover, cow, crop, cross, crowd
cry, carry, cup, cut

D

dad/daddy, dance, dangerous, dare, dark
database, date, daughter, day, dead
deaf, deal, dear, December, decide
deep, desk, Dialog(ue), different, difficult
dinner, dirty, disagree, discover, discuss
do, doctor, dog, dollar, door
draw, dream, dress, drink, drive
driver, drop, during

E

each, ear, early, east, egg
eight, eighteen, eighth, eighty, either
elder, elderly, eleven, eleventh, else
empty, end, England, English, Englishman
enjoy, enough, even, evening, ever
every, everybody, everything, everywhere, example
excuse, exercise, expensive, eye

F

face, fact, fail, fall, family
famous, far, farm, farmer, farther
fast, fat, father, February, fee
feed, feel, few, field, fifteen
fifth, fifty, fight, fill, film
find, fine, finger, finish, fire
firm, first, fish, five, fix
flag, flat, flower, fly, focus
food, fool, foot, football, for
foreign, forget, form, forty, found
fourteen, fourth, free, fresh, Friday
friend, friendly, frighten, from, front

fruit	full	fun	further	future

G

game	garden	gate	get	girl
give	glad	glance	glass	go
god	gold	good	goodbye	grade
grant	grass	great	green	grey/gray
ground	group	guess	guest	guide
gun

H

hair	half	hall	hand	happen
happy	hard	hardly	hat	hate
have	he	head	headache	health
healthy	hear	heart	heavy	Hello/hullo
help	her	here	hi	high
hill	him	himself	his	history
hit	hold	holiday	home	homework
honest	hope	horse	hospital	hot
hotel	hour	house	how	hundred
hunger	hungry	hurry	hurt	husband

I

I	ice	idea	if	ill
important	in	instead	interesting	interested
into	invent	island	it	its
itself

J

jacket	January	jet	job	join
joke	July	jump	June	just

K

keep	key	kill	kind	kiss
kitchen	knee	knife	knock	know

L

lady	lake	language	large	last
late	later	laugh	lay	lazy
lead	leadership	learn	learner	least
leave	left	leg	less	lesson
let	letter	library	lie	life
lift	light	like	line	list
listen	little	live	long	look

| lose | lot | loud | love | lovely |
| low | luck | lunch | | |

M

machine	mad	make	man	manner
many	map	march	mark	market
marry	match	mathematics/math	matter	may
maybe	me	meal	mean	meat
medicine	meet	meet	meeting	member
mend	message	meter	middle	midnight
mile	milk	mind	mine	miss
mistake	mister/Mr.	mistress/Mrs.	Monday	money
monkey	month	moon	more	morning
most	mother	mouth	move	movie
much	mum	music	my	myself

N

name	near	nearby	necessary	need
neither	news	newspaper	next	nice
night	nine	nineteen	ninety	ninth
no	nobody	noise	noisy	none
noon	nor	north	nose	not
note	nothing	November	now	number
nurse				

O

o'clock	October	of	off	offer
office	often	oh	oil	okay/O. K. /OK
old	on	once	one	oneself
only	open	orange	order	other
ought	our	ours	ourselves	out
outside	over	own		

P

page	pain	paint	pair	paper
pardon	parent	park	part	party
pass	past	pattern	pay	pen
pencil	people	perhaps	person	phone
photograph/photo	phrase	pick	picture	pie
piece	pig	place	plan	plane
plant	plate	play	player	pleasant
please	pleasure	plenty	pocket	point

poison police policeman pool poor
popular possible post potato pound
pour practice practise prepare present
price problem professor program(me) promise
proud prove pull pupil push
put

Q

quarrel quarter question quick quiet
quite

R

radio rain raise rather reach
read ready real receive record
red refuse remember repair repeat
reply report require rest restaurant
result return rice rich ride
right ring rise river road
rock role roof room rose
round rule run

S

sad safe sail sailor salt
same sand Saturday save school
science sea season seat second
see seldom sell send sentence
September serious set settle seven
seventeen seventy several shade shadow
shall shape sharp she sheep
shine ship ship shirt shoe
shop short should shout show
shut sick side silly simple
sing single sir sister sit
site six sixteen sixty skin
skirt sky sleep slow small
smell smile smoke snow so
soft some somebody something sometime
sometimes somewhat son song soon
sorry sound soup south space
speak spell spend spoon sport
spring square stamp stand star
start state station stay stick

still	stone	stop	store	storm
story	straight	street	strong	student
study	stupid	such	suddenly	sugar
suit	summer	sun	Sunday	supper
support	sure	surprise	sweet	swim

T

table	take	talk	tall	taxi
tea	teach	teacher	tear	telephone/phone
television/TV	ten	tend	term	terrible
test	than	thank	that	the
theatre/theater	their	theirs	them	themselves
then	there	these	they	thick
thin	think	third	thirsty	thirteen
thirty	this	those	though	thousand
three	through	throw	Thursday	ticket
tie	tight	till	time	tired
to	together	tomorrow	tonight	too
tool	tooth	top	train	travel
trip	trouble	trousers	truck	true
try	Tuesday	turn	twelfth	twelve
twentieth	twenty	twenty-first	twice	

U

under	up	upon	us	use
used	useful	usual	usually	

V

village	visit	visitor

W

wait	wake	walk	wall	want
war	warm	wash	waste	watch
water	wave	way	we	weak
wear	weather	Wednesday	week	weekend
welcome	well	west	wet	what
wet	what	when	where	whether
which	white	who	whole	whom
whose	why	wide	wife	wild
win	wind	window	winter	with
without	woman	wonderful	wood	word
work	worker	world	worry	worst

would   write   wrong

Y

year	yellow	yes	yesterday	yet
you	young	your	yours	
yourself	yourselves	youth		

Z

zero   zoo

II. Phrases

a few	at night	come out
a good deal	at once	day after night
a little	at present	do / try one's best
a lot (of)	at school	each other
a number of	at the beginning of	enjoy oneself
a piece of	at the same time	even if / though
a set of	be able to	ever since
after a while	be afraid of	fall asleep
after class	be busy doing sth.	fall ill
after school	be busy with sth.	fall in love with
again and again	be covered with	far away
agree with sb.	be full of	first of all
ahead of time	be good at	for ever
all over	be used to	for example
all right	be/get ready for	from now on
all the time	because of	get away
arrive at / in	belong to	get back
as if / though	both...and	get down
as long as	by air	get in
as soon as	by sea	get off
as usual	by the way	get on
as well as	call for	get out
as...as	care for	get up
ask for	catch cold	give back
at all	come back	go away
at home	come down	go back
at last	come from	go for a walk
at least	come in	go home
at most	come on	go to bed

go to school	keep on doing sth.	pay for sth.
go to sleep	knock at	plenty of
go to the cinema	laugh at	put down
hand in	less than	quite a few
have a cold	let in / out	right away
have a good time	listen to	right now
have a look	long ago	see off
have a talk	long ago	send for
have a walk	look after	set off
have breakfast	look at	set out
have classes	look for	set up
have got to	lots of	side by side
have lunch	make use of	so far
have supper	more or less	so that
have/take a rest	neither... nor	sooner or later
hear from	never mind	stand up
help sb. with sth.	no longer	such as
hundreds of	no more	take a look
hurry up	not any longer	take a seat
in a hurry	not any more	take away
in a minute	not... until	take care of
in a moment	of course	take down
in a short while	on holiday	take off
in a word	on one's way to	take out
in front of	on the left	take place
in other words	on the right	talk about
in the beginning	on the way	the day after tomorrow
in the middle of	on time	the day after yesterday
in time	once again / more	the other day
instead of	one after another	think a bout
join in	one after another	think of
just a minute	one another	thousands of
just a moment	one by one	throw away
just now	or so	turn into
just then	out of	wait for
keep on	pay attention to	

APPENDIX III

Glossary

符号说明：达到《高职高专教育英语课程教学基本要求》B级应掌握的词汇：★
达到《高职高专教育英语课程教学基本要求》A级应掌握的词汇：▲
大学英语4~6级词汇：♨

A

★ a.m. （缩）上午，午前	U3
★ ability *n.* 能力，才干	U1
★ aboard *ad. & prep.* 在船上，在飞机上	U3
▲ absorb *v.* 吸收，吸引	U1
▲ accompany *v.* 伴随，陪同	U7
♨ accordance *n.* 一致，和谐	U1
♨ accountant *n.* 会计师，会计员	U8
♨ accuracy *n.* 正确，精确	U3
▲ accurate *a.* 正确的，精确的	U3
★ across *prep.* 横过；越过	U2
★ activity *n.* 活动，活跃，行动，行为	U1
★ addition *n.* 加，增加（物）	U5
★ adult *n.* 成年人 *a.* 成年的，成熟的	U5
★ advance *n. & v.* 提高，提升；前进	U5
★ advanced *a.* 先进的，高级的	U1
★ advantage *n.* 益处	U2
▲ adventure *n.* 冒险，惊险活动	U3
★ advice *n.* 忠告，建议；（商务）通知	U6
★ advise *v.* 劝告，建议	U6
♨ adviser *n.* 顾问；指导老师	U6
★ affect *v.* 影响，感动；侵袭	U8
★ agreement *n.* 同意，一致；协定，协议	U4
▲ agriculture *n.* 农业	U8
♨ agriculturist *n.* 农学家，农场经营者	U8
★ aid *n. & v.* 帮助，辅助	U1
★ alike *a.* 相似的，类似的	U2

- ★ alive *a.* 活着的，活泼的 　　U5
- ♨ ally *n.* 同盟国　*v.* 与……结盟 　　U4
- ♨ Amerind *n.* & *a.* 美洲印第安人（的） 　　U4
- ▲ amuse *v.* 逗……乐（笑），给……娱乐 　　U7
- ★ apartment *n.* 公寓，单元住宅 　　U1
- ★ appear *v.* 出现；出版，发表；看来（好像） 　　U4
- ▲ appointment *n.* 约会，指定 　　U5
- ★ appreciate *v.* 感激，欣赏；涨价，升值 　　U8
- ♨ arch *n.* 弧，拱；拱状物 　　U2
- ▲ arouse *v.* 唤起，引起 　　U1
- ▲ artificial *a.* 人工的，人造的；假的 　　U5
- ★ artist *n.* 艺术家，画家 　　U1
- ★ aspect *n.* 方面；样子，外表 　　U1
- ▲ assign *v.* 指派，布置，指定 　　U8
- ★ association *n.* 协会；联合 　　U4
- ★ astronaut *n.* 宇航员，太空人 　　U3
- ★ attempt *n.* & *v.* 尝试，企图 　　U3
- ★ attractive *a.* 吸引人的，有魅力的 　　U3
- ♨ attribute *v.* 加于，归结于　*n.* 品质，属性 　　U8
- ♨ auspices *n.* （复）主办，赞助 　　U4
- ♨ automatically *ad.* 自动地 　　U8

B

- ▲ background *n.* 背景，后台 　　U4
- ♨ bake *v.* 烤，烘 　　U7
- ♨ balloon *n.* 气球 　　U2
- ♨ band *n.* 乐队；带，镶边 　　U4
- ★ bare *a.* 赤裸的，无遮蔽的 　　U6
- ♨ barn *n.* 粮仓 　　U7
- ♨ bean *n.* 豆，豆类 　　U5
- ▲ behalf *n.* 代表；利益 　　U4
- ★ belief *n.* 信任，信仰，信心 　　U4
- ♨ believable *a.* 可相信的，可信任的 　　U4
- ★ bell *n.* 钟，铃　*v.* 系铃于，装钟于 　　U6
- ★ bend (bent, bent) *v.* （使）……弯曲；专心于　*n.* 弯曲 　　U7
- ★ beneath *prep.* 在……之下 　　U2
- ★ beyond *prep.* 在……的外边，远于；超出　*ad.* 在更远处 　　U8
- ♨ bilingual *a.* 能说两种语言的 　　U6

★ billion *num.* 十亿		U3
▲ bite *v.* & *n.* 咬；刺痛		U6
♨ blacken *v.* 变黑，使……变黑；诽谤		U7
★ blank *a.* 空白的；无表情的　*n.* 空白，空格		U6
♨ blunder *v.* 做错　*n.* 错误，失误		U1
★ board *v.* 上（船、车、飞机）　*n.* 木板，纸板；董事会		U8
★ bother *v.* 打扰，烦扰		U7
★ bottom *n.* 底，底部；基础，根底		U3
♨ bowwow *n.* 狗吠声		U6
★ brain *n.* 脑，头脑		U5
▲ breathe *v.* 呼吸；吸口气		U2
♨ breed (bred, bred) *v.* 繁殖；教养　*n.* 品种，种类		U8
♨ breeze *n.* 微风		U2
♨ briefcase *n.* 公文包		U1
▲ broadcast *v.* & *n.* 广播，播音		U1
♨ brook *n.* 溪流，小溪		U2
♨ bubble *n.* 水泡，泡沫		U2
♨ bulb *n.* 灯泡		U7
♨ bunch *n.* 捆，束，团		U2
★ burst (burst, burst) *v.* 爆发，爆裂		U6
★ bury *v.* 隐藏，埋葬		U6

C

♨ cabbage *n.* 卷心菜，甘蓝		U5
♨ cabin *n.* 船舱，小屋		U3
▲ cable *n.* 电报，电缆		U7
★ campus *n.* 校园		U7
♨ candle *n.* 蜡烛		U7
▲ captain *n.* 船长，机长；首领，队长		U3
♨ castle *n.* 城堡		U6
★ cause *n.* 原因，起因　*v.* 引起		U2
♨ CD = compact disc *n.* 光盘		U1
▲ centigrade *a.* 摄氏的　*n.* 摄氏		U2
★ central *a.* 中心的，中央的；主要的		U4
★ certificate *n.* 证明，证书		U3
♨ charming *a.* 妩媚的，迷人的		U2
▲ chase *v.* & *n.* 追逐，追赶；跟踪		U7
★ cheat *n.* & *v.* 欺骗		U6

♨ checkup *n.* 检查，身体检查；审查，鉴定		U3
★ cheer *v.* & *n.* （使）欢快，发出（欢呼）；干杯		U6
▲ cheese *n.* 奶酪，干酪		U4
★ chief *n.* 首领，长官，主任 *a.* 首席的，主要的		U4
♨ chore *n.* 杂事，杂活		U8
★ church *n.* 教堂，教会		U8
♨ civil *a.* 国内的；文明的；公民的		U4
♨ clay *n.* 粘土，泥土		U7
▲ clerk *n.* 职员，办事员，管理员，店员		U4
★ club *n.* 俱乐部，社；棍棒		U4
★ coast *n.* 海岸，海滨地区		U4
★ collect *v.* 收集，聚集		U3
★ compare *v.* 比较，比作		U3
▲ complicated *a.* 复杂的，难解的		U8
♨ computerize *v.* 使计算机化，用计算机处理		U8
▲ conference *n.* （正式）会议，讨论会，协商会		U1
★ confirm *v.* 批准，确认，进一步证实		U4
★ congratulation *n.* 祝贺，恭喜		U1
★ connect *v.* 连接，联合		U7
★ constant *a.* 持续的		U2
★ consult *v.* 商议，请教；向……咨询		U6
▲ context *n.* 上下文，文章的前后关系		U1
▲ contribution *n.* 贡献，捐献		U7
▲ convenience *n.* 方便，便利；方便的用具、器械等		U8
★ convenient *a.* 便利的，方便的		U3
▲ cooperation *n.* 合作，协作		U1
★ cope *v.* 应付，处理		U6
★ copper *n.* 铜；警察		U5
★ corner *n.* 角落，（遥远的）地区，偏僻处		U1
★ count *v.* 数；计算 *n.* 计数，总数		U3
♨ countryside *n.* 农村，乡下		U8
★ craft *n.* 船，飞行器；工艺，手艺		U3
♨ crank *n.* 曲柄 *v.* 转动（曲柄）		U7
♨ crawl *n.* & *v.* 爬行，缓慢行进		U6
▲ credit *n.* 信用，信誉；荣誉，赞扬；学分 *v.* 记入贷方		U1
▲ crew *n.* （全体）乘务员；船员，水手		U3
▲ cultivation *n.* 培育，耕作；培养，教养		U8
★ cultural *a.* 文化的		U1

245

D

- ★ daily *a.* 日常的　*n.* 日报　　　　　　　　　　　　　　　　U4
- ★ damage *n. & v.* 损害，伤害　　　　　　　　　　　　　　　U8
- ▲ dash *v.* 猛冲，猛撞　*n.* 破折号；冲撞　　　　　　　　　U6
- ▲ datum *n.* 数据，信息，资料　data（datum的复数形式）　U3
- ★ deal (dealt, dealt) *v.* 处理，应付　*n.* 交易　　　　　　U6
- ★ decision *n.* 决定，决策　　　　　　　　　　　　　　　　U7
- ▲ definition *n.* 定义，解说　　　　　　　　　　　　　　　U1
- ★ degree *n.* 度，程度　　　　　　　　　　　　　　　　　　U2
- ▲ delegation *n.* 代表团；授权，委托　　　　　　　　　　　U5
- ★ deliver *v.* 交送，投递；发表　　　　　　　　　　　　　U8
- ♨ deliverer *n.* 递送人　　　　　　　　　　　　　　　　　U8
- ▲ delivery *n.* 交货，递交　　　　　　　　　　　　　　　　U3
- ▲ demonstrate *v.* 展示，示范；证明，论证　　　　　　　　U7
- ★ deny *v.* 否认，拒绝　　　　　　　　　　　　　　　　　　U8
- ♨ descendant *n.* 子孙，后裔　　　　　　　　　　　　　　　U4
- ★ describe *v.* 记述，描写　　　　　　　　　　　　　　　　U3
- ★ description *n.* 记述，描写；叙事文　　　　　　　　　　U3
- ▲ despair *v. & n.* 绝望，失望　　　　　　　　　　　　　　U6
- ★ destroy *v.* 破坏，摧毁　　　　　　　　　　　　　　　　U2
- ▲ detector *n.* 探测器，发现者　　　　　　　　　　　　　　U8
- ★ develop *v.* 发展；使成长，生长；显现出　　　　　　　　U4
- ★ development *n.* 发展，开发，研制；生长，进化；新成就　U8
- ★ device *n.* 装置，设备；设计，图案　　　　　　　　　　　U8
- ▲ digital *a.* 数字的，数码的，用数字显示的　　　　　　　U8
- ♨ dim-witted *a.* 笨的，傻的　　　　　　　　　　　　　　　U1
- ★ discover *v.* 发现　　　　　　　　　　　　　　　　　　　U3
- ★ disease *n.* 疾病，弊病　　　　　　　　　　　　　　　　U8
- ♨ dismay *n. & v.* 沮丧，惊慌　　　　　　　　　　　　　　U6
- ★ display *v. & n.* 展示，展览；陈列　　　　　　　　　　　U3
- ▲ dispute *v.* 争论，辩驳　　　　　　　　　　　　　　　　U4
- ★ distance *n.* 远处，距离，间隔　　　　　　　　　　　　　U7
- ♨ dock *n.* 码头，装货坞　　　　　　　　　　　　　　　　　U8
- ★ dull *a.* 迟钝的，呆笨的；不活跃的　　　　　　　　　　　U5
- ▲ dumb *a.* 哑的，无说话能力的　　　　　　　　　　　　　U1
- ★ dust *n.* 灰尘，尘土　　　　　　　　　　　　　　　　　　U3

E

★ eager　*a.* 热切的，渴望的		U3
♨ eagerly　*ad.* 热切地，渴望地		U3
★ economic　*a.* 经济（上）的，经济学的		U1
♨ economist　*n.* 经济师，经济学家		U7
★ effectively　*ad.* 有效地，有力地		U1
♨ efficiency　*n.* 效率，功效		U8
★ efficient　*a.* 效率高的，有能力的		U8
♨ efficiently　*ad.* 效率高地，有能力地		U8
▲ effort　*n.* 努力，成就		U8
★ electrical　*a.* 电的，用电的，电动的		U6
★ electricity　*n.* 电；电学		U2
▲ electronic　*a.* 电子的		U1
★ e-mail　*n.* 电子邮件，电子信函		U1
♨ empire　*n.* 帝国，帝权		U3
★ employ　*v.* 雇佣；使用		U8
★ employee　*n.* 职工，员工，雇员		U8
★ employer　*n.* 雇主，老板		U8
★ enclose　*v.* 放入封套，装入		U3
★ engine　*n.* 引擎，发动机		U3
♨ enjoyable　*a.* 令人愉快的，可享受的		U8
♨ enlighten　*v.* 启发，启示，开导		U3
★ entertain　*v. & n.* 招待，款待		U6
★ entrance　*n.* 进入；入口		U1
★ environment　*n.* 环境，外界		U1
♨ environmental　*a.* 环境的，周围的		U8
★ equally　*ad.* 同等地；公平地		U6
★ equipment　*n.* 装备，设备		U4
★ establish　*v.* 建立；证实；制定		U4
European　*n.* 欧洲人　*a.* 欧洲的		U5
★ exactly　*ad.* 准确地；正好		U2
♨ exceptionally　*ad.* 特别地，例外地		U2
★ exchange　*v. & n.* 交流，交换		U1
★ expect　*v.* 期待，期望；料想		U7
★ experimental　*a.* 实验的		U5
★ expert　*n.* 专家，能手　*a.* 熟练的，有专长的		U4
★ explanation　*n.* 解释，说明；辩解		U4

♨ explanatory *a.* 说明的，解释的	U1
▲ exploration *n.* 探险，探测	U3
▲ explorer *n.* 探险者；探测员	U3
★ expression *n.* 词组；表达	U4

F

♨ fable *n.* 寓言；虚构的故事	U6
★ facility *n.* 设备，设施，便利，简易	U7
★ fair *n.* 展览会，交易会 *a.* 公平的；（肤色）白皙的；（头发）金黄的	U1
♨ fairy *n.* 妖精，仙女 *a.* 仙境的，幻想中的	U3
★ false *a.* 错误的，假的，虚伪的	U1
★ familiar *a.* 熟悉的，常见的 *n.* 密友，熟客	U4
★ fanatic *n.* 狂热者，入迷者 *a.* 狂热的，入迷的	U3
★ fare *n.* 车旅费；机票，船票	U3
★ fax *n.* 传真	U7
★ feather *n.* 羽毛，翎毛	U5
♨ fertilizer *n.* 肥料	U8
♨ fiction *n.* 小说；虚构	U3
★ firm *a.* 坚固的；严格的 *n.* 商号，公司	U2
★ flash *n. & v.* 闪光，闪现	U2
★ flat *a.* 平的，平坦的；浅的；单调的	U3
♨ fleece *n.* 羊毛	U7
♨ flicker *v. & n.* 闪烁不定，忽隐忽现	U7
★ float *v.* 漂浮，浮动；飘扬	U2
★ flow *v.* 流动，川流不息	U2
★ fog *n.* 雾，尘雾	U2
♨ forecast *n. & v.* 预测，预报	U2
★ former *a.* 以前的，从前的	U1
▲ foundation *n.* 基础，根本；地基；基金，基金会	U1
▲ frame *n.* 结构，框架	U5
★ freeze (froze, frozen) *v.* （使）结冰；凝固，冻僵	U2
★ frequently *ad.* 常常，经常	U1
♨ fresh *a.* 新鲜的，淡的	U2
★ fridge *n.* 电冰箱	U6
★ freshman *n.* 新生，大学一年级生	U1
♨ furnace *n.* 炉子，熔炉	U7
★ further *a.* 更远的，进一步的 *ad.* 更远地，进一步地	U7
★ future *n. & a.* 将来（的），未来（的）	U3

G

★ gain v. 获得，赢得 n. 利益，收获 U7
♨ galaxy n. 星系，银河 U3
★ game n. 游戏，比赛；（复）运动会 U5
★ general a. 一般的，综合的 n. 一般；概要；将军 U4
♨ generator n. 发电机，发生器 U7
♨ glitter v. & n. 闪光，闪烁 U6
★ global a. 全球的，世界的；球型的 U1
♨ globalization n. 全球化 U1
★ glow v. 发光，发热 U7
★ gradually ad. 逐渐的，逐步地 U8
★ graduate v. 毕业 n. 毕业生 U8
♨ graduation n. 毕业，毕业典礼；刻度，等级 U7
▲ gram n. 克 U3
♨ gramophone n. 留声机 U7
▲ grand a. 豪华的，盛大的，主要的 U5
★ gray/grey n. & a. 灰色（的） U2
★ guidance n. 指导，教导 U1

H

♨ hail n. 冰雹 v. 向……欢呼 U2
♨ hailstone n. 冰雹块 U2
♨ hairpin n. 发夹 U7
★ handbag n. 手提包 U5
★ happen v. 碰巧，偶然 U6
★ harmful a. 有害的，伤害的 U8
★ harvest v. & n. 收获，收割 U8
♨ hay n. 干草 U8
♨ hedge n. 树篱，矮树 U7
▲ hi-tech a. 高科技的 U8
♨ Holland n. 荷兰 Hollander n. 荷兰人 U4
♨ hollow a. 空的，空心的 U3
★ however ad. 可是，然而；无论如何，不管怎样 U2
♨ humid a. 潮湿的，湿润的 U2

I

♨ ice-drop n. 冰滴 U2

♨ idiom *n.* 成语，习语，土语	U1
♨ idiomatic *a.* 惯用的，合乎语言习惯的	U1
♨ imaginable *a.* 可想像的，可能的	U1
▲ imagination *n.* 想像力，幻想	U3
★ imitate *v.* 模仿，仿效	U1
★ impatiently *ad.* 不耐烦地，无耐性地	U6
★ importance *n.* 重要（性），重大	U1
♨ impress *v.* 留下印象；盖印	U8
★ include *v.* 包括，包含	U5
★ increase *v. & n.* 增加，增长，增大	U3
▲ indicate *v.* 指出，显示；预示	U5
♨ indigo *n. & a.* 靛青色（的）	U2
▲ individual *n. & a.* 个别（的），个体（的），单独的	U1
★ influence *n. & v.* 影响，感化	U1
★ initial *n.* 首字母，姓名（或组织名称）的开头字母 *a.* 最初的	U4
♨ inorganic *a.* 无机物的	U5
▲ insect *n.* 昆虫 *a.* 虫子一样的	U5
★ inspect *v.* 检查，视察	U4
♨ inspection *n.* 检查，视察	U4
★ instruction *n.* 教导，指示	U1
▲ intelligence *n.* 智能，智力，聪明	U5
▲ intelligent *a.* 聪明的，有才智的；[计] 智能的	U3
♨ internationalization *n.* 国际化	U1
★ internet *n.* 因特网，国际互联网	U1
★ interview *n. & v.* 采访；会见；面试	U3
♨ intonation *n.* 语调，声调	U1
★ invention *n.* 发明，创造	U3
★ inventor *n.* 发明家，创造者	U3
★ invitation *n.* 请帖，请柬；邀请	U5
♨ irregular *a.* 不规则的，无规律的	U1
★ island *n.* 岛，岛屿	U4
♨ isolation *n.* 隔绝，孤立	U1
▲ Italy *n.* 意大利	U5

J

♨ jingle *v. & n.* （发出）铃铛声	U6
★ journey *n.* 旅程，旅行	U2
★ judge *v.* 判断，裁判 *n.* 法官，裁判员	U1

★ junior a. 年少的；地位低的 n. 晚辈；大学三年级学生 U6

K

★ kilogram n. 千克 U3
★ king n. 国王 U6
★ kingdom n. 王国 U6

L

★ ladder n. 梯子 U3
♨ lamb n. 羔羊，羊肉 U7
♨ lampblack n. 灯烟，灯黑 U7
★ land n. 土地，大陆   v. 登陆，着陆 U3
★ last v. 持续，维持   a. & ad. 最后（的），最近（的） U2
▲ laughter n. 笑，笑声 U7
♨ league n. 里格（长度名，英美约为3英里）；同盟，联盟；协会 U3
▲ lean (leant, leant) v. & n. 倾斜；依靠；屈身 U5
▲ leap n. & v. 跳跃，跃进 U3
♨ leather n. 皮革，皮革制品 U5
★ leisure n. 空闲，休闲，安闲 U8
★ lightning n. 闪电 U2
★ likely a. & ad. 很可能（的）；有希望（的） U1
▲ load v. 装载，装货   n. 装载量，工作量，负荷，负载 U8
★ lonely a. 孤独的，寂寞的；偏僻的 U3
★ lovely a. 可爱的，有趣的 U6
★ lower v. 放下，降低，减弱 U4
♨ lunar a. 月球的；阴历的 U3

M

★ machinery n. [总称] 机器，机械 U8
▲ magnificent a. 宏伟的，华丽的 U5
★ mail n. 邮件，邮政   v. 邮寄 U1
★ manager n. 经理，管理人员 U7
★ mankind n. 人类 U3
▲ marvelous a. 奇妙的 U2
★ master v. 掌握，精通   n. 主人；教师；大师 U1
★ material n. 材料，物资   a. 物质的，实质的 U5
♨ maximum a. 最高的，最大极限的   n. 最大量，最大限度，极大 U2

★ mechanical	*a.* 机械的，机械学的，力学的；机械似的，呆板的	U8
▲ medium	*n.* 媒介，媒体　*a.* 中等的，半生的	U1
♨ melt	*v.* 融化，溶解	U2
★ memorize	*v.* 记住，记忆	U1
★ metal	*n.* 金属	U5
★ method	*n.* 方法，办法	U8
★ mice	*n.* mouse的复数形式	U6
♨ Midwest	*n.* 中西部（地区）	U8
★ mile	*n.* 英里（=1.609千米）	U2
★ military	*a.* 军事的	U1
★ mine	*n.* 矿，矿井　*v.* 挖掘，开采	U5
♨ mineral	*n.* 矿物，矿石	U5
♨ minimum	*a.* 最低的，最小的　*n.* 最低值，最小限度	U2
▲ minister	*n.* 大臣，部长	U6
▲ mission	*n.* 使命，任务；代表团，使团	U1
♨ mist	*n.* 薄雾	U2
▲ mobile	*n.* 移动电话　*a.* 可移动的	U7
▲ moisture	*n.* 潮湿，湿气	U8
★ monitor	*v.* 监控，监视　*n.* 班长；监控器	U8
♨ monster	*n.* 怪物，妖怪	U3
★ mouse	*n.* 老鼠；鼠标	U6
▲ multimedia	*n.* 多媒体	U4
♨ murmur	*v. & n.* （发出）咕哝；怨言；低沉连续的声音	U6
♨ mute	*a.* 哑的，无声的　*n.* 哑巴	U1

N

★ nation	*n.* 国家，民族	U8
★ native	*n.* 本地人，土著　*a.* 本国的，本族的；土产的	U1
★ natural	*a.* 自然的；天赋的；正常的	U5
★ neighbor	*n.* 邻居，邻国	U7
★ nest	*n.* 巢，窝　*v.* 筑巢，巢居	U7
★ net	*n.* 网，网络；净利，实价	U7
★ network	*n.* 网络，网状物	U7
♨ nickname	*n.* 诨名，绰号	U4
★ noble	*a.* 高贵的，崇高的　*n.* 贵族	U6
♨ non-living	*a.* 非生物的	U5
▲ nonsense	*n.* 废话，胡说	U3
♨ non-stop	*a.* 直飞的，中途不停的	U8

- ★ notice *n.* 启事，通知，布告   *v.* 注意到   U1
- ♨ nylon *n.* 尼龙   U5

O

- ★ obey *v.* 服从，顺从   U4
- ★ object *n.* 物体，目标；宾语   *v.* 反对，抗议   U5
- ★ observe *v.* 观察，观测；遵守；评述，说   U2
- ★ obvious *a.* 明显的，显而易见的   U5
- ♨ obviously *ad.* 明显地   U5
- ★ ocean *n.* 海洋，大洋   U2
- ★ official *a.* 正式的，有根据的；官方的   *n.* 官员，公务员   U4
- ★ okay *a. & ad.* 对；好；可以   *n. & v.* 同意，认可   U4
- ★ operate *v.* 操作，控制；作业，运行；经营，管理；对……动手术   U8
- ★ operation *n.* 操作，运转；经营，业务；运算；手术   U8
- ★ opinion *n.* 意见，砍伐；评价；鉴定   U4
- ★ opposite *a.* 对面的，对立的，相反的   *prep.* 在……的对面   U6
- ♨ orbit *n.* （天体的）轨道 *v.* 沿轨道运行，把……送入轨道   U3
- ♨ orchard *n.* 果园   U8
- ★ organization *n.* 组织，团体，机构   U4
- ♨ originate *v.* 起源，发生   U5
- ♨ outer *a.* 外部的，外层的   U3
- ♨ overcast *a.* 阴天的，阴暗的   *n.* 覆盖，阴天 *v.* （使）阴暗   U2

P

- ★ p.m. （缩）下午，晚上，午后   U3
- ★ pack *v.* 捆扎，把……打包   *n.* 包，小盒   U8
- ★ package *n.* 包，包裹；包装用物   U4
- ★ paragraph *n.* 段落   U1
- ★ part *v.* 送别，分手   U8
- ★ particularly *ad.* 尤其；独特地，显著地   U8
- ★ partly *ad.* 部分地，几分   U5
- ★ partner *n.* 伙伴，伴侣   *v.* 与……合伙，与……组成一对   U5
- ♨ pasteurize *v.* 消毒，灭菌   U8
- ★ peace *n.* 和平，安宁   U6
- ★ percent *n.* 百分比，百分数   U1
- ♨ perseverance *n.* 坚持   U1
- ♨ phonograph *n.* 留声机，唱机   U7
- ★ phrase *n.* 短语，词组   U4

★ pilot n.飞行员，领航员 v.驾驶（飞机等），领航		U1
★ pipe n.烟斗；管道，输送管 v.以管道输送		U7
★ plain a.普通的，平坦的 n.平原，平地		U2
★ plastic n. & a.塑料（的）		U5
★ pleasure n.愉快，高兴		U5
★ point v.指出，指向；瞄准 n.要点；分数		U6
★ political a.政治的，政治上的		U4
▲ pollution n.污染		U2
♨ polytechnic n.职业学院，工艺学校 a.工艺的		U7
★ popular a.流行的，通俗的，受欢迎的		U4
★ population n.人口		U8
★ position v.定位，安置 n.位置，职位；立场；阵地		U8
★ postcard n.明信片		U6
♨ postcode n.邮编		U7
♨ powder n.粉末		U3
★ power n.动力，电力，功率		U7
★ practical a.实际的，实践的，实用的，应用的		U7
★ praise v.赞扬，表扬 n.赞美，称赞		U7
★ president n.总统，校长，董事长，总裁		U4
★ pretend v.假装，装扮；假设		U3
♨ previous a.在前的，早先的		U5
★ princess n.公主，王妃		U6
★ process v.加工，处理 n.过程，程序，步骤		U8
♨ prod v.戳，刺激		U7
★ produce v.生产，产生，制作 n.产物，农产品		U7
★ product n.产品，产物；乘积		U8
▲ productive a.多产的，有成果的；生产的		U8
★ profit n.利润，益处 v.有益于，有利于；得到，获益		U8
♨ profound a.深刻地，渊博的		U1
★ program (UK) programme n. & v.（安排）节目，（编）程序		U1
▲ promote v.促进，发扬；提升，晋级		U1
★ proposal n.提议，建议；计划		U4
★ propose v.提议，建议；提名，推荐；计划		U4
▲ prosperous a.繁荣的，昌盛的		U1
★ protection n.保护		U8
★ proud a.骄傲的，自豪的，妄自尊大的		U3
★ provide v.提供		U7
★ public n.公众 a.公共的，公众的；公立的		U4
♨ publicly ad.公开地，公然地，当众地		U7

★ pure *a.* 纯粹的，纯正的，纯洁的 U4

R

★ railroad *n.* （UK railway）铁路 U4
♨ rainbow *n.* 虹 U2
♨ raindrop *n.* 雨滴，雨点 U2
▲ raw *a.* 生的；未加工的 U5
♨ rayon *n.* 人造丝，人造纤维 U5
★ realize *v.* 认识到，了解；实现，实行 U1
★ reasonable *a.* 合理的，有道理的 U4
★ recent *a.* 近来，最近 U3
★ reception *n.* 招待会；接待，接受 U5
♨ recite *v.* 背诵，朗诵 U7
★ refrigerator *n.* 电冰箱，冷藏库 U8
★ regard *n.* & *v.* 关心，注意；重视，尊敬；致意，问候 U3
★ reliable *a.* 可靠的，可信赖的 U1
★ reply *n.* & *v.* 答复，回答；报复；答辩 U6
★ reporter *n.* 记者，通讯员 U3
★ responsible *a.* 有责任的，可依赖的，负责的 U8
★ result *n.* 结果，后果 *v.* 导致，引起 U2
★ resume *v.* 再继续，重新开始 U3
♨ retell *v.* 复述，重讲 U1
★ reward *v.* 报答，酬劳 *n.* 奖金，报酬 U1
♨ rhyme *n.* 韵律，押韵；押韵的诗词 U7
♨ roar *n.* & *v.* 吼叫，怒吼 U3
★ robot *n.* 机器人，遥控设备，自动机械 U5
★ rocket *n.* 火箭 *v.* 急速上升 U3
★ role *n.* 作用；角色 U3
★ Roman *n.* & *a.* 罗马的，罗马人（的） U5
♨ Rome *n.* 罗马 U5
★ root *n.* 根，根部 *v.* （使）生根，扎根 U6
★ rough *a.* 汹涌的；粗暴的；粗糙的 U4
★ rub *v.* 擦，摩擦 U7
★ Russian *n.* 俄语，俄国人 *a.* 俄国的，俄国人的 U3

S

★ sail *v.* 航海；翱翔 *n.* 帆，篷 U4
★ sailor *n.* 税收，海员 U4

▲ satellite	n. 卫星，人造天体	U8
▲ scatter	v. 撒，散布；驱散	U2
★ scene	n. 场面，景色，情景，布景	U3
★ scholar	n. 学者	U4
★ scientific	a. 科学的	U3
♨ scissor	n. 剪刀　v. 剪，剪去	U5
♨ Scottish	a. 苏格兰（人）的	U4
♨ scratch	v. 搔，抓；刮擦，涂抹	U6
▲ seal	v. 封，密封　n. 封条，密封	U7
♨ seashore	n. 海岸，海滨	U4
♨ seep	v. 渗进，渗入	U2
▲ senior	a. 年长的，地位高的　n. 长辈；大学四年级学生	U6
★ settle	v. 定居，安家；解决，决定	U4
♨ settler	n. 移民，移居者；殖民者，开拓者	U4
★ shadow	n. 影子，阴影；阴暗	U2
★ shake (shook, shaken)	v. & n. 摇动，振动	U3
★ shape	n. 形状　v. 形成	U2
★ shiny	a. 闪亮的，刺眼的	U4
♨ shuttle	n. 梭，梭状物　v. 穿梭	U3
★ silence	n. 寂静，沉默	U3
★ silently	ad. 寂静地，沉默地	U3
★ silver	n. 银子　v. 镀银	U5
★ similar	a. 相似的，类似的	U8
★ simple	a. 简单的，朴素的；率直的；易受骗的	U6
▲ sincerely	ad. 真诚地	U8
★ site	n. 站点；地点，场所	U5
★ situation	n. 情景，境遇；位置	U6
♨ sleet	n. 雪雨，雨夹雪	U2
♨ slippery	a. 滑的	U2
★ smart	a. 精明的，灵巧的，巧妙的	U3
♨ sniff	v. 嗅出，闻；用力吸气	U7
♨ snowflake	n. 雪花，雪片	U2
★ soap	n. 肥皂	U2
★ sock	n. 短袜，鞋内衬底	U5
★ softly	ad. 柔软地，温柔地	U6
★ solution	n. 解决方法；溶解，溶液	U6
♨ son-in-law	n. 女婿	U6
♨ sophomore	n. 大学二年级生；有两年经验的人	U1
♨ sour	a. 酸的；刺耳的；讨厌的	U4

★ source *n.* 水源，来源		U2
★ southern *a.* 南方的，南部的		U4
★ Spain *n.* 西班牙		U4
★ speed *n.* 速度　*v.* 加速		U3
♨ splash *n. & v.* 溅，泼		U3
▲ splendid *a.* 壮丽的，辉煌的；极好的		U6
★ spread （spread, spread）*v.* 伸展，传播；扩散，撒		U4
★ spring *n.* 泉，源泉；春天；发条　*v.* 跳跃，触发		U2
♨ squeak *v. & n.* （发出）尖叫，吱吱叫		U6
★ stare *v.* 盯，凝视		U7
▲ starve *v.* （使）……饿死		U6
▲ statistics *n.* 统计，统计表		U1
♨ steadily *ad.* 稳固地，稳定地		U7
▲ steady *a.* 稳固的，稳定的　*v.* 使……稳定，使……稳固		U7
★ step *v.* 走，举步　*n.* 脚步，梯阶，步骤		U3
★ stocking *n.* 长袜		U5
♨ stopover *n.* 中途停留		U8
♨ storey *n.* （层）楼		U3
★ stranger *n.* 陌生人，外地人；门外汉		U6
★ stroke *v.* 抚摸　*n.* 击，敲		U6
♨ stunt *v. & n.* 阻碍，妨碍		U1
♨ submarine *n.* 潜艇，海底动物　*a.* 水下的，海生的		U3
★ suburb *n.* 市郊，郊区		U8
★ succeed *v.* 成功；继承，接替		U8
★ successful *a.* 成功的，圆满的		U3
▲ sunlight *n.* 日光，阳光		U2
★ surface *n.* 表面，外观		U2
♨ surprisingly *ad.* 出乎意外地，令人惊奇地		U3
★ sweat *n.* 汗；水珠，湿气		U7
♨ swell *v.* 膨胀，肿胀		U2
▲ switch *n.* 开关，电键　*v.* 转换		U7
★ system *n.* 系统，体系；制度，秩序；规律，方法；公司，集团		U2

T

★ tail *n. & a.* 尾巴（的），尾部（的）		U6
♨ tale *n.* 故事，传说；谎话，谣言		U3
▲ technician *n.* 技师，技术员		U8
★ technology *n.* 技术，工艺（学）		U1

▲ telescope *n.* 望远镜		U3
★ temperature *n.* 温度，气温		U2
♨ terrific *a.* （口语）极佳的；令人恐怖的		U3
▲ thread *n.* 线，思绪		U7
▲ thunder *n.* 雷，雷声 *v.* 打雷		U2
★ tightly *ad.* 紧密地；牢固地；严格地		U7
♨ tinfoil *n.* 锡箔，锡纸		U7
★ tiny *a.* 极小的		U2
★ tongue *n.* 舌头；口语		U1
★ topic *n.* 主题，话题		U1
★ tower *n.* 塔，城堡		U5
♨ tractor *n.* 拖拉机		U8
★ trade *n.* 贸易，交易，买卖 *v.* 交易，用……进行交换		U1
♨ trader *n.* 商人		U4
★ transfer *v. & n.* 转移，迁移；转让，过户；调动，转学		U8
★ translation *v.* 翻译，译文		U1
♨ transmit *v.* 传达，转送；传导，发射		U3
★ transport *n.* 运输，运输工具 *v.* 运输，输送		U1
★ traveler *n.* 旅行者，旅客		U3
♨ trench *n.* 深沟，渠		U7
♨ tribe *n.* 部落，宗族		U4

U

♨ underwater *a.* 水下的，水中的		U3
★ uneasy *a.* 拘束的，不自在的；忧虑的，担心的		U7
★ unfair *a.* 不公平的		U6
★ unless *conj.* 如果不，除非		U2
♨ unpleasant *a.* 令人不快的，讨厌的		U4
★ usage *n.* 用法，使用		U1

V

★ value *n.* 价值，估价，评价 *v.* 估价，评价，重视		U8
★ various *a.* 不同的，各种各样的		U8
♨ vat *n. & v.* （装进）大桶，大缸		U8
♨ vegetable *n. & a.* 蔬菜（的），植物（的）		U5
♨ violet *n. & a.* 紫色（的），紫罗兰（色的）		U2
★ vocabulary *n.* 词汇（量）		U1
★ vocational *a.* 职业的		U7

♨ volunteer v.自愿　n. & a. 志愿（的），志愿者（的）　U6

W

♨ waist n. 腰部；衣服的上身　U5
▲ walkman n. 随身听　U1
▲ web n. 网，环球网；蜘蛛网　U5
▲ website n. 网址　U5
♨ wed v. 嫁，娶，结婚　U6
♨ westward a. & ad. 向西（的）　U4
♨ whisker n. 胡须，腮须　U6
★ widely ad. 普遍地，广泛地　U1
★ wire n. 金属线　U2
★ wisdom n. 才智，英明，学问　U4
★ wise a. 明智的，英明的，博学的　U4
★ wooden a. 木制的　U6
★ wool n. 羊毛，毛织品　U5
♨ worm n. 虫，蛆虫；蚯蚓　U5
▲ wrap v. 缠绕，包裹；遮蔽　U2
♨ wrinkle v. 起皱　n. 皱纹　U7

Y

♨ Yankee n. & a. 美国佬（的）　U4

Idioms and Expressions

a flash of　一道，一线
a number of　一批，若干　U3
agreed on　对……意见一致　U4
along with　与……一起　U1
and so on　等等
appear on the scene　出现，登场　U4
artificial intelligence　人工智能　U6
as a result　所以，因此
as soon as possible　尽快　U1
as well as　也，又；以及　U3
as well as　以及，除……以外，也，又　U5

at least	至少	U4
at the age of	在……年龄	U3
at the bottom of	在……的底部	U3
be (fully) prepared for	为……做好（充分）准备	U1
be alike (to)	与……相似（类似）	U2
be assigned to	分配于；指定为	U8
be attributed to	把……归结于；归功于	U8
be aware of	对……清楚/了解	U1
be connected with (to)	与……连接；和……有联系	U8
be dressed in	穿着	U5
be familiar to	为……所熟悉	U4
be familiar with	对……熟悉	U4
be interested in	对……感兴趣	U7
be made from	由……（原料）制成	U5
be made of	由……组成，由……制成	U2
be not sure about	对……没有把握	U5
be obvious to sb.	对某人是清楚（明显）的	U5
be on one's guard against	提防，谨防	U1
be popular among	在……流行或受欢迎	U4
be proud of	为……而骄傲（自豪）	U7
be regarded as	看待，当做	U3
be responsible for	对某事负责	U8
be responsible to	对某人负责	U8
be similar to	与……相似	U8
bite one's way through	咬穿……而过	U6
blow away	刮走，吹走	U6
both...and	既……又，两者都	U3
break apart	断开	U7
break one's promise	违约	U5
bring in	获得；引进；产生	U8
build...into	把……建成	U1
burst into	爆发；闯入；突然出现	U6
burst out	爆发	U6
burst through	冲破	U5
by any chance	万一，或许	U5
call for help	求救	U1
call for	邀约（某人）；拿取（某物）	U5
carry on	进行；处理；坚持下去	U7
catch... out	发现（某人的）错误	U1

chase after 追逐，追赶	U7
cheat sb. into doing sth. 欺骗某人做某事	U6
come across 偶遇，偶然碰到	U1
come on the scene 出现，登场	U6
connect...to/with 与……连结，与……相连	U7
cope with 处理，应付	U6
deal with 处理，对付，安排	U6
do harm to 对……有害	U7
fairy tale 神话，童话	U3
fall in 掉下，坍塌	U7
far from 远没有，远未	U8
feel at home 如在家中；没有拘束	U1
find one's way to/into 进入	U2
fit into 装进，放进……合适之处	U1
from the corners of the earth 来自世界各地	U1
general public 公众，大众	U4
get ...right 把……做对	U1
get in touch with 与……接触	U1
get in 收获	U8
get on (well) with... 在……进行得（很）顺利	U1
get used to 逐渐适应，逐渐习惯	U2
give one's best regards to 向……问好/致意	U8
go a long way 大有作为	U7
go on a journey 旅行	U3
go out 出外；熄灭；过时	U7
graduate from 毕业于	U8
hang around 聚在附近	U1
happen to (do) 碰巧做，偶然发生	U6
have a checkup 进行体格检查	U3
have a good command of 精通，掌握	U1
I.O.U = I owe you 欠条，今欠到	U2
in a bunch 一团，一束	U2
in accordance with 根据，按照；与……一致	U1
in addition to 除……以外，又	U5
in addition 此外，另外	U8
in agreement 同意，与……一致	U4
in all 总计，一共	U8
in dismay 处于沮丧状况	U6
in honor of 向……表示敬意，为……欢迎	U5

in no time 立即，很快	U6
in one's leisure time 在空闲时	U8
in search of 寻求，查究	U8
in sight 看得见	U3
in silence 无声地，沉默地	U3
in spite if... 虽然……但是	U4
in the dark 在黑暗中；秘密地	U8
in the distance 在远处	U7
insist on 坚持	U1
instead of 代替，而不是	U2
keep one's eyes open 睁大眼睛，注意观察	U2
keep one's promise 守约	U5
lay a solid foundation of 在……打下坚实基础	U1
lift off 起飞，发射	U3
living thing 生物	U5
look forward to 盼望，期待	U1
look into 展望；调查；看……的内部或深处	U3
look like 看起来像……，似将	U2
look up 查词	U1
Lost and Found 拾物招领处	U1
lunar landing craft 登月舱	U3
make a contribution to 对……做出贡献	U7
make a trip to 到……旅行	U3
make up 编造，虚构；弥补；化妆	U4
millions of 数以百万计的；无数的	U2
mother tongue 母语	U1
move about 走来走去，四下活动	U3
name...after 以……命名	U3
neither...nor 既不……也不	U3
no wonder 难怪，不足为怪	U1
non-living thing 非生物	U5
not a bit 一点也不，毫不	U7
not only...but also 不仅……而且	U4
now and then 时而，不时	U7
on behalf of 作为……的代表；为了……的利益	U4
on line 在线	U5
on one hand 一方面	U4
on the other hand 另一方面	U4
once upon a time 从前	U6

one's native language 母语，本族语	U1
one...after another 相继，一个又一个	U7
outer space 外层空间	U3
per annum = per year	U2
physical labor 体力劳动	U8
pick up 学会（语言）；捡起；加速；挑选；用车接人	U1
play a joke on 对……开玩笑	U4
play a part in 在……方面起作用	U8
play a role in 在……发挥作用；扮演……角色	U3
point out 指出	U6
point to 指着，指向	U7
pull up 拔起；阻止，使停止	U2
rely on 依靠，依赖	U1
right away 马上，即刻	U3
rocket ship 火箭宇宙飞船	U3
RSVP 法语缩写词，请帖用语（=please reply）	U5
run after 追赶，追逐	U6
run for 竞选	U4
see through 看穿，识破	U2
sell one's idea to 向……兜售其主意	U4
send out 送出，发出	U3
shake hands with 与……握手	U3
show around 带领……参观	U7
sooner or later 迟早，早晚	U4
space shuttle 航天飞机	U3
splash down （宇宙飞行器在水面上）溅落	U3
stare at 凝视，盯着看	U7
succeed in （干……）成功	U8
swell up 肿胀起来	U7
take advantage of 利用	U2
take care 保重	U8
take in 吸收；接受；收容；理解	U8
take it easy 别着急，沉住气	U5
take on 具有；接纳；呈现；承担；流行；穿上；雇用	U4
take...for granted 认为……是理所当然的	U1
think out 想出，解决	U6
try out 试验，试行	U7
turn off 关上（电器、自来水、煤气等）	U3
turn on 打开（电器、自来水、煤气等）	U3

turn to 转向；求助于；开始行动	U6
turn...into 使……变为	U1
under the auspices of 由……主办	U4
USD=U.S. dollars STG=British sterling pounds	U2
use one's brains 动脑筋，想办法	U5
wash away 冲走，冲跑	U6
web site 网站	U5
what's more 此外，另外	U4
word for word 字对字地，逐字地	U1
work on 从事于；继续工作	U7
work out 想出，做出，计算出	U5
work with 同……一起工作；对……起作用	U2
would rather...than 宁愿……不愿，与其……倒不如	U4